# PRAISE FOR OTHER WORKS BY TIMOTHY WYLLIE

"Although Timothy is no longer with us in the conventional sense, he is very much alive in the latest of his Rebel Angels series. As millennium-spanning actors in this ongoing cosmic play, we are amused, stimulated, and entranced."

GORDON PHINN, AUTHOR OF *YOU ARE HISTORY:*
*THE SOUL, THE HIGHER SELF, AND*
*OUR SHARE OF DIVINITY*

"In a time of unfolding mysteries, Timothy Wyllie has written beautifully [in *Dolphins, ETs & Angels*] of his own fantastic adventures in a universe larger than our aspirations and richer and more complex than all our dreams."

JEAN HOUSTON, AUTHOR OF
*THE HERO AND THE GODDESS*

"Timothy Wyllie's multivolume narrative, of which *Rebel Angels in Exile* is part, is a masterpiece of writing. It is essential reading for any who would explore the cosmic dimension of mercy suggested in the parable of the prodigal son and the role of those often known as starseeds in its manifestation upon this and many other worlds."

ROBERT DAVIS, DIRECTOR OF
THE DAYNAL INSTITUTE

"*Confessions of a Rebel Angel* is Timothy Wyllie's magnum opus. This saga is brilliant, arresting, and fulfilling; a true story of the esoteric secrets that fester in the human heart that are now awakening the human spirit. Georgia, a juicy and witty rebel angel, comes to us through Wyllie's engrossing and engaging prose—a totally balanced story of humankind's evolution and struggles with the forces of the dark and the light. If you want the real truth about the fallen angels, read this book!"

BARBARA HAND CLOW, AUTHOR OF
*AWAKENING THE PLANETARY MIND*

# Revelations
### of the
# Watchers

## THE
## UNFOLDING
## DESTINY
### OF THE
## REBEL ANGELS

## TIMOTHY WYLLIE

Bear & Company
Rochester, Vermont

Bear & Company
One Park Street
Rochester, Vermont 05767
www.BearandCompanyBooks.com

Text stock is SFI certified

Bear & Company is a division of Inner Traditions International

Cataloging-in-Publication Data for this title is available from the Library of Congress

ISBN 978-1-59143-368-2 (print)
ISBN 978-1-59143-369-9 (ebook)

Printed and bound in the United States by Lake Book Manufacturing, Inc.
The text stock is SFI certified. The Sustainable Forestry Initiative® program
promotes sustainable forest management.

10  9  8  7  6  5  4  3  2  1

Text design and layout by Virginia Scott Bowman
This book was typeset in Garamond Premier Pro and Gill Sans with Baskerville and
Copperplate used as the display typefaces

To send correspondence to the representative of the author of this book, mail a first-
class letter to the author c/o Inner Traditions • Bear & Company, One Park Street,
Rochester, VT 05767, and we will forward the communication, or visit
**www.timothywyllie.com** for direct contact options.

*At the center of the universe is a loving heart that continues
    to beat
and that wants the best for every person.
Anything that we can do to help foster the intellect and
    spirit
and emotional growth of our fellow human beings, that is
    our job.
Those of us who have this particular vision must continue
    against all odds.
Life is for service.*

FRED ROGERS


*When you reach the end of what you should know,
you will be at the beginning of what you should sense.*

KAHLIL GIBRAN, *SAND AND FOAM*


*There are hundreds of paths up the mountain,
all leading to the same place,
so it doesn't matter which path you take.
The only person wasting time is the one who runs around
    the mountain,
telling everyone that his or her path is wrong.*

HINDU PROVERB

# Contents

Foreword: Timothy's Spiritual Legacy,
Continued Forever                                          xi

An Update for the Reader

Introduction: The Nature of Nurturing                      1

Challenging Questions Addressed, Deception and Self-
Delusion, Intuition and Certainty, Georgia's Intentions,
and the Variety of Starseeds

**1**    Tangled Lies and the Path to Awakening             5

A Necessary Deprogramming, the Indwelling Spirit, Animal
Fear, Caligastia's Rage, Starting a Business, Sleeping Around,
and Rigveda

**2**    Free Congregation and Adventure Relived            29

The Albatross, Visions of a Desert People, Aboriginal
Dreamtime, the Face on Mars, an Acid Test, Lost at Sea,
and Entheogenic Wisdom

**3**    From Ancient Secrets to a Modern
Entheogenic Breakthrough                                   47

A Forty-Thousand-Year Story, the Walk-Ins, an Aboriginal
Corroboree, Pituri, Atlantis Restored, Entheogenic
Shamanism, and Poseidon's Influence

## 4 The Reason of Experience 69

Atlantis, the Nile Valley and Sumer, Polytheistic Cults,
Nommo and Mali, James's Three Wives, Dolphin Telepathy,
and an English Inquisition

## 5 Deeper Secrets of a Deeper Being 90

The Blessings of Rebellion, the Toroidal Multiverse,
Scientific Priests, Introduction to Ketamine, Talking with
Angels, and Egyptian Mysteries

## 6 A More Perfect "Intelligence" 111

Nommo and Oannes, Angelic Coordination, Rare Cetacean
Insights, Rescued by Dolphins, Planetary Amnesia,
and a Seraph's Insights

## 7 Synchronous Existences and Understandings 131

Multiverse Completion, a New Symbiosis, Agondonters,
UFO over New York City, Calligraphic Humor, Phinsouse,
and Zandana's Fourth Density

## 8 Interdimensional Vision 150

A Magisterial Son, Tourists from Andromeda,
Lake of Glass, the Prince's Spy, Talking with Angels,
and Loving Your Enemies

## 9 The Interconnectedness of Us All 173

An Invasive Scan, Gradual Disillusionment, a Young Sorceress,
*The Helianx Proposition,* Starseed Relationships, and
the Commodore Speaks

## 10 Of Scrims and Where the Action Is 196

Extraterrestrial Substances, Peeling Away the Scrim,
Solonon, the Andromedan Starship, the Heart of Creation,
and the Fourth Dimension

## 11 Hidden Intentions 214

Serpents, Nagas and Dragons, the Deta Factor,
Aerial Battles, Akhenaten's Rule, and the Wounded Mother

## 12 What Lies Beneath Our Fears 236

Nonviolent Resistance, Catharsis, the Basis of Religion,
the Left-Hand Path, Yazidi Cosmology, the Peacock Angel,
and Brutal Thoughtforms

## 13 The Related Spirit of Events 261

Midwayer Conflicts, Threatened with Extinction, Machiventa
Melchizedek, the Conference-in-Spirit, a Rebellion
Reconciled, and Hypnotic Locks

## 14 Dissembling the Lies and Rebuilding from the Ashes 282

An Astral Encounter, Self-Healing, Amdon the Shepherd,
Machiventa Melchizedek's Mission, the Dome of the Rock,
the Healing Grotto, and Small Miracles

## Afterword: An Exciting Future 306

True Angelic Collaboration, Starting a Second Life,
the Islands and the Ocean, and the Experiment Continues

➤·◄

## Appendix 310

The Angelic Cosmology

## Glossary 314

## Index 323

## About the Author 335

# Timothy's Spiritual Legacy, Continued Forever

## An Update for the Reader

When *The Secret History of the Watchers* was published, I alerted the readers that Timothy had passed on from this life in October 2017. I shared the "succession plan" that Timothy and I had discussed in regard to carrying on this series and explained his spiritual legacy even further in his previous book, *The Rebel Angels among Us*.

My name is Daniel, and Timothy and I shared a "surrogate" father and son relationship. As he and I discussed the future of his work, Timothy directed me to "reach as many people as possible" through his writing, art, and music. He simply stated that if folks felt sufficiently moved and/or inspired by his creativity, then he wanted those creations in their homes.

I am still following that directive, and my desire is to let you, dear reader, know that Timothy's works continue on. Whether it is through his books, his art, or through the multitude of people he has inspired, he lives on—and he will continue to.

As you'll read in the afterword, Timothy was very excited about getting into the next volumes with Georgia. I honestly have no idea if Georgia will work with someone else to get these out . . . whether it is about bringing conclusion to the last thirty-plus years of Timothy's life, or starting with someone else.

Timothy penned copious writings. They are not formal books, but they are nevertheless beyond mind-blowing, and there is a good possibility—God willing—that I will organize them into something Timothy would want shared. His forte was not organization, so please be patient!

Timothy's website is up and running and is being updated as I go through his photos, writings, and other creations. Please feel free to visit it at www.timothywyllie.com.

As I mentioned in the previous book, the website now has both the information and the functionality to order an art print directly from the site. Folks can also contact me for additional information on originals (or anything else Timothy). I do not maintain Timothy's originals, which are in the care of Timothy's lovely "artner," June Atkin, but she and I work together closely, and I am glad to serve as an intermediary for her.

I helped Timothy with his books in the past (mostly in a support and editing capacity). Editing these last three books has been a sheer joy. As I read their words, I've heard Timothy's voice—and fondly recall seeing Georgia's cheeky "face" waking me up in the middle of the night when I lived with Timothy near the turn of the century. There is nothing like being in a deep sleep, sensing something hovering over you, then opening your eyes, and seeing eyes glaring back but six inches from yours . . . followed by a screeching "HELLOOOO!!!" at 3:00 a.m.

That memory will always be emblazoned in my mind when I think of Georgia, and Timothy and I were always in contact after that. So, again, I absolutely loved reading their words. Even if I knew some of the stories, others I didn't—and all of it has inspired me to "come back to center," as Timothy often advised me to do.

The Inner Traditions staff—and the remarkable June Atkin—deserve such praise and gratitude for their unfailing patience, love, and support. I am a husband, father, and professional, and I coach ice hockey and lacrosse to youngsters. Time is hard to find! Whereas most authors are always on standby and at the ready, I wasn't able to be. But Inner Traditions supported me anyhow. I had to again *become* Timothy while still being Daniel, and they bent over backward to help me bring Timothy's final books to life. I thank and love them all for it.

And thank you, dear reader, for your inquisitive nature and for supporting someone I love so dearly. I hope my efforts to bring Timothy and Georgia's wisdom to you has proved meaningful. I wish you nothing but the best in life, and would share one last "Timothy-ism" with you: "Know that you are right where you need to be. Calm yourself and know that everything is as it should be. If you find yourself in a situation you see as 'negative,' find the positive lesson in it that you are there to learn."

All blessings to you. I hope you enjoy this—the last volume of Georgia's *Confessions*.

DANIEL MATOR

## Note to the Reader
## Regarding a Glossary of Terms
## and the Angelic Cosmology

In this work the author has coined or provided specialized definitions of certain words, some of which are derived from *The Urantia Book,* a key source text. A complete list of these terms and their meanings has been provided in the glossary at the back of this book for your ready reference. The reader will find a brief overview of the Angelic Cosmology, also drawn from *The Urantia Book,* in the appendix.

# The Nature of Nurturing

Challenging Questions Addressed,
Deception and Self-Delusion, Intuition and
Certainty, Georgia's Intentions, and the
Variety of Starseeds

As I start this, the eighth volume of Georgia's *Confessions,* I've now had the opportunity to do a number of radio interviews and answer readers' letters. I've done this ever since the first volume of my collaboration with rebel angel Georgia, *Confessions of a Rebel Angel,* was published in October 2012. In this, I've found that there are several questions that seem to reoccur. While in most cases Georgia has already addressed these questions in her narrative, many people are curious to know what I, Timothy, think and feel about collaborating with a discarnate Watcher.

I have to admit that writing these books with Georgia was a complete surprise. It really was the last thing I expected—even though I've been working consciously with the angels for more than thirty years. There was never even a hint that this project awaited us in the future. And yet now it feels absolutely right. It is the intuitive and logical outworking of everything that deeply interests me. I had no idea that all those years of training—a training I didn't even know I was receiving—was leading me inexorably to this unusual collaboration.

Georgia isn't one of my two companion angels, both of whom I've come to know well over the years. And yet she says she has been with me throughout this current lifetime and, as it's turning out, a number of other previous incarnations as well. I accept that in many ways she knows me better than I know myself, which she is constantly demonstrating in the anecdotes she uses that are drawn from my life.

Can I be certain of all this? How can I be sure Georgia is a Watcher and not merely a figment of my imagination? How do I know Georgia isn't fooling me for her own covert purposes? How do I know I'm not fooling myself? These are a few of the questions that need some answering, and from me, not Georgia.

First, I should make it clear that life is never about certainty. If anything, demanding certainty is the delusion—science should have taught us that. When no one can be certain of waking up alive the very next morning, it would be foolish to demand certainty in such a delicate collaboration.

However, there's another form of knowing—intuition—whether something feels right. This is nothing like George W. Bush's infamous "gut feeling." Intuition is a far more subtle affair, and not quite as easily accessed as this so-called gut feeling . . . that simply echoes the state of the person's third chakra. Is it really surprising that George Bush—a man so evidently at war with himself—would project his self-hatred onto others and use his gut feeling to justify the killing of thousands upon thousands of people? And just to prop up his wilting self-esteem! That is not intuition.

Intuition has taken a lot of knocks recently as science, with its statistical methodology, tries to demonstrate that it knows best. But what isn't so readily factored in is that intuition is much like a muscle; if it's not used it will atrophy. And although we all use our intuition without being aware of it during our everyday lives, it's really only when we call on our intuition consciously that we can learn to trust the inner voice.

Asking our intuition for its counsel and then following through is a great deal more challenging than it sounds—particularly when the rational mind is telling us otherwise. It's not that intuition will be invariably correct but that in following intuition's counsel we can make our mistakes—and not the mistakes of those we credit for knowing more than us.

Having come to know Georgia over the course of my life, I've no reason to doubt she is a Watcher, as she says she is. Of course, she could be somebody or something else entirely; I'm not naive. Yet with seven books behind us, she has remained consistently who she is. Her narrative is coherent and deeply meaningful, and she is constantly surprising me with insights entirely new to me. If she is indeed setting me up for some hidden reason of her own, then she has shown no sign of it so far. Frankly—with what I know about her—harming me is the last thing she would want to do. It would be entirely out of character for the Georgia I've come to love and respect to want to take advantage of me. I feel confident about that.

Am I fooling myself? There's always a possibility, but if I am, I'm doing a damn fine job of it. I'm learning loads. This goes back to the certainty issue. How certain do I need to be that I'm not fooling myself? One hundred percent? Ninety percent? Seventy-five percent? Thought of in these terms, the question makes little sense. Certain enough, has to be the answer, I guess. What's the worst that could happen if I am deluding myself, or even if I'm being fooled by Georgia? I guess I'll have a red face at my afterlife review!

The short answer is that—after knowing Georgia as well as I do after the past four years of working so closely with her—I choose to take her at her word as to her claim of identity. It also serves me to consider her as an autonomous entity who has an existence separate from mine—and yet who can communicate with me through my inner imaginal world. Of course, it has also helped that since my near-death experience (NDE) I've been aware that angels are existentially real beings.

The concept of writing so closely with a discarnate entity was never as strange to me as it might be for someone lacking the long training and preparation the angels have been putting me through for these past fifty years. But this is all head stuff. Ultimately, the authenticity of Georgia's words can only be assessed on their coherence and their relevance. She doesn't appear to crave the agreement of other people.

As far I understand, she's narrating her half-million-year story to better understand for herself what has occurred on this world to shape it the way it is.

As for my story, she hopes I will gain some wisdom from her insights but—more than that—she believes her words will resonate with other rebel angels who are currently incarnated into mortal bodies and will help wake them up to who they truly are.

A word about starseeds: I've noticed Georgia has sometimes used *starseed* interchangeably with the clumsier *rebel angel incarnate*. I suspect she'll have more to say about this alternate name as we go along, for it's my impression the word *starseed* also refers to ET Walk-Ins, star people, and others of an extraterrestrial heritage who adopt human incarnation or use human bodies. Whether these starseeds, too, share the lineage of the rebel angels will be for each of them to discover for themselves.

I'd imagine that most of Georgia's readers are starseeds of one kind or another. Earth is a complicated planet facing a crucial stage in its evolution and—according to Georgia—this is the place to be. I'll have to wait for what Georgia has to say about the variety of starseeds. However, if her words resonate with you, I trust it will serve you to know something of the spiritual roots of the rebel angels and the history of the planet. It has certainly served me.

# 1

# Tangled Lies and the Path to Awakening

A Necessary Deprogramming, the Indwelling Spirit, Animal Fear, Caligastia's Rage, Starting a Business, Sleeping Around, and Rigveda

The arctic winds that howled down from Canada during the bitter cold spring of 1978—icing the trees in Central Park and whipping down the West Side avenues from Columbus to Riverside Drive—had finally yielded to the warming rays of an April sun.

It had been a wretched few months for the six who had left The Foundation Faith of God and established their own splinter group they had dubbed "The Unit." Although the split had been difficult—that was clear to me—there were breakthroughs, too. However, they'd been harassed mercilessly by those still in the main First Avenue community who had set the police on them; they'd been called traitors and betrayers; and they'd been taken to court by the Foundation. Mein Host had even suffered a vicious psychic attack. Yet they had all come through, they believed, stronger and wiser for overcoming the obstacles.

I believe the other five would have agreed with my ward, after the long deprogramming sessions they held every free evening, that Mary Ann—their erstwhile Goddess—and the Four, her direct proxies, had overplayed their hand and revealed the worst of themselves. In fact they had behaved shamefully. However, in this way, Mary Ann's vengeful actions only confirmed for the six of them the rightness of their decision to finally cut their ties with the community.

In both Dominic and my ward's case, this meant that thirteen years of complete devotion and daily dedication to Mary Ann and the group was now behind them. The other four had lived in the community for less time—ranging between five and nine years—so in some ways it was easier for them to make the break. They weren't carrying the baggage that Dominic and Mein Host, both longtime Luminaries, needed to come to terms with and release before they could comfortably reenter society. They had long since cut their ties with the outside world—the "World of Men," as they'd called society in general back in the day—and always with a sardonic twist. Now they needed to entirely reassess their relationship with a world they'd previously disparaged, ridiculed, and on which they'd turned their backs.

I found it interesting to observe the contrast between these two men, Dominic and Jesse (my ward, as he was known at the time in the Process . . . "Father Jesse"), who were both in their thirty-eighth year. I was intrigued to see how they were conducting themselves throughout this intense period of deprogramming they put themselves through. Although both of them were angry and horrified to hear some of what went on in the community, of which they hadn't been aware at the time, each approached and attempted to resolve the troubling issues, with rather different results.

My ward, for example, knew nothing of Mary Ann's constant, malicious efforts to separate Dominic and his wife, Victoria. Their marriage was one of the very few Absorptions—the weeklong period allowed to couples in the community to explore their mutual sexuality—to blossom into a loving, committed relationship. Yet it sounded like Dominic always had to plead with Mary Ann to permit them both to stay in the same Chapter together. He told the others that this would invariably subject him to the Oracle's scathing comments about his neediness and his being "led around by his short and curlies"—a favorite expression of hers.

Dominic and Victoria had a couple of children together, and the kids had been held over in the Children's Chapter after The Unit had made their exit. There was a jittery sense, whether or not true, that the two young children were being held hostage and were being used as leverage to try to get the couple to go back to the main community.

Dominic and the others, in their turn, knew little—or nothing—about all the sexual shenanigans that had gone on in the early days of the community. And only one of them knew about the sad demise of a baby—apparently from crib death—that had occurred some years earlier in the New Orleans Chapter. The sad event had been covered up for fear people would think the worst of the group.

Rachel, one of those in The Unit who had lived only in the main community for about four years, had a story to tell that revealed yet another duplicitous aspect of Mary Ann's personality. Here, for example, is how Rachel expressed her break with the community in my ward's 2009 book (*Love, Sex, Fear, Death: The Inside Story of The Process Church of the Final Judgment*, page 17). She wrote:

It was actually Mary Ann who made the first large crack in my devotion to The Foundation. As a junior member, and being on the lowest rung of The Foundation hierarchy, I was never permitted to meet Mary Ann. That privilege—to gaze upon the countenance of the Most High—was reserved strictly for the Luminaries.

With time, that started to bother me. Here I was, a total convert. I had handed over my entire life to the group. Not just all my worldly possessions, which included one of the day's sexiest cars—a Mazda rotary engine sports car—money, art, etc., but most importantly, my free will. I was told when and what to eat, to sleep, was sent into the street to raise money and was completely controlled 24/7.

It seemed wrong to me that I could not even know what "The Matriarch," as she was called, looked like. So I wrote to her, asking in a much more diplomatic and worshipful way than this, why couldn't I meet my leader? I got back a note card on the finest, thickest, embossed paper, in a large, strong and confident hand, saying essentially that I had it wrong. That she was just a "friend" of The Foundation and not its leader.

It was such an obvious lie and it had a profound effect on me. For her to deny she was the leader—while living in luxury on the toils of all the members, sending pronouncements from on high that affected all our lives—struck me as so out of integrity that I had to question The Foundation as a whole. My temerity to write to her must have had some repercussions on those above me, because it elicited anger at me from some of the Luminaries I had close relationships with as well. So, for me, this became the beginning of the end.

Rachel was a worldly and free-spirited New Yorker in her mid-thirties when she joined the community. She'd had to fight her impulses to prove herself worthy—usually a six-month process that she'd failed the first time around and was required to start again. Thus it had taken her almost a year to get in. Joining the community was a very considerable step for a woman who would herself admit that she had been a most unlikely candidate in the first place.

Her "failure" was merely to smoke a little pot one evening just before her six-month probation was up. She had promptly owned up to her transgression and found her honesty rewarded with having to start her probation period all over again.

As the stories and the secrets poured out in The Unit's evening sessions—far more than need repeating here—the members were constantly being faced with the discomforting duality. Was Mary Ann simply a con woman, always out for herself, who'd fooled them all? Or was she a harsh and demanding incarnate Goddess whom it had been a privilege to serve? Did she herself believe in her "pronouncements," as Rachel called them, or had she merely been "baffling them with bullshit" all along, without any care or compunction?

And then again, could it ever have been that simple?

No one had any doubt that Mary Ann was truly at the center of the action—although, she might have lied in her reply to Rachel's letter.

However, could their Oracle really be pinned down to a simplistic all good or all bad?

It was this question that lay at the center of the issue dividing the way in which Dominic and my ward dealt with these apparently opposing realities. Dominic—who admitted to having been fooled once by a con man back in Australia when he was in his late teens—became quite convinced he had been deceived once more. I believe, from my ward's brief and intermittent contact with him, that this is an opinion he holds to this day.

I observed in my ward's case that over time—when the anger and self-recrimination had been brought out and released—his resolution to this paradox lay in simply making this Manichean duality irrelevant. I could see that he tended naturally to choose to focus primarily on the totality of the experience itself, as well as all the wide variety of experiences he'd garnered in his thirteen years in the community.

He would ask whether it really mattered that much at the end of the day if all those experiences were the result of following a woman who actually was an incarnate goddess, or a woman who was believed by others to be divine, or a woman who merely believed herself to be a goddess—or indeed, just an outright con woman? The experiences were the experiences, whatever the reason given for them.

After all, these were the sort of experiences he would have been unlikely to have had over the normal course of an architect's life back in London. Although he wouldn't be able to express it until much later—it takes time to assimilate a cult experience—I've heard him express more than once his basic gratitude for his years in the Process.

I was struck by my ward's choice to follow this path of owning the experiences themselves for what he learned from them. I don't think this is a resolution that would so easily have occurred to me had I been as betrayed as Mein Host must have felt.

But then again, as I write these lines it came to me how remarkably similar is the situation in which I find myself in my relationship to my Lord Lucifer. It is a tribute to my simplemindedness that I have never really appreciated this obvious parallel until this very moment. I can only wonder if and how this insight might allow me a deeper understanding of the nature of Lucifer—and possibly even yield the yet deeper meaning of the angelic revolution.

What this approach did not appear to mitigate in Mein Host's life were some of the more practical aftereffects of all those years in a closed community. He found the sudden expanded multiplicity of choices that were now available to him to be quite surprising. For example, in a supermarket even a straightforward matter like choosing a breakfast cereal proved quite impossible to deal with. It was all too much. He hadn't been in an American supermarket for ten years—it had never been his function to do the community's shopping—and that was when an explosion of differing brands hit the shelves. And this was just the tip of an iceberg of indecision.

Entering a mystery school, a traditional monastic order, or a religious cult means, in essence, exchanging the hundred and one daily choices faced in everyday life for the one totally life-changing choice of commitment to the community.

It clearly wasn't an easy matter for my ward to fully reclaim himself.

I have to admit I was amused as I watched him one afternoon on the sidewalk outside his apartment building. He was obviously going out on an assignment, with some purpose. Yet I saw him walking; first one way, then reaching the middle of the block, then suddenly stopping. He paused, turned, and walked back a few paces, only to turn again and set out with more determination. Then he stopped again and walked back, before finally—after this went on half-a-dozen times, back and forth, back and forth—he appeared to make his decision and headed off toward the subway at Central Park West and 85th Street.

Leaving the community after so many years was one matter. Being able to discern what to shrug off and release—and what to keep as having authentic continuing value—was going to be quite another.

* * *

I completed the previous volume with a brief exploration of what I called "Prince Caligastia's monotheism."

I hoped to emphasize the contrast between the Prince's imposition of himself as the single Supreme God and the monotheism that the Multiverse Administration's first mission brought with them and taught in their city of Dalamatia. (The Multiverse Administration, or MA for short, is the celestial administration.) In this latter case, their teaching was of an Invisible God who was not only the Creator of all life—the universe and everything—but had also idiosyncratically chosen to reside in, and accompany, all mortal beings on their life's journey.

This is the Atman, the Indwelling Spirit, the Divine Spark, the Thought Adjuster of the Urantia cosmology. This aspect of the Creator has many names in many different cultures, because the presence of this Indwelling Spirit is a palpable spiritual experience available to all human beings if and when they are ready to embrace it. This, the teachers will have said, has held true for all time on all third-density worlds.

They might even have added (but I never heard any of the staff admitting this) that they, too, once possessed an Indwelling Spirit. This was when they were mortals on the worlds of their origination but were required to undertake this mission without the privilege of an Indwelling Atman. These they had left on Jerusem with the promise of being reunited with their Indwelling Spirit when they returned to the capital planet after completing their mission. As I have shown, it was one of the consequences of the planetary isolation that the sixty rebel staff members died prematurely, as the loyalist staff were also prematurely removed from the planet.

The Prince's staff, prior to the revolution, might even have dared to confide in the more advanced of their students that this indwelling of the Great Spirit in mortal beings is one of the true mysteries of the Multiverse. I've heard it reported that even the Melchizedek Brothers have no way of accounting for this most disarming of miracles. I'm aware I must have said this before, for it remains an astonishing fact for a simple Watcher to absorb.

You should understand that celestials—all the great ladder of beings who stand between you and the Most High—do not possess an Atman. It is for this reason that the process of mortal ascension is so central to the purpose of the material Multiverse. To put it in the most direct terms, as a mortal being it is your Indwelling Spirit that the celestials primarily serve in their efforts to engage with your personality and bring purpose to the mastering of your animal nature.

In the early years, the great truth of the Indwelling Spirit should have been known to all who were touched by the teachings of the staff. And by "early years" I mean well before the Lucifer Rebellion broke out some 297,000 years after our mission had arrived on the planet and upturned life as we knew it.

However, a purely expedient decision made by those of the Prince's staff particularly concerned with extending the MA's religious teachings had produced a destructive blowback. This has had some disastrous consequences over the millennia. When the College of Revealed Religion made the decision to couple the natural animal terror of the unknown possessed by most early humans with a fear of God, they laid the basis for the lamentable lie that continues to be used by ruthless priests to terrify their flocks. And as for the staff teaching the fear of God merely to make their own task easier when trying to control these unruly humans, you wonder? This, I have come to believe, was at the core of the fragmentation of the staff's original brief to create a unified and unifying world religion. It also fed directly into the rebel midwayers' assumption of their roles as faux divinities. They'd invariably found it easier to frighten human beings into following them, and they certainly had the capacity to carry out their threats.

Introducing the Creator as a god to be feared also gave Caligastia a convenient whip to use when he illegitimately declared himself God of this World. By that time enough people had been primed to fear God, which allowed him to move in and make his play.

It was as the fifth millennium before Christ was shading into the fourth that Prince Caligastia was starting to renew his efforts for the campaign to declare himself the sole Supreme God.

The Prince's previous efforts had rung too hollow to his rebel midwayers for his claim to take much hold among them. This time I reckoned the Prince was trying to take another tack by reaching out to various indigenous tribes in the Middle East. I suspected he might have believed this would be a last, desperate attempt to pull off his long dreamed-of coup. Then, through the influence of the converted tribes, he would be able to take effective control of the whole world.

You might think that as a Planetary Prince, Caligastia would already be in control—as the well-being of the world and its expanding population was still his responsibility. By the end of the fifth millennium, however, almost all of his natural authority had slipped through his fingers. If we are to believe Prince Caligastia, this had been through no fault of his own. I've frequently heard the Prince ranting on endlessly about how all his plans for helping the planet and its human population had been consistently thwarted by the MA. But he *would* say that, wouldn't he?

The Prince had been infuriated, for example, at the terrible ruin visited on his golden island of Atlantis—not once, but twice—and after all his ambitious plans to develop a truly advanced civilization. He'd always complained that the MA had it in for him—that they were singling him out from all the other Planetary Princes for especially harsh treatment. He would have known, I'm sure, that the comet predicted to destroy the people of Mu and their world could have easily been diverted by the MA's Energy Beings had they deemed it correct to do so.

He was particularly vicious in his lambasting of "the MA's lazy little drones" back on Jerusem who had done nothing to petition for an intervention by the Energy Beings, and again, not once, but twice. I don't believe that in his narcissistic fury the Prince ever fully absorbed that the devastation wrought by the comet must have necessarily been sanctioned on levels a great deal higher than that of his "lazy little drones" back on Jerusem.

Caligastia was never particularly close to Lucifer. I think he naturally felt far more affinity for Satan, his immediate superior.

It was Astar, one of my sister Watchers, who passed on that she'd overheard Caligastia cursing out Lucifer—not in his presence, of course—for not lending his weight to the Prince's demands for the MA to redirect the comet. He blamed Lucifer for his callous indifference to his plight, for being the one who could have persuaded the MA's senior bureaucrats to change their minds. But, no! Not a word back from him. Lucifer had done "absolutely nothing! Nothing!"

Astar had done a passable job of mimicking the Prince—her beautiful, soft face hardening in fury. "Wasn't Lucifer the System Sovereign?!" she wailed with just the right mix of the Prince's self-righteous anger and self-pity. "Lucifer could have pulled it off . . . he had the power. He could have done it if he'd really wanted to . . . but he never liked me. He never liked me! Right from the beginning . . . yes, right from the start. Right back then, Lucifer turned his back on me! He turned his back! Couldn't have cared less! After all I'd done for him . . ."

And so it went, said Astar, rolling her shining eyes on and on. Then, giggling, she told me that the Prince was so consumed with his rage that he seemed completely oblivious to Lucifer having been replaced by Lanaforge as System Sovereign on Jerusem soon after the revolution. The fact that Lucifer had been rendered essentially powerless in the affairs of the System since the revolution was either irrelevant to the Prince in his fury, or he was sounding to me in a far worse state than I remembered from our recent encounters in Göbekli Tepe.

Astar and I agreed, before we parted, that Caligastia's evil temper— and his propensity to blame anyone and everyone for his own troubles— did not bode well for this new monotheism he was imposing upon the Semitic tribes in southern Palestine. We knew the Prince had no choice but to work through his midwayers. He was unable to directly affect third-density reality, and the midwayers themselves were far too spoiled by their libertine independence to fall easily under the Prince's waning control.

Astar reckoned that Caligastia was mighty fortunate—yes, that's how she expressed it—to have found a midway clan prepared to cooperate with him. I have previously called them the Jehovah, although the clan wouldn't be known as a singular deity of that name until the mid-second millennium.

This small clan of midwayers had originally settled in the mountainous regions straddling southern Palestine and east across the Dead

Sea to present-day Jordan. The clan was known among their own order to be particularly authoritarian in the way they conducted their affairs. Unlike many other clans of midwayers, the Jehovah functioned best under the controlling figure of their patriarch.

Astar had thought it significant that the Jehovah were among the few midwayers who had fallen so completely under Caligastia's spell as to agree to serve as a front for him in his claim of absolute sovereignty. Apparently it had been their autocratic manner and clan structure—together with the strict laws by which the clan lived—that had made them vulnerable to a yet more powerful master than their own patriarch.

It was never going to be a simple matter to harness a fearful and belligerent people under the banner of a single all-powerful deity when they were surrounded by tribes with very different and mainly pantheist beliefs. This multiplicity of gods and goddesses—and the many beliefs they spawned—were the consequence of many millennia of rebel midwayer godplay. These self-proclaimed divinities weren't about to willingly relinquish their power—certainly not to serve under the Jehovah—whatever their Prince might have demanded.

You can infer from this how complicated and challenging the obstacles were to Caligastia's work with the Jehovah and, through them, with the tribes. There were short periods during which the Jehovah, through their priests (there always seems to be priests!), were able to galvanize and unify their people. Yet it was never long before a famine—or perhaps a plague, or a battle with a neighboring tribe, or simply the superior magic of another priest's god—would quickly disperse the unifying spirit of Caligastia's monotheism, and they would need to start all over again.

No, it wasn't going to be a simple matter to spread Caligastia's monotheism. There would be many lapses over the next millennium before the cult started catching on with the nomadic tribes roaming the lands east of the Mediterranean. By the mid-second millennium, this would become formalized into the religion of the Jewish people.

I report this, knowing full well I might risk offending my Jewish readers by associating the foundation of Judaism with the self-interested machinations of the corrupt Caligastia, but let's not forget the Nigredo stage of the alchemical process. Although the Prince's form of monotheism may have been initially founded of his ill-conceived megalomania, by the second millennium the Jewish people would discover themselves to have been chosen as host to one of the MA's most esteemed celestial teachers. This would be a certain Machiventa Melchizedek, who would be known as the High Priest of Salem during his ninety-four years of active service.

Oddly enough, the Jewish people would not have been chosen for this unique privilege but for Caligastia's monotheism. Despite its faults, it was thought to have more affinity with the MA's theocratic mandate than with any of the other belief systems of the time.

It would be an irony not lost on us Watchers to witness the MA outfox Caligastia yet again—when the Prince's monotheism became the platform upon which Machiventa Melchizedek would build a ministry that would span the world.

\* \* \*

The statement "You can take the man out of the Foundation, but it's far harder to take the Foundation out of the man!" proved true in Mein Host's case—yet in a somewhat more positive sense than the clichéd phrase suggests.

He must have become so accustomed to focusing his life on work during his years in the community that when he started his company in New York he continued to think nothing of putting in eighteen-hour days, week after week, to get the company off the ground. He clearly derived a lot of pleasure from building the business. He was fortunate to find himself to be the right man, with the right system, at the right time—and to be surprisingly successful from the very start.

DW Viewpacks Ltd., his mother's audiovisual company, had been marketing the photographic slide, filmstrip, and transparency storage system he'd thought up for Diana twenty years earlier. The company had been selling throughout Europe—but his system hadn't yet reached America.

These were the days before computers stored digital images from digital sources. The profusion of 35 mm color slides—and all those 4 × 4-inch, 4 × 5-inch, and 8 × 10-inch transparencies—made it almost impossible to store and conveniently access them. Transparencies are images; they are designed to be seen and not packed away in boxes or stored in carousels.

All major corporations maintained active audiovisual departments. Museums and art galleries needed to keep visual records; advertising and PR agencies collected thousands of images; and professional photographers of all types churned out color slides in massive numbers for even the simplest of projects. To my ward, it must have seemed like picking ripe apples off a tree. On a sales call to some vast—and inhumanly efficient—multinational corporation, he would frequently find every flat surface in their audiovisual department covered with loose slides and color transparencies. Mixed in were their unreadably labeled little boxes—generally upturned and spilling their slides willy-nilly over light table and floor.

My ward's slide storage system was so absurdly simple and obvious that once a client had seen it for themselves, there was invariably a moment of illumination and a slapping of brows. One day had been a particularly successful one in terms of sales for my ward; he'd scored sales on seven out of the eight sales calls he'd made. That evening I heard him joking with Marion that he was starting to collect the various different eureka moments his clients had when they "saw the light."

"And d'you know the most common reaction, Marion?"

"Their minds got blown?" she replied.

"Today five of the eight said some version of the same thing after I'd shown them a Viewpack. Know what they said? 'I could have thought of that!' That was their reaction . . . they could have thought of it! Yet here we were in their own art department, sitting at this light table literally awash with loose slides . . . and they're telling me they could have thought of it. Well, yes, of course they could have, but they didn't, did they?"

"And they had the filing cabinets right there! In front of their very noses!" Marion said, laughing. She knew how simple his system was and how the clients must have felt. After all, a Viewpack 24 was simply a transparent sheath with pockets for twenty-four slides, with the metal bar found in a Pendaflex file slipped into a groove, which allowed the Viewpack to hang in a normal filing cabinet.

"After they had their 'ah-ha!' moment, they'd look at me while holding up the Viewpack. Then they'd look at their bank of filing cabinets. When they looked back at me it was almost like they resented me for stealing their idea! Can you believe it?"

"But they didn't," Marion said, half listening. She'd heard this before.

"In the twenty years since I invented the thing—and in all the places I've been—I have never once seen anyone else come up with the idea . . . if it's so damn obvious!"

Marion added, "But people are buying it. I bet they love the accent."

"Oh sure, that's going fine, Marion, but it's not the point. The people are nice enough, I guess. A few of them are very interesting, but most of 'em are corporate drones. I feel like a fish out of water standing there in my business suit and going through the same spiel again and again . . . trying to change it slightly each time to keep myself interested. I'm starting to think I'm just not cut out to be a businessman. I can do it, sure, but I really don't enjoy it much."

"Haven't you committed yourself for five years?" Marion asked, surprised. She hadn't heard him say *that* before.

"I told Diana I'd aim for five years, but if after three years it's not working out we'd renegotiate. We agreed on that."

There was a long pause. Marion would have known of my ward's reluctance to let his mother down. Indeed, and although that had been a long time ago, he'd found it impossible to tell Diana the truth about life at Charterhouse—the distinctly upper-class school into which she'd so cleverly maneuvered to enter her son. He'd never been able to bring himself to tell her that existence there was brutal, stupid, and hypocritical and that much of his life was a living hell. He was a lot older now, and selling Viewpacks certainly wasn't a living hell. But I could tell it was starting to bore him, even as the first year of his commitment was drawing to a close.

I believe it was at this point that I knew—even as my ward was still clearly determined to fulfill his obligation—that running a business, however financially rewarding, would never satisfy his artistic soul or his questing nature.

It would take him another two years to arrive at the same conclusion for himself. However, those two years would turn out to be rich in a manner that would shape his future life in ways he would not have been able to recognize at the time.

Although he didn't know it, his companion angels were already laying the path that has brought him—thirty-two years later—to collaborating with me in writing these words.

Marion had attached herself to Mein Host with the grip and determination of a limpet and appeared as oblivious to the harsh currents of life as our little marine mollusk ignores the wild currents seeking to tear it off its rock. My ward even allowed himself a brief sexual dalliance with Valerie, one of the other members of The Unit, whom he'd always admired from a distance. I knew he'd entered into this relationship not only to satisfy his sexual desire now that he was no longer celibate but also to try to drive a wedge between Marion and himself.

If Marion took any notice of this deliberate ploy, she did not betray it in any way that my ward was able to read. She simply became more clingy and worked that much harder to sexually suck him dry. Mein Host had made it clear from the start that he wasn't prepared to make love with Marion. If she insisted in expressing her service by blowing him, however, that was a different matter. I've heard him say she accomplished this with palpable enthusiasm and no lack of skill—after responding well to my ward's helpful suggestions. Thus he wouldn't be true to himself to turn her away. That's what he said: "I wouldn't be true to myself," if he was to refuse her desire to pleasure him.

I recognized in this a desperate need to be true to himself in the face of Marion's intense and needy desire to throw herself at him. I knew he didn't want to repeat with Marion what he had done with Mary Ann. I'd heard him describe this as "giving myself away to a woman just because that's what she wants."

If this was unfair to Marion, who for reasons of her own had pledged herself to Jehovah to care for Mein Host, then that couldn't be helped. He'd had no part in her pledge. He didn't even know about it until she blurted it out one day when they were in The Unit. This was four years after she made the vow to her god. The difficulty lay in the fact that Marion, while not that bright, was particularly devout by nature. She was raised in the Jewish faith, and devotion came naturally to her when she transferred her allegiance to the community's version of Jehovah. To Marion, Jehovah wasn't an archetype or a convenient label for a personality type . . . Jehovah was a very real god indeed. And Jehovah was famously not a god to appreciate an empty vow.

There was nothing my ward could say that would deter Marion, and I've heard him express how awkward he felt because pushing her out of his life meant she'd have to break her sacred vow. He would have been aware by this time that she'd only left the community because of him—and her need to continue to fulfill her pledge. The sad irony was that of all the people in the community, Marion—for the ten years she was in the group—would have been considered by the others as one of the most committed and the most "gung ho" of all the members. Marion really should have stayed with the community. That's where she belonged.

I could tell it weighed heavily on my ward to find himself responsible—through no fault of his own (as he saw it)—for this woman whom he didn't even *like* and who'd given up her chosen life in the community to be with him.

For a young man who, for the previous thirteen years with few exceptions, had been celibate, it was natural to want to indulge in some of the pleasures he'd missed out on in all that time. I know he also hoped that his various affairs—and he was quite open about them with Marion—would help her make the decision that he wasn't really worthy of this sacred vow of hers.

More precisely I have heard him say he had slept with seven

different women during this period and that nothing seemed to make any difference to Marion's dedication to her vow. Sure his taking other lovers aggravated her—despite the arguments in which he'd try to get across that she didn't own him. After all he hadn't asked for this sort of dedication, and no one had the right to impose themselves on another person. This was true even if they'd promised their god to do so, and especially if that person didn't really want it. But of course—in Marion's straightjacketed mind—she made it clear that her vow to Jehovah far outweighed any objections my ward could come up with, however unfair it might seem to him.

If openly sleeping with so many different women had not put her off, then what was Mein Host to do?

*  *  *

If I'm thought to be focusing more on activities in the Middle East than in the rest of the world—as well as the emphasis I place on life around the Mediterranean basin—then please keep in mind a couple of key factors.

I can only really report on what I've observed, what I've overheard, and what I speculate, and I tend to be drawn to where the energy is most vital and progressive. I am also addressing my ward in this narrative, and he is someone with a Western educational and cultural background. As well, I imagine that most (but not all, I hope) of my readers will probably share Mein Host's cultural background.

However, with that said, I will add a few brief notes on observations that either a sister Watcher or I had made in other parts of the world. It was perfectly true, for example, that throughout the fifth and the fourth millennia, the population of the Asian continent—as well as the subcontinent of India—were both expanding far more rapidly than in the West.

There'd been periodic efforts in China to unify the clans and tribes under a single power, but they'd invariably failed. The very act of trying to bring the different tribes together all too often produced the friction that drove them apart.

The great coastal cities of India—first built after the Lemurian diaspora and that had then dominated the subcontinent for thousands of years—had disappeared under the rising sea levels of the tenth millennium. This had left the increasingly densely populated country in social chaos. India would become further fragmented as hostile and conflicting warlords—as well as rampant banditry—challenged any real chance for social advancement on the subcontinent.

The expanding population of southern China was starting to settle into what must have been one of the first of the feudal societies of the modern era. Feudalism simply added, if I'm to be cynical, a slightly more formalized approach to the mutual distrust and belligerence displayed by the feudal lords. Over the centuries, the power would flip like a hot potato between the various feudal lords and their clans as one after another gained its moment in the sun.

In spite of that—if I were to contrast the conduct of those Far Eastern extended family clans and their feudal lords with the tribes in the Western World—the most noticeable difference was the comparative lack of aggression among the clans in the Far East. Mind you, it was only a comparative lack of aggression, because what I have observed of the tribal conflict in the Middle East has been so exceptionally violent.

Granted, the feeling was subtle. Yet it seemed to me that those generations of feudal lords in China were invested in achieving a balance—uneasy though it might have been—among the various, different clans. They were more invested in this than they were in the constant drive for supremacy that Caligastia had been stoking with such determination in the West.

At the time, I attributed this greater desire for a peaceful coexistence that I found in China as most likely due to what may have remained of the teachings of Vanu and Amadon. I believed that the ancient teachings must have still carried a resonance. This, I believe, was demonstrated by the widespread prevalence of ancestor worship throughout the East—a belief that continues to this day.

I say I attributed this at the time to Vanu's teachings—and I'm sure they must have helped—because I didn't know then that both China and India were being used by the MA to seed some of those clans with rebel angels at early stages in their reincarnational cycles.

I've previously referred to the difficulties and challenges faced by a starseed over the course of their first half dozen mortal lifetimes. It wouldn't have been altogether surprising, for example, to find rebel angels during their early incarnations in physical vehicles that would currently be labeled as autistic. Other starseeds might choose the briefest, and sometimes the most violent, of lifetimes. Rebel angels at the start of their cycle will frequently decide on short, brutal lives to accelerate their spiritual progress. They will choose this route as a way of burning off karma as rapidly as possible. The more advanced among them may well choose to use their incarnations for acts of self-sacrifice, so that others might learn and grow in spirit from their lives and deaths.

If it is a challenging and painful affair for an angel to assume mortal incarnation, this uncomfortable limitation also holds true for extraterrestrials willing to spend time on a third-density planet. However, as physical beings, it's a rather less stressful process for those from other material worlds.

There is a race of semiaquatic beings, the Nommo—on a world in the Sirian star system—that requires the members of their race who are willing to incarnate in a human vehicle to first spend a lifetime (or multiple lifetimes) in a cetacean vehicle. And I have previously noted the problems those Walk-Ins from Andromeda had when they were unable to cope with the confusion of energies in Manhattan. And these were material beings!

In truth there is no real preparation for the impact of a third-density world on an angel's subtle energy system—and her far weaker emotional body.

If I'm belaboring this point—and I am aware I've noted this before—it's to remind myself, as much as the reader, of some of the inherent demands of a human incarnation.

It is all a question of the multiplicity of complex choices.

As a Watcher, for example, I have never needed a particularly resilient emotional body to fulfill my functions as an angel. Before the rebellion I'd never had any reason to spend much time in Earth's astral regions, let alone get close enough to human beings to become empathically affected by their unpredictable and extreme, emotional mood swings.

This all changed after the angelic revolution.

If I were to stay at my post—and not be relocated with so many others of my kind to the so-called prison planets—I realized I would have to throw myself, as much as any Watcher can, into the emotional bandwidth of human life. I believe the formula is simple: the more challenging the emotional choices available to an individual—and more importantly, how wholeheartedly those choices are exercised—the stronger and more resilient will be that individual's emotional system.

I feel myself most blessed, for example, to have this working relationship with my ward because it allows me to experience his emotions as mine. Thus it toughens me up by proxy. Although I have to admit, I won't really know the truth of this until I, too, am privileged to be able to claim a mortal lifetime.

It is only now—when I've needed to gather my thoughts for this narrative—that I've been shown further details about the return of the rebel angels. I've previously confessed to being surprised at observing that cluster of starseeds serving on Atlantis—and in very lowly positions, too, as far as I could make out. Slaves, many of them. Frankly, I think I'd prefer autism to slavery!

I hadn't spent the time in Asia that I had in the West, so I didn't take much notice of this impulse I observed toward greater harmony among the Eastern tribes while it was actually going on. Yet in retrospect it seems clear to me that the burgeoning early Chinese cultures—and the advances made in medicine, the arts, and in social engineering—were the product of a combination of Vanu's teachings and the later influx of starseeds.

I say "Vanu's teachings," but, of course, Vanu's actual teachings had long since become lost to time and to the inevitable erosion of information in an oral culture. Yet such was the coherence of those ancient teachings that I found something of the truth of them had become embedded in the psyche of the people. This allowed a more peaceful location for a normal human lifetime. For this reason, southern China—during the fourth and third millennia (or so I've been told)—was being used by the MA for the placement of small groups of rebel angels during their early mortal lifetimes.

The various different tribal cultures that had developed throughout the Indian subcontinent by the fourth millennium, on the other hand, presented a somewhat more complicated scenario than China. There had long been a mixing of a wide variety of beliefs in India, coming from both East and West and spreading along the Silk Road.

I gathered, too, that India during this same era was thought to be a fitting environment for fostering the mortal life of rebel angels—who were at a more advanced stage in their reincarnational cycles. And here was the difference between the two continents.

In India there were far fewer starseeds per generation than in southern China during the same time frame. In India, the rebel angel starseeds were generally further along in their cycles. So as individuals, some of them were able to make a profound impact on the spiritual life of the people on the subcontinent.

This would lead to a gradual accumulation and codifying of their beliefs in the Vedas, primarily as an oral tradition that flowered throughout northern India and becoming—by the mid-third millennium—the basic teachings of the Hindu faith. As any written records of those early times have long ago disintegrated, this has given the impression that the "Vedic Age" blossomed somewhat later than it really did.

Academic religious historians, dependent as they are on existing written texts, believe the Vedic belief system peaked between 1,500 BCE and 1,200 BCE; but the truth is that those who followed the Vedic path in the fourth and third millennia were far stronger and more committed to their faith than those of later eras.

An oral tradition can be an inherently powerful and effective medium for the reliable preservation and transfer of a continuing thread of knowledge. A storyteller would move from village to village weaving his sacred tales to villagers who knew the stories just as well as the teller and would chant and sing the words along with him. The sacred knowledge embedded in the stories would then be distributed broadly throughout a population. Because of the villagers' active participation there was also a far greater emotional investment in recalling the information accurately.

When an oral tradition starts to be written down and recorded in texts, the knowledge becomes restricted only to those who are able to read. This then becomes a turning point in the early times of any literate society, when the shaman and the storyteller get replaced by priest and priestess—with all that that entails.

Written knowledge can then offer a tempting tool used by the unscrupulous to establish their status. It can also be the dawning of deceit when texts become changed or distorted to serve the demands of the time. As a result, many fragments and written texts from those ancient times will just as easily confuse the modern mind.

For example, one could use the aforementioned example of those academics who have claimed that the Vedic Age flourished in Northern India from 1,500 BCE to about 600 BCE. And yet the Rigveda—one of the very oldest of the existing sacred texts (as a result of etymological analysis)—is believed to have been composed by a number of voices sometime in the mid-second millennia. My collaborator's research places it sometime between 1,700 BCE and 1,100 BCE. Yet the extant texts were actually written down in the fifth century BCE—as the Vedic Age was winding down. It was also the time that Buddhism was gaining traction, so there would likely be every reason for the Vedic scribes to place more emphasis on the immediate relevance of the Rigveda for those turbulent times.

Admittedly the materials used for writing throughout this period—birch bark and palm leaves—were extremely fragile and liable to disintegrate in tropical climes. Thus it's hard to say with any certainty exactly when, in fact, the Rigveda was actually composed. Naturally the scribes who wrote it down would have recorded the manuscripts in a manner linguistically familiar to them, so that doesn't really establish their origination.

Perhaps I can put this confusion to rest for my ward's clarity of mind, even if it will have little relevance as a citation for the academic.

I observed the original sources that came to be the Rigveda first gathering among the seminomadic tribes of the fourth millennium. Despite the constant movement of the tribes throughout the region— from Persia and the Caspian Sea to the mountains of Kyrgyzstan through Central Asia and south to the Punjab—it was in the Punjab that the teachings composing the Rigveda eventually took hold. These sacred teachings were then augmented by many generations of storytellers. I am told that certain astronomical references to stellar events and planetary alignments in the Rigveda can now be shown, thanks to computers, to have occurred in the fourth and third millennia.

I have indulged in this digression on the origination of the Rigveda to emphasize the significance of the latter part of the fourth millennium as a melting pot of different beliefs and cosmologies. I never witnessed any direct contact among those tribes subject to Caligastia's strict monotheism and the mountain nomads who were composing the Rigveda at around the same time. However, a few lines from the Rigveda's "Hymn of Creation" demonstrate how very different were the two conceptual frameworks. On the one hand, there were the absolutist claims of Caligastia's Jehovah with all his angry threats and claims of jealousy. On the other, as charmingly illustrated in the "Hymn of Creation," we find a delightfully honest tribute to cosmic ambiguity.

> *Then even non-existence was not there, nor existence,*
> *There was no air then, nor the space beyond it.*
> *What covered it? Where was it? In whose keeping?*
> *Was there then cosmic fluid, in depths unfathomed?*
> *But after all, who knows? And who can say whence it all*
> *came, and how Creation happened?*
> RIGVEDA 10.129.6

*The gods themselves are later than Creation, so who*
*knows truly when it has arisen?*
*Whence all Creation had its origin, he, whether he*
*fashioned it or whether he did not, he who surveys it*
*all from the highest heaven, he knows, or maybe, even*
*he does not know.*

RIGVEDA 9C–129

Whether or not he who surveys Creation from the highest heaven truly knows when it had its origin is an insight no more available to me now than it would have been to the Jehovah of the fourth millennium, for all his grandiose claims. Such knowledge, if it truly exists, is far above the pay grade of a Midwayer, a Watcher, or a Planetary Prince.

I can say with certainty, however, that Creation did not find its origin in a big bang.

# 2

# Free Congregation and Adventure Relived

## The Albatross, Visions of a Desert People, Aboriginal Dreamtime, the Face on Mars, an Acid Test, Lost at Sea, and Entheogenic Wisdom

The Unit closed its doors in the spring of 1979, and by this time Marion had managed to insert herself not only into my ward's bed, but she was also helping him out with his Viewpack business. She knew how to make herself useful, did our Marion. She packed up and labeled Viewpack parcels; kept the books while my ward was out making sales calls; sat in the rental van fending off traffic wardens while he was making the weekly deliveries; and she otherwise ran various essential errands. She was starting to make herself indispensable, which I imagine must have concerned my ward and his plans to liberate Marion from her vow.

They'd moved from the apartment they shared with the four others on Central Park West to a smaller place on West 85th Street. It was a block west of Central Park. Marion had found the place, which was small in the manner of most New York apartments. However, it was on the ground floor with access to a private back garden and had a finished basement—perfect for storing all the Viewpacks on metal racks. Apart from one tiny bedroom only a couple of feet larger than the double bed, the single spacious living room and the basement became the offices of DW Viewpacks America. Having almost no personal possessions between them, the apartment—designed ideally for a single person— would turn out to work perfectly for the three years my ward lived there.

Once again he had tried to make a break with Marion before moving, but she'd woven herself so fully into his life by this time that expedience won the day and they moved in together.

I believe Mein Host thought that by throwing himself so wholeheartedly into his business, eventually Marion would get bored and leave him for good. Whether or not that may have worked was rendered irrelevant by a plan he'd been quietly hatching since he'd been a member of The Unit.

There had come a time in The Unit when donating no longer paid the bills. Besides, I don't believe they thought it any longer correct to raise money on the streets for a church they no longer supported. Each member of the little group now needed to find a way of making her or his own money as best as they could in a brutal and expensive city.

Marion had hung out her shingle as a psychic counselor, as had three of the other young women in The Unit. As such they continued to do the empath readings that they had developed in the community. And Marion was good at it, there was no denying that. She was empathic enough to help her clients, in most cases, and would bask in the love that her counseling seemed to evoke from them.

One of Marion's clients was a young man whom I'll call Adrian, who'd recently become the boyfriend of Rachel, the sixth member of The Unit. There had never been any love lost between Marion and Rachel, and yet Adrian's progress as a result of Marion's therapy was undeniable, and for many months all went well. His relationship with Rachel deepened as a consequence of Marion's help, and Rachel, who was mature enough to be cautious around men, had started to let down her guard to allow herself to fall in love with Adrian.

Adrian was a tall and exceptionally handsome young man in his late twenties, with the dream of becoming an actor. He would get a few small jobs, but handsome though he was, he didn't really possess the inner strength to pay his dues. He was the sort of man who desperately needed a strong woman in his life to galvanize him to action and tell him what to do—and even then he was likely to wilt at any moment.

It must have been only too obvious to Mein Host that Adrian was a far more appropriate match for Marion than he'd ever been. Adrian actually seemed to blossom as a result of Marion's pushy, busybody ways. This was a manner that had served her well in the community, as well as with the sort of clients who were drawn to her counseling services.

Mein Host, while obviously appreciating strong and confident women—he had grown up with one—obviously disliked it if the woman in question tried to boss him around. Bossiness had never been part of his leadership style; he found charm worked much better. So Marion's high-handed manner—which had gotten more obnoxious after she'd left the community, as I'd frequently observed—infuriated my ward.

I believe it was when Mein Host realized this obvious potential connection between Marion and Adrian that he started taking every opportunity to encourage Marion's interest in the man. It was clear how much Adrian needed her, and my ward was pretty sure that Adrian was already in love with her.

Marion, however—whose integrity would have insisted on keeping the client/counselor relationship all aboveboard—continued to resist acting on his lavish embellishments of Adrian. As the weeks turned to months—and despite Adrian continuing to flourish as a result of his therapy sessions—it looked like my ward's machinations behind the scenes weren't going to prove effective in transferring the focus of Marion's obsessive attention over to Adrian.

There came a day—some seven months after Mein Host and Marion had moved the business to the West 85th Street apartment—when she confessed to having started an affair with Adrian. She claimed to have been responsible about stopping the counseling sessions before they'd started their affair, as if by choosing to be ethically responsible she could assuage the guilt betrayed by her emotional body.

Frankly I was amused to watch my ward's reaction to this revelation. He couldn't afford to appear too jubilant. Nor, obviously, did he want to display any hint of an emotion that might discourage her from her attraction to Adrian. To add to the situation's emotional complexity— as well as to further his intention of making sure Marion left him with the feeling that she had honorably fulfilled her vow to Jehovah—he had to get across that she'd be moving on to somebody who needed her more than he did. This meant he would have to display a shocked reaction to her confessing the affair—as she would have expected— while simultaneously appearing reluctant to lose her. Yet he'd have to do all that without putting her off from taking the step he'd hoped for all along.

It had been important for my ward that Marion not feel chucked out of his life. She had done her best for him; it really wasn't her fault he didn't get along well with her. The woman had been useful to him as a personal assistant in the community. However, he was clearly averse to the sort of partnership for which she was pushing.

He'd long been aware that Marion's bossy manner was merely a veneer covering an insecure and frightened child. He was kind enough to understand that she needed—for her self-esteem—to emerge from their relationship feeling that it was *her* decision to leave. I overheard him once describe his actions during this period as "putting a little passive aggression to good use."

Yet having admitted her growing attachment to Adrian, Marion still seemed resolute in her vow to serve Mein Host and continued to make no move to leave the apartment. The situation at this point became so emotionally charged that it was painful for me to get too close to any of the players. I should add—at my collaborator's insistance—that he wasn't particularly proud of the deceptive lengths he had to go to to get out from under Marion's formidable grip. It was an impossible situation in which he found himself. He was faced with a determined—but not too bright—woman who'd pledged to her god Jehovah to serve him all his days. This situation was never going to be easily dislodged.

However, there was a curious incident that occurred during this purgatorial period that, in its own way, defined all too clearly for each of them who was who and what was what. My collaborator hasn't known this until now. Yet it was this incident that precipitated Marion's decision as to where to finally place her considerable energy.

When I observed earlier that Adrian lacked a certain inner grit, I was only stating what would have been painfully obvious to Marion over the course of his therapy. She had complained about Adrian's lack of emotional strength to my ward on a number of previous occasions. However, he still appeared surprised to find her concerned enough to ask him to help her in toughening Adrian up. Of course it was in my ward's interest to go along with her wishes if it would hasten her exit from his life.

It was possible that Marion thought this was a way of keeping both men in play, but she wasn't a duplicitous woman—so it was more likely to be a sincere request. Yet she could just as well, in her mind, have been throwing down the gauntlet between the two men; may the best one win her. Marion was a young woman with an unreasonably high opinion of herself, so I wouldn't put this beyond her romantic imagination. Given all this, the way the incident played itself out was more revealing than perhaps she might have wished.

It seemed that Adrian, doubtless under Marion's orders, was hoping to push himself through his fears and wanted Mein Host—whom he knew had some previous experience with entheogens—to accompany him on what Adrian had built up to be the most important trip of his life.

Adrian scored some blotter acid and had arranged for his family's vacation house on the Connecticut coast to be empty the following week. He did this so they could trip in peace—as well as provide a familiar and safe environment for Adrian.

The scene was being set for an event that would test Mein Host's mettle to the limit. It would reveal Adrian to himself in a way he could never have imagined, and it would finally decide in Marion's mind which of the two men needed her most.

* * *

It is certainly a curious fact that all three of the major Western monotheistic religions not only emerged from desert people but also developed in very much the same region of the world. It's really rather odd. Why not China? Why not America?

Of course I feel bound to include the Prince's mission and the city of Dalamatia on the Persian Gulf, as well as the second mission's two gardens. One garden was on a peninsula at the eastern end of the Mediterranean and the other was in Mesopotamia. Given this, I find the need to question what exactly it has been about the Middle East that has made it so spiritually potent to this day.

There is a certain centrality to the region geographically from which ideas could potentially disperse most efficiently throughout three contiguous continents. It wasn't a region affected by the periods of glaciation, which would have seriously impeded the first two missions had they been placed in more vulnerable locations. It may also have been—as some have suggested—that deserts are pure, uncluttered, and favor thoughts of the transcendental. Yet when the first mission decided to build its city on the Persian Gulf, the Arabian Peninsula was still a verdant and fertile land.

As I explored this odd coincidence, it came to me that once the Prince's mission made its decision to locate in the Middle East, then all the subsequent intraterrestrial missions would potentially benefit from piggybacking on the work of the previous ones. This in itself would have been enough to have attracted Caligastia and many of his rebel midwayers to that region in their campaign of sabotaging the MA's missionary efforts.

As I trust I have demonstrated in this narrative, there was much else happening in different parts of the world. The Islands of Mu, for example, couldn't be farther away from the activities in the Middle East. North and South America, too, remained relatively isolated from what was occurring in the Middle East until the second millennium.

The Aboriginal natives of Australia had been completely isolated since the last ice age when the rising sea levels overran the land bridge connecting the island continent with New Guinea. This meant that the Aboriginal tribes had remained completely unaffected by anything that was happening in the Middle East—or anywhere else for that matter. This lasted from the tenth millennium BCE until the eighteenth-century European voyages of discovery some twelve thousand years later.

This long period of isolation from the belief systems springing out of the Middle East throughout that era also carried the advantage of attracting minimal attention from the Prince and his rebel midwayers.

When the original tribes migrating south through the Philippines about sixty-five thousand years ago crossed the land bridge to Australia, they traveled in small familial clans. They had no idea what a vast continent awaited them.

The clans naturally tended to follow the coastline to the east and west in both directions before turning south to ultimately encircle the island. Over the course of this long circumambulation, they had grown in number as more and more migrants arrived. The clans had grown in size and scope as the earlier arrivals then expanded into tribes that started to venture farther inland.

Unlike any migrant people I've observed, the Aboriginal tribes had the advantage of understanding that the land they had adopted was in fact one extremely large island, and that—as far as they'd discovered—it was also uninhabited. The early people of all cultures had a close relationship with the earth, and the isolation and insularity of the Australian Aboriginal tribes and the bleak vastness of the interior conspired to give them a particularly intimate understanding of the landscape.

The nomadic tribes grew in number over the millennia until there were well over six hundred of them. Each had its own language and tribal traditions, and all followed their annual migratory patterns to and fro across the continent. With no compelling reason to unify, the tribes continued their nomadic lives with remarkably few intertribal conflicts for the next fifty millennia. With no Prince Caligastia and few rebel midwayers to stoke their aggressive ambitions—and with no territory to conquer (the usual reason for any intertribal hostility)—they had to work out how to coexist for themselves.

Given that the tribes lacked a common language, they evolved a sophisticated form of communication based on elaborate dances—often in emulation of the local animals—and chants with which they evoked the topography of the landscape through which they passed. These ultimately became the song-lines down which their shamans and sages were able to travel in their altered states of consciousness.

I found it intriguing that regardless of all those different languages, there appeared to be a general agreement among most of the tribes of what became known as Dreamtime. I've since attributed this tribal familiarity with the astral realms—as well as with the fourth dimension—to the credence and power given over to the shaman, the sorcerer, and the magician.

Nomadic tribal life was always simple, even if it wasn't always easy. Living off the land could have its challenges, yet on the whole, much of the continent was rich with game so food wasn't an issue. The cycles of nomadic life would tend to follow the seasons and the movement of the animals, but in the case of the Aboriginal tribes of Australia, there was a far higher level of personal conscious awareness and a sense of responsibility for maintaining the integrity of the land they'd been given. These would have been the tribes who would have had some ancient memory of Vanu and Amadon, if not some of their teachings. They were always more focused on tribal relationships—and on keeping up tribal traditions and rituals—than they were driven to exert power over others or develop a technology with which they might achieve this more effectively.

Of course they weren't entirely blameless. There were the normal feuds you would expect of a spirited people—such as thefts (especially of another tribe's womenfolk). And yet there was never the organized violence that characterized the tribes in the Northern Hemisphere under the control of Caligastia's midwayers.

Idiosyncratically, for all their hundreds of languages, the Aboriginal people were great communicators with much to share. This became formalized into a system of corroborees whereby the different tribes were able to interact.

The corroboree was the core of an intertribal tradition of gathering together for a day (or five) of festivities when a couple of tribes crossed paths on their annual migration routes. The news and gossip was shared through dance and music, while the genetic vigor of the tribes was sustained by the young men and women of the different tribes who were able to interact with one another in this festive setting. In the purely material sense, the lives of the Australian Aborigine had changed very little over all those millennia.

They became masters of adapting to their environment. They demanded little of their surroundings but good hunting and sufficient water. Their surroundings were simple. They evidently experienced themselves as an integral part of the living landscape by playing an active role in sustaining the natural world through their songs and rituals.

Then over time, having mastered their relationship with their surroundings—and with no real concept of material progress in the Caligastian sense—they were able to discover a deeper and more authentic apperception of the inner realms. Some of the tribal shamans also developed a sophisticated spiritual technology for traveling out of their bodies, which allowed them familiarity with a number of extraterrestrial races.

Mein Host recalls a conversation he had with Marilyn Ferguson, author of *The Aquarian Conspiracy,* soon after images of the "Face on Mars" first started appearing in the press. She said she'd been talking to an Australian Aboriginal elder who told her casually they knew all about the so-called face, because they'd seen it when they'd traveled out-of-body to Mars.

The Australian Aborigine was a far more subtle and sophisticated human being than the British colonists could ever have admitted when they stole their country.

When Mein Host was spending time in Australia in the 1980s, his companion angels guided him one early evening to a rundown café off the beaten track. It was a modest affair, with about twenty locals lazing around tables. Each table had its own red-and-white checked plastic tablecloth, its candle stuck in a Chianti bottle, and a glass ashtray— overflowing with cigarette butts, burned matchsticks, and bottle tops.

The front of the café was open to the lane outside, and the sound of the sea drifted up from the massive Pacific Ocean breakers beating on the beach at the base of the cliff beyond the lane and the dunes.

There was a subtle sense of expectation in the place that my ward commented afterward felt as though some of the people there might have had some idea of what was coming. He also said he was surprised to see an unusual racial mix, with more than half of those present clearly of Aboriginal background. Under normal conditions in a regular café, he said, there might have been one or two Aborigine, if that. The local Aborigines generally preferred to keep to themselves.

There was some movement over by the counter as one of the men—a dark-skinned Aborigine perhaps in his early forties—hoisted himself up onto one of the barstools, one elbow on the counter, and a large didgeridoo gripped in his left hand.

The chatter in the small room died down as the first deep, tentative rumble from the didg set the glasses and cups on the shelves behind the counter into a tinkling accompaniment. A whispery jingle from the cups' sympathetic resonance brought some quiet laughter from the tables at the front before the deep roar of the grandfather didg over-whelmed the tinkle.

Three or four more locals slid quietly into the back of the café and found a bench seat to perch on. A skinny young waitress—blond hair tied up in a bun, her face sallow with eyes rimmed red by smoke and exhaustion—lethargically slid between the tables to collect their orders. The didg shifted tone, and suddenly the animals of the outback were resonating down the didg. Their purring calls and all their barks and growls were slyly embedded within the vibratory structure of the sound itself. It felt like the animals were coming to join the small crowd.

A couple of weeks earlier, when my ward had been shopping in an open mall in Coff's Harbor, he had come across a young Aborigine sitting on the ground. The aborigine's back was against a shop window, and one of his legs was outstretched with the end of a didgeridoo perched on his toe. My ward had stopped to listen on a nearby bench and rolled himself a cigarette before sitting back with his eyes closed, the smoke from his rolly drifting languidly in the humid heat of an Australian summer.

When the young man was sure of Mein Host's attention, out from the didg came not the sounds of the birds and animals of the bush, but all the sounds of city life. There was the roar of a truck accelerating from a stop, the gear changes clearly audible. Next was the warning beep beep beeping of a bus backing up. This folded into the throaty boom of a cruise ship's foghorn, which then segued into the staccato whine of a passing police car's siren—complete with full Doppler effect. This was followed by the crash of a garbage truck lifting—and then noisily dropping—the contents of a wheelie into its capacious belly. There were the familiar jackhammers, the car horns, the rattle of an escalator, the incomprehensible shouts of a boy selling newspapers, the honks of a variety of car horns, the shriek of a child, and a burst of a drunken woman's laughter with a hysterical edge to it. All this and more poured out of the man's didg for my ward's obvious wonderment.

He said afterward that in all his time in Australia he had never heard a didgeridoo played this way. My ward felt that by incorporating all the mechanical sounds of city life into the rhythms of his didg, what the young Aborigine was really doing was reclaiming and owning the small Westernized coastal town of Coff's Harbor. He was trying to snatch back what had been stolen from his race after the arrival and the subsequent occupation by the British, first as a prison colony, and then as a brutal colonial outpost of an empire upon which the sun was soon to set.

In emulating the sounds of a technological society on his didgeridoo—in the same way as he might have reproduced the calls of the wildlife had he been playing his instrument in the outback—he was drawing a sonic equivalence. The shrieks of a flock of parrots became the shrill bleats of car horns, a woodpecker rat-tat-tatting on the trunk of a eucalyptus tree became the rattle of a distant jackhammer, the cackling call of a kookaburra echoed a sudden burst of a woman's drunken laughter, and the gobbling of a bush turkey became the rheumy cough of a homeless man. All these sounds of town and country—evidently as far as the young didg player was concerned—became a single, uninterrupted sonic landscape.

"It was the most brilliant piece of sonic assimilation I've ever heard," my ward summed up later to his Aussie girlfriend.

* * *

Mein Host may have had his reservations about accepting Adrian's request—and Marion's encouragement—to take LSD with the younger man. Yet I've heard him say he was trusting that the entheogen would guide them to some form of resolution.

Thus it was on a pleasantly warm afternoon in early September that Adrian and my ward dropped acid in the living room of Adrian's family's clapboard vacation home.

The cottage was a couple of blocks from Long Island Sound, and the water could be seen glimmering through the trees and intervening cottages. The roads were unpaved and covered with loose gravel—a fact that became more painfully significant as their adventure progressed. The place appeared to be a destination for blue-collar workers who had vacation cottages here. They evidently hadn't warranted the local council's blessing of well-paved roads.

While they were quietly chatting and waiting for the acid to come on, Adrian suddenly pointed at a canoe they could see resting on its side in the enclosed porch.

"That's what I want to do!" Adrian stood up, his face a mask of enthusiasm. He was clearly pushing himself.

"Later, perhaps, when we're over the peak," my ward said sensibly.

"No, c'mon, man, let's do it now." He was already moving toward the door.

"Hold it, Adrian! Hang on a sec. We came here so you'd be in a safe place for the trip. Now you want to go to sea in a pea-green boat?"

"A kayak, it's a kayak, not a boat," Adrian was fossicking around in the porch for the oars. "C'mon, man. It's cool, don't worry about me. I'll be fine . . . Ah! Here . . . the oars."

"Is this what you planned all along? Did Marion put you up to this?" My ward got to his feet when he couldn't hear Adrian's reply, and moved toward the porch. "You really want to do this? Go out on the sound when we'll be totally fucked up?"

"We can leave our shoes and everything in the house. They'll be safe here."

"Really? This is something you really want to do?" Mein Host repeated—he obviously had his concerns. He was no stranger to acid, but he'd not done LSD since the early 1960s, and I thought he was wise to be cautious.

"You're absolutely sure about it, Adrian? Here, look me in the eye and tell me you're fine with this, it's what you want . . ."

"Hey man, it was my idea . . ." Adrian straightened up to his full height; he was six feet ten inches tall.

"So what if it was Marion who told me to do it." Adrian was looking into my ward's eyes. "So what! It was *my* idea, she just okayed it. It's what I want. I really, really want to do it, okay?"

"Then . . . so be it, Adrian. So be it." Mein Host grinned at his use of the phrase, so familiar from his days in the community when it was their reply to the greeting "As it is."

As they stood face-to-face, I found it fascinating to see the difference in the two men's mien. They were both unusually good-looking men. Each was in his physical prime: Adrian with his dark hair and male model prettiness, his tanned face beading with sweat. Then there was my ward—light to Adrian's dark, and his profile more hawk than human—his frame a taut and sinewy contrast to Adrian's soft and somewhat endomorphic frame.

My ward said afterward that he thought taking the kayak out was a crazy thing to do, yet as it was the only time he had ever heard Adrian expressing what he wanted with any real conviction, he went with the flow. This was evidently to be a part of the toughening up of

Adrian—an aspect of which necessarily involved being challenged and tested by the younger man. My ward had been out in canoes a few times before in his life, but he was certainly no expert. He said he reckoned Adrian must have been out hundreds of times when he was growing up, so he should know what he was doing.

"C'mon, grab the other end, I'll take the front," Adrian said, throwing the oars into the kayak. They then awkwardly maneuvered it out of the porch and into the bright sunlight.

Kayaks must be heavier than they look, and it was evident once they got off the patchy front lawn and onto the gravel road that Adrian's choice to carry the front end was based on long experience. He could see where he was going and was able to avoid any particularly sharp pieces of stone on the road. Mein Host, at the back, could see nothing of what lay ahead, and his feet were taking the punishment.

He said afterward that the acid was just starting to come on when he was trudging along behind Adrian, the stones cutting into his feet. The kayak was evidently getting heavier by the step, and Adrian was showing no signs of stopping before they got to the water. My ward said it was no time to show any weakness. If Adrian could do it, then he was damn well going to have to deal with it, too!

He later told Marion it was at that point he had one of those acid brain waves. He said it came rapidly in a series of gestalts; a tactile memory of how he'd learned to control his body temperature in a New York heat wave; images of Buddhist monks running full-tilt down a rocky incline; a fakir he once knew who stuck skewers bloodlessly through his cheeks; mountain goats leaping from one impossibly small ledge to another; donkeys picking their way confidently through rubble, unable to see where to place their hooves and yet never stumbling; and all this culminating, so he said, in the idea of distributing his consciousness throughout his body. He saw no reason—given the clarity of the acid— why his bare feet couldn't perfectly well see for themselves where they were going.

"They were that part of me down there, weren't they!" he joked. "They're on ground level. They should be able to see what to avoid."

This made me laugh because all I saw and heard of this revelation as it occurred was my ward murmuring over and over under his breath: "Feets . . . Feets . . . Feets we needs you now," to a sloppy funkadelic backbeat.

And surprise, surprise! By the time they finally reached the water, his feet had done their work well! Once he'd started his chant, his "feets" had come through completely unscathed. However, they were to find that there was no real beach, just a small strip of more gravel. As it was midweek, the place was deserted. There were also no boats visible on the sound.

My ward, up to his knees in water, held the kayak steady while Adrian clambered onto the front seat. He grabbed the oars, one in each hand, and stuck them firmly into the seabed in the shallow water on either side of the kayak before motioning for my ward to get in.

It was one of those windless late summer days when the sound was so calm they might have been paddling on a lake of glass. They didn't talk much while Adrian—in the front seat and presumably with the acid breaking over him—paddled vigorously. Straight out from the coastline the little boat sped over the placid water—Adrian urging greater and greater efforts, on and on, farther and farther—until they finally tired and let the kayak drift with the current. They relaxed and closed their eyes, bathing their faces in the soft sunlight and allowing the acid to take them where it would.

They'd both been so taken up with the speedy edge of the acid that neither had the slightest idea of where they were going. It was only after their little interval of meditation that they finally turned to look back and saw that the land had completely disappeared. They'd been drifting, too, so it appeared they didn't even know in which direction the land should have been, had it been there. They were totally lost on a blank sea.

And they were stoned out of their minds.

Now, Long Island Sound is not an impressively large body of water, but they'd found themselves where the sound was at its widest. Neither shore—neither the Long Island coastline nor the Connecticut side—was visible. This probably would not have been of great concern to a savvy sailor with his compass and some idea of where the sun ought to be. But our two heroes were not savvy sailors, and with a healthy headful of acid they clearly had absolutely no idea where they were—or in which direction to paddle.

The sun was beginning to drop lower in the sky as the Earth turned. They'd been out on the water for about four hours and already a soft, early evening breeze had picked up.

Mein Host still doesn't know what it was that set Adrian off, but what began as a series a half-stifled whimpers coming from the front seat soon resolved into phrases the poor man repeated over and over, locked in an endless loop of fear.

"What's going on, man? What's happening?" On and on went the sobbing voice of a terrified three-year-old. "What's going on, man? What's happening?" Again and again and again.

My ward could see Adrian trembling and zonked out of his head in front of him and felt the whole kayak shaking beneath him. Adrian was now slumped over, a large man reduced to a lost and frightened little child, mewling in abject panic. There was no point in being angry with the poor guy, and there was no cajoling or consolation offered that stopped his looping whimper and that would bring him back into his body.

Mein Host was on his own.

"Just the way I like it," he told Marion later. "I knew I had to stay fully conscious and use the acid, not fight it. I'd managed it with the stones, so I reckoned I should be able to ask the acid to help us find our way home."

"What d'you mean get the acid to help you?" Although Marion liked to put on a good front, she had an instinctive fear of entheogens—so much so that when Adrian suggested it she'd initially opposed the idea.

"There's a flow to any entheogen," my ward was explaining. "You can fight it or you can trust it and allow the acid to take you where it will. That's what I did without really knowing I was doing it. I started paddling gently, trying to keep my cool—with Adrian a useless lump in front of me still rabbeting on about 'where are we and what's happening?'"

I could see a flash of anguish cross Marion's expressive face, yet she leaned forward all the same, curious to know what happened next.

"I noticed the kayak had turned into the breeze, and although it made paddling slightly harder, I made sure to keep the wind in my face . . ."

"And Adrian?" Marion interrupted.

"It was awful . . . he just went on and on. It was useless. I don't think he pulled out of it until we could see a coastline on the horizon. He didn't believe it at first, until we got closer. Then he started recognizing landmarks, and that's what got us home."

"So he did okay in the end . . . he got you back."

"We had a chance to talk it through after we'd arrived at the house and we'd come down a bit. I think what it did for him was to give him the actual experience of being absolutely terrified and yet finding there was nothing, in fact, to fear. It was about trust."

"Yeah, right," Marion said slowly. "He doesn't really trust himself."

"It was that, Marion, but also I think he was just totally terrified of being terrified. I doubt if he'd ever felt that frightened. This gave him the chance to see that he was stronger than his fears. Let's see now what he does with that knowledge."

What he didn't confide in Marion was how the experience had been for him. I saw he had noted in his journal that one of the previous times he'd been in a situation of extreme potential danger, he felt he'd lost his wits. He said at that time—when Hurricane Inez was about to blow down one of Xtul's monastery walls, which would have crushed him where he sat—that he felt as if he was being possessed by an overwhelming death wish.

In facing a somewhat similar situation—this time lost on Long Island Sound in a fragile little craft with a painfully panicked passenger—he had been able to reach deeper into himself and maintain his psychic equilibrium.

In much the same way that he was grateful for the speedy reflexes the acid gave him, so also did he give credit to the acid for getting them home. It was Albert Hofmann's "medicine for the soul," as the good doctor called LSD-25 in an interview just before his hundredth birthday. This medicine of the soul had been born from Hofmann's almost incidental discovery that by extracting ergotamine from ergot fungi, he could then synthesize his mind-opening medicine.

It wasn't long after this event that Marion was finally able to make her decision to be with Adrian, whom she married within the year. She'd left the apartment within the week, and, as Mein Host said, he was "finally mercifully free of Marion and all her good intentions."

My ward may not have liked the woman much, and he and Marion had absolutely nothing in common but what she did for him. However, it was Marion's good intentions that had made her eviction so challenging.

Call it deceptive manipulation, diplomacy, or the realpolitik of relationships, but my ward's strategy had needed to be subtle so that each of them would emerge from the fray with whatever each of them most wanted and what would serve them best.

Mein Host evidently did not enjoy having to go behind other people's backs to covertly manipulate the relationship—even if he could justify it by his desire that Marion wouldn't be crushed by forsaking her vow to Jehovah.

His intuition about Adrian being a more suitable match for Marion than him has been borne out by the fact that the couple have remained married to this day.

And Mein Host, to his credit, made sure never again to find himself in a situation in which he would have to resort to such covert manipulations.

# 3

# From Ancient Secrets to a Modern Entheogenic Breakthrough

## A Forty-Thousand-Year Story, the Walk-Ins, an Aboriginal Corroboree, Pituri, Atlantis Restored, Entheogenic Shamanism, and Poseidon's Influence

In the rundown little café, the man put his didg aside and started talking . . . except it wasn't quite talking. It seemed to become more of a spoken chant as the words came pouring out.

At first it wasn't clear, even to me, what he was talking *about*. When a couple of the elderly locals chimed in, however—echoing and emphasizing certain names and phrases—it became clear the man was reciting the oral history of his tribe, with all its bells and whistles.

He interspersed his recitation with some evocative blasts on his didg. This was as much to give his listeners time to absorb the complex knowledge he was imparting as it was to collect his own thoughts before launching back into his narrative. It was really a superbly fluid and proficient display of storytelling on an epic scale—as full and rich as Homer's *Iliad,* as emotionally charged as the *Odyssey,* and yet many times longer . . . and a great deal more cosmic.

On and on it went, with barely a pause. The audience was oddly attentive. It was as if each member of the audience knew they were witnessing a rare and special event and that they felt it was a privilege to be there. In the one brief break after a couple of hours, the storyteller kept to himself, smoking a cigarette, while the audience—now swollen to more than thirty—seemed unusually quiet for a group of Australians.

What emerged over the next seven hours of nonstop narrative clearly astonished my ward.

The small café was crowded—with additional arrivals standing at the back—when the Aborigine's story started unfolding again, hour after hour, to a rapt audience. Of particular interest to my ward was the didg player chanting on about the "star people from the Pleiades." He told of these star people who would sometimes come down and occupy the body of one of their tribe and then live alongside them.

What particularly surprised and amused my ward was the reason given for the arrival of the star people on Earth. He has never been completely sure he'd heard the words correctly, so now I can confirm for him that he got the gist of the story quite right.

He had pricked up his ears when he heard the Aborigine chanting about the star people and the Pleiades, but he didn't know what to make of it. It wasn't a situation in which he could have interrupted the flow to ask his questions, so let me set his mind at rest.

The Pleiadeans hadn't arrived in their silver ships this time— or in their massive space-arks as they had when they'd evacuated the Lemurian survivors. No, these Pleiadeans came in ones and twos. They might be thought of as Walk-Ins in contemporary terms, yet with a couple of key exceptions.

Walk-Ins have always been used sparingly down through the centuries by various off-planet races with a concern for this world. I'm aware, as I am sure they are, that the Courts of Uversa are known to frown on the practice. If the Walk-In spiritual technology becomes overused it can easily threaten the evolutionary integrity of the planet in question.

I can't speak for the court, of course, but from what I've observed the legal beagles on Uversa must be prepared to overlook its usage if employed quietly and frugally. I have noticed, however, a certain increase in numbers of Walk-Ins since the end of World War II, another indication that matters are reaching a head in this world.

Walk-Ins, I should add, are not permitted to interfere in any substantial way with the natural social and technological advancement arc of the planet in question. Recently, I have observed that the Walk-Ins my ward has come to know have most frequently been rebel angels, with a partially conscious awareness of their previous lifetime. These people generally experience themselves as Walk-Ins, and yet on arriving here— as holds true for all other incarnate angels on the planet—they assume mortal identity.

Under normal circumstances, a Walk-In will take over the physical body of a human being when that person has used up the body and is usually at the point of a premature death. The timing of this exchange would have been decided upon prior to their incarnation, and a contract that would serve both party's spiritual growth would have been agreed upon as well.

A Walk-In's life is never an easy one—especially in the years it takes to assimilate and burn off the karma of the previous occupant. Their missions—once they have walked-in—tend to be personal and redemptive, rather than public. In the few cases my ward has come across in which Walk-Ins have tried to introduce, for example, an advanced invention that might have overly impacted the collective, they have invariably been met with insurmountable obstacles or collective ridicule.

The star people that the Aborigine was describing were rather different. They had no ambition but to relax into the ways and rhythms of the tribe. They were acknowledged for who they were and greeted as such by the rest of the tribe. As the star people generally made it their practice to walk into a dying adolescent male, they grew up and were known to the tribe, occasionally even becoming the tribe's shaman.

What Mein Host hadn't been able to understand at the time was the reason given for the presence of these star people. That had produced some laughter among the Aborigine in the crowded café. The star people liked to explain some version of having walked-in to reconnect with the natural life. They hailed from one of the more advanced fifth-density worlds within the Pleiades cluster, and the chant made it sound as if they'd come here on holiday. It was this idea of being here on a vacation that had drawn the sardonic laughter.

My ward said afterward that he felt it was an unusual and expected privileged to have been there and that he felt he was being let into something that had been kept hidden from the skepticism of the Europeans. This "something," he said, was what made the Australian Aboriginal conceptual framework even more significant and fascinating.

What the long, seven-hour narrative allowed Mein Host was an insight into a race of human beings that had somehow managed to retain traces of an oral history stretching back more than forty thousand years. Shamefully it had been only in the past two hundred years that almost everything of the old sacred ways and traditions were lost.

I say "almost everything" because of what I learned over the course of my ward's friendship with Bill Smith and others of the Komilaroi tribe of the northern tablelands of New South Wales. Mein Host had come to know some of the elders of the tribe about a year before he heard the oral history of the people from the didg player that evening in the café. Thus he'd already had some glimpses into their spiritual maturity.

What he, not surprisingly, learned from Bill Smith—one of the younger and most progressive (*in the right way* —*TW*) of the tribal elders—was the typically tragic story that had befallen all the indigenous tribes. This included the diseases, the brutality of the British, the campaigns of extermination, all of which is too broadly known now for me to belabor the horrors. What has barely ever been acknowledged by the colonists has been the loss of so many tribal traditions and all the sacred knowledge embedded in the ancient rituals.

While the mainly British treatment of the Australian indigenous population over the past two centuries is no longer a shameful secret, the treatment they still receive today remains almost as shameful as it ever was. Perhaps it's even more so because the Australian governments of the late twentieth century really should have known better. (*Some small steps have been taken by officialdom in the past twenty years to improve the lives of the aboriginal people. —TW*)

In any event, Bill Smith was one of a new generation of vigorous, well-educated, younger tribal leaders who was determined to try to reclaim the sacred rituals. He told my ward that about seventy years ago the elders of their tribe had simply given up on passing the sacred knowledge down the generations. The horrors had become too much, the injustices too intolerable, and their demonization by the invaders too degrading for a fine, proud race. They'd just given up and were faced with the inevitable disappearance of their sacred traditions—and, most likely, the extinction of their own race, too.

Bill Smith claimed, however, some seventy years later, that he and his tribal colleagues had caught the vital importance of the situation just in time and had managed to persuade the few living old-timers to share, before they died, what they recalled being taught as children. At that time, there was only one carrier of this information remaining: a ninety-year-old man on his last legs. They recorded from him all he knew.

Bill had proudly said he felt that they almost threaded it together. And already, Bill said, it had raised the morale of the tribe. This my ward had seen for himself when he was able to join one of their corroborees.

The corroboree was held at Valla Beach, near the NSW coastal town of Nambucca Heads. It had rained earlier in the day, and yet the two enormous stacks of firewood the younger members of the tribe had been piling up all afternoon surprisingly flared into a blaze at the strike of a match.

Here is how my ward noted down his experience in his journal. He wrote:

> The ground was damp and sweet-smelling. About twenty-five people stood around in an irregular oval formed by two large blazing

bonfires. The booming of a couple of didgeridoos and the arrhyth-
mic snapping clack of the click sticks pulsed over the background
surge of a stormy surf beating against the beach on the other side of
the nearby dunes. The bonfires crackled and spat sparks and thick
smoke, lighting up two large men—very nearly naked and covered
with ample amounts of what appeared to be ocher or white clay.
Both were dark-skinned and muscular, barefoot, and dressed only in
working shorts, and between them they seemed to be carrying on a
wonderfully intricate line of patter.

The oldest of the two I recognized as Bill Smith—although it
was momentarily dyscognitive to associate the quietly respectable,
besuited man I'd previously met with this vision in what looked like
war paint. The other man—perhaps in his mid- to late thirties—was
radiantly fine-faced and full-bearded. I later learned this to be Ray
Kelly Jr.

At first I couldn't quite make out what was happening. The dialogue was fast, and my ear hadn't yet grown used to the accent. Both
men were bounding around—sometimes upright, sometimes on all
fours—while constantly keeping up the line of patter between them.

I had a moment of wondering if I was going to be a painful witness to that saddest of affairs in which indigenous people perform
their rituals before the uncomprehending and patronizing eyes of
their more "sophisticated" Western brethren.

I could not have been more wrong!

I was simply not prepared for the true sophistication of the
Aboriginal worldview as it was to emerge over the course of the corroboree. Nor was I prepared for the degree of compassion and forgiveness, nor indeed the pure sense of fun radiating out of these two
glorious men. Their leaping and gamboling suddenly started making
perfect sense, and within moments I was being swept along by the
energy and humor of it all.

It was a multilevel dialogue—many levels of which I could only
vaguely discern but not understand. I found myself drawn into a succession of teaching stories, with one flowing naturally into another.

As I fell into the rhythms of the corroboree and learned to make out the words from the accents, it came to me that I was hearing the downright funniest, coolest, hippest line of patter I've ever encountered—well on a par with Richard Pryor or Robin Williams at their wildest—and this mainly from Ray Kelly Jr. There was a weaving, too, of what were evidently traditional stories along with a completely extemporaneous line of spontaneous repartee. It was very, very funny. In the kindest way they put us all on, and while they were at it, they put themselves on, too. The whole occasion was a massive joke, and both of the men exuded a deep sense of joy and well-being. They were not mocking their own traditions at all, but by frequently making themselves the victims of their own jokes they broke down the barriers separating them from us, the spectators.

In Aboriginal life there are few, if any, spectators. Everyone in the tribe is involved, and I'm told that each person in the tribe has something they do better than anyone else—or who knows a piece of information entirely personal to themselves. I suspect there are no passive survivors in the Australian bush. As I listened, I became aware of a larger picture emerging from the teaching parables and fluid one-liners—of a people who had somehow managed to find ways of maintaining their spirit through the most inhumane of colonizations.

Mein Host has written more fully about this corroboree in his 2001 book *Adventures among Spiritual Intelligences,* but one of the teaching stories particularly amused me. So here it is, again in my ward's words:

Another story started, one that tells of the discovery of the European honeybee by the first Aborigines to ever encounter them. Apparently the indigenous Australian bees have a negligible sting so—after 39,800 years of bushcraft—there was considerable surprise and pain at stumbling upon this new species. Ray had us out there in the center as a gum tree forest, our limbs waving in the wind while the story unwound. It culminated in both Ray and Bill throwing themselves around in a paroxysm of bee stinging.

I could see that whatever story they got into they totally identified with the characters, whether human or animal. When Bill played a kangaroo, he became Kangaroo: sniffing, tense and watchful, with big sad eyes. In the bee story, I could almost see the swarm of angry insects and feel the stickiness of the stolen honey. And in the emu dance that followed, Ray was uncanny. He became Emu so entirely that I all but saw his tail feathers.

The corroboree with Bill Smith, Ray Kelly Jr., and the men, women, and children of the Komilaroi tribe remains one of the supreme experiences of Mein Host's life—one that opened him up to the wisdom of the indigenous people of the world. He says there were four centrally important insights he was permitted that have stayed with him.

Aborigine are amazing. They have a long history of a familiarity with off-planet life and have a knowledge of the solar system based on their out-of-body travels. The Aboriginal people—taken as whole and during the tens of thousands of years prior to the invasion of the Europeans in the eighteenth century—were also probably the most consistently emotionally and spiritually advanced race on the planet. As well, the Komilaroi tribe, at least, practiced a form of panentheism, as demonstrated by a prayer offered by Bill Smith at a short ceremony before Mein Host had to depart and which Bill wrote out carefully in my ward's journal after the ceremony.

Bill spoke with a strong, deep voice and with an authentic and touching sincerity.

Blessed are You, Biami, Lord God, Maker of all the Universe, Creation of all Creation, Butta Waa GoYu (Big Boss), Maker of the sun, stars, skies, rain, wind, earth, and all that lives within it; all glory and praise are yours. Bless the people of this community. Help and teach us to live together in harmony in our land as one. Because who can own the land? For the land is our mother. Biami is present in all Creation. By His powers, strength, and spirit, there is nowhere on Earth within our land where you can hide from Biami. He sees us and knows our every thought. So take care, and let the spirit of the land breathe, for it is alive and breathing. He reaches out to His Creation and helps us wherever we are.

Stop and listen. Be still. Be a part of your land; look after it. Nurture it so that it will bear fruit and become your home. It is yours only while you care and share with one another, as one with the land. We are only passing through; we are in your hands, Biami. For who can own something that is part of us?

We welcome you to this land, our country. Our fathers' and mothers' spirits join hands with you. For we love you all. Our spirits are now one, and you are safe.

Bill said this prayer in a ceremony to bless the recently acquired land of a dolphin research center on the coast of New South Wales, which overlooked an Aboriginal dolphin dreaming site.

As I suggested, a careful reading of his prayer demonstrates how deeply panentheistic the Aborigine are. There is the Biami, the Father God who infuses all of Creation; there's the living, breathing Earth, the Mother; and there's the recognition that mortals are "only passing through"—truly "sojourners in a foreign land . . . leaving heaven for a new home," as Philo of Alexandria wrote two thousand years earlier in *The Unchangeableness of God.*

Curiously, there is a generosity of spirit that welcomes those of another race to share their land with reverence and care. This raises the obvious question: How would Australia have developed had the whites—when they first started arriving—treated the indigenous people with respect and worked with them to share the land and coexist in harmony?

It's an empty fantasy, of course, but one that has to be proposed and examined so that another such tragedy might be avoided in the future. That's if Bill Smith and Ray Kelly Jr.—and all the other forward-looking Aboriginal leaders—have anything to do with it.

* * *

After that digression on the background and nature of the Australian Aborigines, let me return to the Middle East. But before that my ward suggests I should add one significant fact that has only recently emerged and which tells a great deal about the Aboriginal mind—and which ties into the Middle East discussion.

Ethnobotanists have long believed that the only cultures to not have a history of using entheogens were the Eskimos and the Australian Aborigines. It has only emerged in the past twenty years that the indigenous people of central Australia have had a long tradition of using pituri (*Duboisia myoporoides*) as a sacred substance for their rituals.

Pituri, my collaborator's research reveals, is derived from the leaves of the corkwood tree—containing active alkaloids, nicotine, scopolamine, and hyoscyamine—which can produce altered states of consciousness when smoked.

It's a tribute to what an important part pituri would have played in the sacred life of Aboriginal peoples that, throughout the centuries of European colonization, they had managed to keep their use of this power plant secret. That the corkwood tree is indigenous to Australia would have helped to keep their sacred secret.

I have touched on the use of power plants before, given that they have played such a significant role in the inner life of human beings down through history. I've noted the use of the seeds of the morning glory plant by a shaman on one of the Islands of Mu. However, the rise and spread of shamanism from the Indian subcontinent—where it had been brought originally on one of the Lemurian diasporas—was accompanied by the use of whatever power plant was locally available.

Prince Caligastia, through his midwayers, invariably tried to suppress the use of entheogens in the tribes under his thrall—for much the same reason that most organized religions and many contemporary governments attempt to forbid their use. Entheogens used wisely, or in ritual settings, can reveal the deeper truths of mortal life. As such they will work to release the individual from the deceptions imposed by social, religious, and political officialdom.

It was when shamanism had spread west to the Nile Valley in the fifteenth millennium that the priests attending a nascent pantheon of midwayers began to work with entheogens in their ceremonies. Although the Geb, Nut, Isis, Osiris, and Horus pantheon wouldn't fully emerge as the dominant belief system of the people of Egypt for many millennia, the seeds of the belief were laid in early shamanism.

The Egyptian preoccupation with the underworld—and with the dead—was directly inherited from entheogenic shamanism and the shaman's experiential knowledge of the Afterlife and the astral realms. Osiris—whom they believed was the firstborn son of the earth god Geb and the sky goddess Nut—was their primary deity, and he was worshipped as Lord of the Dead.

Yet there was a curious twist here that only further showed how deeply embedded the shamanic experience was in the Egyptian belief system. Although Osiris was worshipped as god of the Afterlife—and a merciful judge of the dead—he was also known paradoxically as "King of the Living," because the dead were the ones they considered to be truly alive. This insight, as my ward suggests, would have been available only to those with an actual experience of the Afterlife, and that would have been most reliably developed and kept alive through the ritual use of entheogens.

Then came the natural disasters of the thirteenth and twelfth millennia, followed by the disastrous flooding during the tenth millennium—when the glacial melt-off substantially raised the level of the oceans, swamping the coastal cities and forcing the survivors to start all over again.

The great coastal cities—many of which owed their initial creation to the Lemurian traders and explorers who had encircled and charted the globe by 35,000 BCE—had been settled over the subsequent millennia by regular waves of Lemurian migrants. These were the cities—relics of their busted and broken stonework still discernible beneath the ocean off the northwest coast of India, off the Pacific coast of South

America, and off the coast of the Japanese island of Okinawa—that became the dominant cultural centers of the age. When the cities were swallowed by the rising ocean levels of the tenth millennium, it not only killed people by the tens of thousands, but it also started the final collapse of the Lemurian culture—casting a terrible pall of depression over the survivors.

There would be other civilizations that would rise and fall over the following millennia, yet none would match the high culture of those majestic Lemurian cities. When Atlantis emerged as the dominant power it also experienced its own share of natural disasters. Enough of value had survived, however, to rebuild the cities and restore the trading routes that brought the Lemurians the copper and tin that had made them rich beyond measure.

Much of this restoration had been due to the attention Prince Caligastia and his midwayers had given to the island. It had been the Prince's ambitious plans to make Atlantis the center of his operations from whence he hoped to spread his absolutist creed. He had overseen the rebuilding of Atlantis as well as the design and development of larger and more formidable oceangoing vessels that had made the Atlanteans feared throughout the Mediterranean region—as well as up and down the western coasts of Africa and Europe.

Atlantis by the end of the fifth millennium had restored itself—not quite to its former glory, but sufficiently to reimpose its naval primacy throughout the Mediterranean. However, something fundamental had changed in the way that the Atlanteans regarded themselves and how they related to the outside world. Their sailors had always been feared for their acts of piracy—and the Atlantean dominance in the trade of metals had made them indispensable to the region. In itself, this caused them to be resented and envied by those who depended on them.

Then—as I was contemplating the change of mood that had befallen the island—the aether beside me trembled and here again was Astar. I supposed my sister Watcher was drawn in by my concern for Atlantis.

You'll recall that Astar has made a specialty of observing Lemuria through all its history. Then when the Lemurian colonists mixed with the descendants of the scientists whom Caligastia had moved to the island many thousands of years earlier, Astar chose to focus her attention on Atlantis.

We'd exchanged our greetings when Astar—never one to waste her time—spoke loudly in my mind. "Any attention I give you, dear sister, takes me away from making my observations of Atlantis."

I ignored her condescending tone. I was more used to her by now. As our interactions always addressed, if not answered, an issue that was puzzling me, I overlooked her attitude.

"You were correct," she continued, "when you detected that change of mood on the island. Truly, it was profound. The last gasp of the Lemurian culture. That's the way I saw it."

I knew the few remaining Lemurians on Atlantis had become a dispirited lot. As the islands of their ancestors had long sunk beneath the ocean, and then Atlantis had suffered its own share of natural disasters, they must have felt as if they were cursed.

"That was the start of the rot." Astar's tone changed, as it often did when she realized I was cleverer than she'd thought. "They no longer practiced the age-old rituals inherited from the times of Vanu and Amadon. They had ceased their worship of Father Sky and Mother Earth in their anger at the catastrophes they'd suffered."

"But hadn't the city been rebuilt using ancient Lemurian building construction techniques?" I wondered. "Why would they have done that if they'd rejected their gods?"

"Because it was at that point that Caligastia's midwayers had taken over Atlantis and created what essentially became a shadow authority. Poseidon—the secondary midwayer who, you'll remember, had fallen under Caligastia's control—had been given authority over the island by the Prince; more to get rid of him . . . to exile Poseidon as far away as possible from whatever Caligastia was brewing up at the eastern end of the Mediterranean."

Now *that* I hadn't known.

"Oh yes, indeed." Astar's tone was firm. "Poseidon was one of the secondaries who'd given Caligastia the most trouble. He couldn't seem to stop himself, Poseidon; he was always in competition with the Prince . . . who couldn't stop *himself.* At the time I thought Caligastia was very clever to have exiled Poseidon to Atlantis, but now—with what's happening on the island—I suspect the Prince is starting to doubt the wisdom of his action."

This was the sort of gossip I found most fascinating and why I'm inclined to tolerate Astar's condescension. So much of human history unfolds as a consequence of the feelings and actions of single individuals, whether mortal or midwayer. If I caught Astar's drift correctly, it was either Caligastia's baleful influence that was responsible for the profound mood shift, or the Prince had ridden in on the waves of cynicism following the collapse of their religious beliefs.

Had I known that Poseidon had taken a local woman for a wife soon after arriving on the island, and between them they'd spawned five sets of twins? Or that these twins had grown up to become the kings of what Poseidon had proudly called his New Order? And that this New Atlantis—now named in honor of Atlas, the firstborn son of Poseidon and Kleito—had reequipped itself once again to threaten the Mediterranean world?

Had all this occurred while I was last on Zandana?

How could these changes have happened so fast?

Astar broke into my thoughts. "When did you last observe life on the island?" She didn't wait for an answer before hurrying on. "Isn't it obvious? Poseidon, as a secondary midwayer, had one great advantage over the Prince: he could spend as much time as he wished in a materialized form. Poseidon had children with a mortal woman and yet he could appear as a god before his people. He could appeal to his people as a god and as a supermortal. The Prince—for all his claims—always had to work through one of his cooperative midwayers . . ."

And they'd invariably let the Prince down.

Unfortunately for the Prince, it appeared that once a rebel midwayer gained ascendancy as a local divinity, he or she frequently ended up claiming the power for themselves. I trust the irony was not entirely lost on Caligastia that by emulating the Prince's lust for power, the midwayer rendered him all but impotent and irrelevant.

"It was this frustration with his midwayers," Astar was speaking in my mind again, "that caused him to not trust them any longer; not most of them, anyway. It's what caused the Prince to focus on the Jehovah clan when he lost control of Poseidon's New Atlantis. He thought he could trust them."

Perhaps I had overestimated Prince Caligastia's influence when I stated earlier in this narrative that, through his rebel midwayers, the Prince indirectly controlled all expressions of religious worship throughout the Middle East.

Astar broke in again. "This is based on an erroneous assumptions." Her tone had turned impatient—I'd forgotten that she was still listening to my thoughts. I felt for a moment she was going to disappear, but no, she had more to say. "It was precisely Caligastia's declining influence over his independent rebel midwayers that had made him place so much attention and energy on the Jehovah."

Astar paused, and I could hear her thinking of the best way to summarize her insights.

"If I called Poseidon's New Atlantis the last gasp of true Lemurian principles," she said finally, "then I'd venture that the Prince's imposing his monotheism through Jehovah on the Semitic tribes of southern Palestine was every bit as much the Prince's final bid for absolute power."

There was more I wanted to ask Astar, but before I could form my question she was gone. I hoped I hadn't put her off with my "erroneous assumptions."

\* \* \*

With Marion finally out of his apartment and happily set up with Adrian, Mein Host was now able to settle into his own natural rhythms.

He had started to draw again since returning to The Unit, but now—with more time on his hands—he was drawing for as many hours as possible every evening after finishing work. To begin with, those hours of getting lost in his drawing made for a relaxing contrast to long days of selling Viewpacks. As the months passed, his art became progressively more a part of his life as he became increasingly engaged with the technical challenges that drawing with a pencil presented.

Yet beneath the daily grind of running the business and the nightly joy of getting lost in drawing, other elements were brewing in my ward's life. Some of these he was aware of; however, the most important of them were being organized beneath his level of consciousness.

The high energy he'd become accustomed to enjoying during his time with the community had served him well in the business, which was steadily flourishing. Soon selling the Viewpack system became second nature to him. He could do it on automatic—although I watched him trying his best to stay fully present. It was not only the common sense simplicity and efficiency of his system that made it so easy to sell. My ward also found that his prospective clients were unusually thrilled to discover it was *he* who had invented the Viewpack system, and they therefore couldn't wait to buy it. He would later joke that it was one of the advantages of selling in a celebrity culture.

Although the business continued to do well, it played a progressively less important part in his life. Thus I won't be focusing on that aspect of his life any longer except to say that—by 1981, three years after he'd started the North American company—he was able to step aside and arrange for a distributor, to take over the accounts. By that time he knew what he wanted to do with his life, so he was able to negotiate a contract with the distributor, whence he'd receive a thousand dollars a month for four years as compensation. This wasn't a large sum by any means, but if he lived modestly he believed he could write the book he felt gestating inside him. I know this because I heard him say more than once that if he couldn't write a good book in four years he would have to turn his attention to something else that interested him.

The three aforementioned years my ward spent in New York City as the owner of a successful small business—and his ability to extract himself at the time he did—went far to stabilize his mind after all the turbulence of life in the community. But those three years also did something else.

I don't think he consciously realized it at the time—so happy was he to be out of the business—but it gave him a confidence in himself I hadn't seen before. He knew, despite the community's dismissive opinion of the "World of Men," that he could make a success of himself in the straight world.

However, he also clearly determined that—as a result of what had started occurring in his life—he would never again bend himself out of shape to fit into the straight world. He wasn't to know until much later in his life that he had inadvertently—as far as he knew—stumbled upon an ancient truth. If a mortal dedicates his or her life to doing what they most love to do, and if what they do is aligned with their highest intention and that of the angels who accompany them, then it becomes the Multiverse itself that bends to accommodate that mortal's progress. The signs of this in a person's life include noticeable increases in synchronicities.

My ward would learn there are a number of provisos to this spiritual law of the Multiverse. Whatever it is that has to be done needs to be done with a whole heart and with complete dedication. It needs to be done with no thought of material reward or public acclaim, and it requires complete personal honesty. Other provisos are that the work will take as long as it takes, and courage is needed to follow one's intuition without hesitation. As well, the scorn of contemporaries—like their shadow of praise—is irrelevant.

Some of these lessons came naturally to him, while some were more of a challenge and took longer to learn. There would be some wrong turns—as there would be some cul-de-sacs—but it was a journey from which once set out on, there would be no turning back.

At this stage I feel I need to restate my contract with Mein Host. As he has written extensively about his life from 1980 until 2010 in a series of books recording his thirty-year exploration of nonhuman intelligences, I see no need to repeat what has already been explored. The exceptions will have to be those times that were too weirdly improbable to have been included in his books. They were too dark or disturbing to have been relevant to his interspecies focus. Then there were the situations that have remained a mystery to him and on which I can perhaps shed some light.

I said earlier in my narrative that I'm not trying to write a history of the world anymore than I'm writing my ward's spiritual biography. Up to this point I have made an effort, with my collaborator's help, to write chronologically, even though it is not my natural mode of expression. From this point on you will find that my narrative will be based more on the associations I make than on the more orderly sequencing you have come to expect from me.

In 1980 my ward passed his fortieth birthday and had become, on the surface anyway, very much his own man. What he wasn't to know at that time was that everything that had been stripped away over his years in the community had revealed a much deeper layer of inner conflict he hadn't yet addressed. And to resolve these issues, he would find that he'd need to return to working with entheogens.

There had been many advances in entheogenic research since the early 1960s despite the increasing government prohibition. Entheogens were just too valuable a research tool to permit fearful and shortsighted politicians to dictate what was permissible. This was especially true when those same hypocritical politicians smiled on the alcohol, cigarette, and arms industries alike.

So the research and development of new entheogens was driven almost entirely underground. All the while, intrepid ethnobotanists were starting to penetrate deeper into the forests and mountains to unearth new, and as yet undiscovered, power plants. Albert Hofmann was isolating and synthesizing psilocybin and psilocin from psychedelic mushrooms. At the same time, chemists at the CIA were trying to isolate novel psychoactive compounds for their own nefarious purposes.

In the late 1960s and early '70s, the Vietnam War made its unique demands on chemistry—and not merely for concocting new and more effective ways of killing people.

What was needed in this case was a battlefield anesthetic; a drug that didn't depress the wounded soldier's breathing system before they reached the hospital. First, phencyclidine—commonly known as PCP—was developed. This worked by popping the soldier out of their body, so there was nobody there to feel any pain. The drug had little effect on the soldiers' breathing, which allowed them to be anesthetized where they fell—but it had the disadvantage of lasting six hours or more. As a result, this delay frequently created complications for subsequent anesthetic and surgical procedures.

Next it was ketamine hydrochloride's turn—a "kissing cousin of phencyclidine," as my ward calls it. It had all the advantages of being short-acting and remarkably safe. In fact, so safe and effective was ketamine that it was used extensively by anesthesiologists in hospitals throughout the 1970s and '80s for minor surgical procedures, often on babies and small children.

Ketamine was marvelously convenient for hospitals because it was so short-acting and dosage-dependent. Because of this, surgeons could turn over patients faster and without the risks incurred by the heavier anesthetic drugs, which required the addition of an oxygen mask and everything that entails the necessary part of the anesthesiologist.

However, by now a new phenomenon was raising its awkward head. Men and women were going into surgery for minor operations that required an anesthetic and emerging from their operations talking of meeting God, speaking to angels, or finding themselves in a flying saucer chatting with aliens. These experiences were intensely meaningful to these patients, and although they could be dismissed as mere drug-induced hallucinations, their persistence became a challenge—and then an embarrassment—for those trying to explain them away. Soon other drugs were used that suppressed any memory of what might have occurred to the patient during their time out of their body.

It was Dr. John C. Lilly (1915–2001) and his colleagues who took special note of ketamine's emergent properties and tirelessly investigated the substance at all dosages. Lilly was a doctor, neuroscientist, psychoanalyst, writer, and philosopher who, as part of the counterculture of the twentieth century, led groundbreaking research into the nature of human and dolphin intelligence and the effects of hallucinogenic drugs on the brain. Dr. Lilly wrote up his findings in a number of provocative books, of which *The Scientist: A Metaphysical Autobiography* is the most deeply informative on his use of ketamine.

Mein Host, with his interest in dolphin intelligence and his attraction to altered states, was drawn to Dr. Lilly's early books. These books focused on dolphins as well as his work studying the mind, as Dr. Lilly did in *The Center of the Cyclone* and in his *Simulations of God*. But it was in reading *The Scientist* and learning of the doctor's experiments with ketamine that my ward determined to find some ketamine and try it for himself. His new girlfriend, Alma Daniel, turned out to be an enthusiastic coconspirator, so between them they formed the intention that if it was correct that the substance should appear in their lives, then so be it. They would experiment with it with respect, and in the spirit of exploration.

Now, here's the rub.

Before he'd read about ketamine in Dr. Lilly's book, my ward had never known the word—or even heard about the substance—and ketamine was not easily found outside the medical community. It wasn't a prohibited substance—as it was considered such a useful drug by surgeons and hospitals—and it wouldn't be discovered by the rave community for another decade. Even the druggie crowd wasn't yet aware of the potential of ketamine, and it had the advantage—as my ward pointed out—of not appealing to users of opiates. A heroin junky, for example, hopes to blot out an unpleasant reality or escape from the tedium of a normal everyday life. Ketamine, being an entheogen, reveals the inner workings of the user's mind—just the opposite of the effect hoped for by the junky.

In short, not only was ketamine almost impossible to find, but it was also an obscure enough substance that most drug users hadn't even come across it. And the few who did know the substance and its potential were more than content to keep quiet about it!

Two days after my ward and Alma had created their intention, my ward's companion angels started moving into action.

It was on a baking hot August afternoon—and Mein Host was striding on his own along West 92nd Street—when he passed an elegantly coiffed middle-aged man coming the other direction and dressed entirely in orange. Being familiar with a few other followers of the rogue Indian guru Bhagwan Shree Rajneesh, he gave the man a polite nod and walked on, giving the Rajneeshy—so he told Alma later—not a jot more thought.

It might well have stayed that way. He had never seen the orange man before in his years living on the Upper West Side. He would be most unlikely to ever see him again in a city of eight million souls.

Yet in a prime piece of angelic coordination that Mein Host called one of the most pronounced synchronicities of his life, there was the orange man later that same afternoon, on the same street. Only this time they were both walking in the same direction.

Falling into conversation and making their introductions, they'd barely walked a full block when their mutual interest in altered states came up, and only another half-block before the orange man started talking about ketamine and the group sessions he ran—mainly for other followers of Rajneesh.

It must have seemed almost miraculous to my ward that their intention had been answered so quickly—or that it had been answered at all! But he didn't know then what he later came to understand: that in certain people's cases it is in the angels' interest to facilitate the means to alter consciousness so they can more easily make contact with that mortal.

It was quickly arranged for my ward to attend the next of the orange man's group ketamine sessions, which would be held in his apartment in two days.

Mein Host—like everyone aware of the new consciousness movement—had met a number of Rajneesh sannyasin and had generally liked most of them. He would not have known this at the time, but many of the followers of the guru were incarnated rebel angels who, like him, were unaware of it. One of Alma's friends, a man she'd known as a child—a family friend with whom she had grown up—had become a sannyasin, and my ward had gotten along well with him.

Orange man would be a little more complicated.

"I liked the guy okay," he told Alma on his return with the good news, "and the K thing happened so fast it blew me away . . ."

"So you're going to the session?"

"Of course, yes. Why not?! Guess what? To add to all the weird coincidences, the guy lives only two blocks up from us on Central Park West!"

Mein Host had been spending more time with Alma after meeting her at a party soon after he'd left the community. Upon sharing a taxi home after the party they'd discovered that they both not only lived on Central Park West, but they also lived in apartments that were only one block apart.

It was a coincidence too obvious to ignore, so this—and the obvious pleasure they found in each other's company—led first to a long, platonic friendship and then later to their becoming lovers. Their relationship would develop and deepen over the years through many periods of closeness—and even longer times of separation. They shared such warmth and intimacy that I've heard my ward call Alma "the love of my life."

When my ward met the orange man that hot August afternoon in 1980, his friendship with Alma was based on their mutual interest in entheogens. Their choice not to sexualize their friendship allowed them the freedom to explore shared altered states and to get to know one another with the psychic transparency permitted by entheogens.

It was evident that Alma was as intrigued with the ketamine experience as was my ward, but neither of them placed much hope that he would emerge from the group session with any ketamine to share with her. If he did, it would be just one more lucky break in this run of good fortune.

He wouldn't have known—or, perhaps, might have been able to anticipate—what a distasteful little dance he'd have to go through before returning to Alma after the orange man's session, clutching a small vial of ketamine hydrochloride.

# 4

# The Reason of Experience

Atlantis, the Nile Valley and Sumer,
Polytheistic Cults, Nommo and Mali, James's
Three Wives, Dolphin Telepathy, and
an English Inquisition

By the mid-fifth millennium, Egypt and the Nile Valley culture—after a long period of dormancy—was starting to show signs of life again. The changing weather patterns had driven many of the people south in search of more habitable conditions. The once reliable Nile River had been regularly drying up and then changing its course, leaving a maze of dusty irrigation channels to return to desert.

The nomadic desert tribes were still living in the shadow of the Great Sphinx, which was already so ancient it was credited as the work of the gods. These tribes started coalescing once again in the Nile Valley as the climate stabilized and the Nile flowed once again in the course it follows to this day.

I sometimes think of Egypt as the center of gravity of the Middle East, and in less salubrious terms as the drain in the middle of the Mediterranean basin. In good times—and the fifth millennium was bringing back the good times—the Nile Valley would draw the best and the brightest from as far as the mountains east of the Caspian Sea and as far south as Afghanistan.

There is a certain predictability to the arc of development of all civilizations. Once a Watcher has seen enough of them rising and falling, they appear to differ only in the length of time they flourish before withering and dying away. I wouldn't be the first to comment on the ever-shortening length of time a civilization assumes its dominant position on the world stage. The reason for this has only become more obvious with the passing of history—it all comes down to the speed of communication.

Most civilizations have started, sensibly enough, in the presence of water. Sensible enough, of course, until the ocean rises and swallows the city—the pearl of that civilization. I've previously written about the river people of Europe and their expansion throughout Europe using the waterways threading through the continent. Similarly it was their kinship and familiarity with the ocean that drew the Australian Aborigines south. Down they came to the coasts of the continent and the many settlements around both the Black Sea and the southern reaches of the Caspian Sea. It is water, after all, that a Mars Rover first looks for in its search for life.

It was the seasonal rise and fall of the Nile—and the torrent that brought nutrients leeched from minerals in the mountains where the Nile found its source far to the south—that ensured the rich harvests on the plains of the Nile Valley. This in turn required the need for food distribution centers. This drew the builders and the craftspeople, then came the makers of implements and artifacts, and tents became houses—with the tribal leadership getting the largest dwellings.

Trading began with the nearby tribes, and news of the work opportunities opening up in the burgeoning Nile Valley traveled fast along the caravan routes. This prompted a steady stream of migrants from the Land of the Two Rivers, who brought with them some of the fruits of this far older Mesopotamian culture. These were a settled people who had been able to develop their agriculture—their growing of grains— in the increasingly arid conditions in southern Iraq. They had domesticated animals and established industries producing anything from elaborate metalwork to elegant pottery to a wide variety of building materials. By the mid-fourth millennium, numerous cities had sprung up in Sumer (the Land of the Two Rivers). This occurred from Ur and Eridu in the south—close to the mouth of the Persian Gulf—with other cities following the rivers all the way north to Sippar.

In Egypt the tribes had coalesced first in the north, in the region of the Nile Delta where the city of Heliopolis would grow some two and a half thousand years later. Here the expanding culture would spread south along the fertile Nile Valley to leave its mark in a later era on the Giza Plateau. They would then expand their reach of the area with their pyramids and temples and the magnificent statuary that would follow the river south as far as Luxor.

If I'm to step back for a moment and survey the fourth millennium as a whole, I would have to confess that what I'd observed was making me increasingly nervous. It looked to me that the three great centers of power—Atlantis, the Nile Valley, and Sumer—although still in their early periods of growth, were already setting themselves up for the con-flicts that would be rumbling through the next three thousand years.

I suppose my nervousness at the time was based on what I had seen in the past—admittedly the distant past in mortal terms—when Caligastia was pushing so hard for technological progress. In this he set side against side and tribe against tribe—and for no other reason than his obsession for revenge against his archenemy Vanu.

Would that vengefulness start all over again? I cringed at the thought. I'd seen this cycle repeat itself so many times before that I could hardly be blamed for anticipating the worst.

However, Prince Caligastia appeared to have changed his tune—if only to modify it slightly. He had failed to develop the means to con-front Vanu. Worse, he had inadvertently provoked a thermonuclear war that laid to waste much of North Africa and the Middle East. With Vanu and Amadon long withdrawn back to System Headquarters, the Prince evidently felt free to use a more subtle strategy.

The atomic war almost eighty thousand years earlier was the result of the Prince's hubris and his misjudgment of human cunning and belligerence. I believe Caligastia had learned to be more cautious after the effects of the war had backfired on him. I'd seen signs he was starting to anticipate the eventual rebellion that would be provoked among those subject to his ruthless oversight. But I couldn't tell whether his intention was to provoke rebellions or to prevent them by supporting the harshest of repressive methods.

I don't believe that it once occurred to Prince Caligastia that the spirit of rebellion was deeply embedded in the spiritual and psychological makeup of human beings. In a very real sense humans were built to rebel. Unless they have been bent out of shape, human beings of every race and era tend to react similarly to oppression and injustice. Indeed it's true that most children seem to grow into having an innate sense of fairness after they mature out of their baby-egotism phase.

Having rebelled with Lucifer against the MA—and then, after attempting to set himself up as the sole divine authority in the world—the Prince appeared oddly blind to the inevitability of the revolutions inflamed by the tyrannies he nurtured. I suspect he had convinced himself that rebellions were solely about power, because the driving element behind his rebellion against the MA was based on power.

What I was starting to grasp—but what I fear Caligastia was never able to understand—was that most human-instigated rebellions were ignited and sustained by a deep sense of injustice on the part of the rebels. Rebellions were seldom primarily about power; they were about the unfair distribution of power. Sure, there might be a few among the leadership of a revolution who lust for power—but the main body of the rebels would almost always be rebelling against a perceived injustice.

Here, I believe, is where Caligastia's pride and extreme narcissism rendered him unable to recognize the Indwelling Spirit in human beings, and he was unwilling to admit that humans were becoming progressively more strong willed and individuated.

The Prince's attempt to impose his control over Atlantis—only to have been usurped by the very midwayers he was working through—was a humiliating failure for a Planetary Prince. It was a dishonor that a prince as proud as Caligastia would be unlikely to forget, let alone forgive.

Thus by the fourth millennium the Prince and his midwayers appeared so deeply embroiled in their own private rebellion that they'd lost sight of any goal but obstructionism. The Prince was focusing most of his time and energy on the Jehovah and the influence they were starting to exert over the nomadic desert tribes roaming throughout the land of the Bible. But the monotheistic cult he was promoting had its many setbacks and was growing far more slowly than the Prince had evidently hoped it would. Monotheism was proving to be a hard sell in a rough-and-tumble world.

Yet should anyone have known it at the time, the fourth millennium was also an era of profound change.

The midwayers were finding it more difficult to influence human behavior, while the priests and priestesses of a heady profusion of polytheistic cults and sects were starting to assert their power. Most of the sonic building technology of the Lemurians—their ability to shape and move enormous blocks of stone, for example—had been lost in the many natural catastrophes of the previous millennia. Despite Caligastia's midwayer-led pressure on the tribes to attempt to emulate Lemurian technology in places such as Göbekli Tepe, the Prince was never able to satisfactorily replicate the great architectural works of the Lemurian civilization.

It appeared that word may have leaked out about events to occur on this world sometime within the next few thousand years of that time. If true, the rumors were predicting an occurrence that would entirely change the Great Game, and that would bring a profound new meaning to what had been transpiring on this planet since the time of the angelic revolution. No Watcher I encountered could quite agree on what this event was going to be. What they *did* seem to agree upon was that it would change everything and that it was going to be influential—far beyond this one planet. This latter proposition piqued my interest because of what I had recently witnessed on one of my travels, which had introduced a new element that surprised me at the time.

I say it surprised me with good reason, because I had the impression the planet was still under quarantine—and that any space-faring extraterrestrials straying into the System would have been warned off. Wasn't that part of the midwayers' function? But of course that begged the question. Which midwayers? The loyalists or the rebels?

It happened that I was drifting idly over one of the west-central African deserts in the region of present-day Mali. I had been moving north, drawn—or so I thought—toward the Atlas Mountains with the idea of observing the growing Berber community.

Mali was one of those regions particularly hard hit by the changing climatic conditions that had desertified so much of the land to the north. The landscape appeared as a featureless, sandy wasteland as I moved over it. I was marveling once again that any human could live under such harsh conditions when I spied a stand of palm trees far ahead. Knowing palm trees meant the presence of water—and an oasis meant the possible presence of people—I allowed myself to be carried there by my curiosity.

Now, I do have to admit this was a bit strange. I have commented on it briefly before, but the effect had seemed to continue. At that time, I put it down to the idea I was being guided and placed, unbeknown to me, into a wide variety of significant situations so I would be able to make a record of them at some point in the future. Happening to be present for one of the visitations of a small group of extraterrestrials from an aquatic world in the Sirius star system only further illustrated this theory.

It amuses me that Mein Host has also experienced something of this phenomenon; the experience of finding himself in a number of unusual—and sometimes significant—situations over the course of his life.

I know he hadn't given it any thought, because he was surprised when Ruth—one of the three wives of his friend James Wharram—demanded to know why he seemed to have all the luck. Why had he had such privileged encounters with dolphins? Why had he been able to talk with an extraterrestrial? And what was the reason the angels talked to him? Why to *him*?

There was a slight tone of skepticism in Ruth's question, which was asked soon after they'd met. She'd read my ward's first book, and—having spent much her adult life at sea—there was a subtext of incredulity as to why *she* hadn't had such privileged encounters with dolphins.

Ruth was the elder of James Wharram's three wives, all of whom lived together harmoniously in a town on the southern coast of Devon. Ruth had been with James since he'd designed and built *Tangaroa* in 1953. It was the first western oceangoing catamaran, and also the first catamaran to make a transatlantic crossing.

James had continued to design and sail catamarans over the years, borrowing from Polynesian boat-building techniques and creating what he has called "flexible and intelligent boats." James has since been hailed as the boat builder who introduced oceangoing catamarans that anyone with skill could easily build from his plans.

My ward had met James Wharram in 1992 at the Third Dolphin and Whale Conference in Hawaii when they found themselves sharing a luxurious hotel room that the conference had provided them with (as they did for all the scheduled speakers) as a perk for participating in the conference. James was a large, flamboyant man, some twelve years older than my ward, with strongly held opinions about anything that came up for discussion. He was confident, loud, and funny. The two hit it off immediately.

On the first day of the conference my ward couldn't help but notice an exquisitely beautiful young black girl attending some of the talks. At lunch it turned out that she was a friend of some of his pals living in Hawaii, who were happy to introduce her as Gwendolyn.

Gwen was exceptionally bright and lively, as well as being breathtakingly pretty. She was tall and slim as a rail, with a long, elegant neck and a modest Afro. She moved like a wraith, happy, it seemed, to be wafted by the prevailing winds. Recently Gwen had been laid off from working as an intern for a research program with dolphins at an aquarium associated with the University of Hawaii. At that time the experiments under Dr. Louis Herman were focused upon whether dolphins were sufficiently conscious to comprehend what was being shown them on underwater television screens.

Apparently they were.

Gwen had joked at lunch: "What the dolphins actually thought about what they'd seen on TV we had no way of knowing. Not that it would satisfy scientific standards, but they seemed to especially like the commercials!"

Dr. Louis Herman is known for making some important observations about dolphins. For example, he has shown the mechanism by which the dolphin eye "sees" functions equally well both underwater and above the surface in the air. As a serious academic researcher, Dr. Herman's methods, according to Gwen, were "laboriously pragmatic in the constant face of the miraculous." She told my ward, much to his amusement, that the good doctor "would regularly get furious with the poor dolphins when they responded to a command before he gave it! He just refused to deal with it . . . to see what was really going on."

As the evening of the first day of the conference drew to a close, it appeared that Gwen—who lived on the other side of the Big Island—had nowhere to sleep, and the hotel, of course, was far too expensive for her. Mein Host was only too happy to offer to share with her the second of the two massively large double beds in the room that the conference organizers had given him and James Wharram.

And young Gwendolyn, not surprisingly, was just as happy to accept.

Do I digress again? Wasn't I about to narrate what I observed in the deserts of Mali? Well I did warn you, patient reader! I was going to allow myself to free-associate more liberally in my narrative as the appropriate incidents come to me. And I'm not finished with young Gwendolyn quite yet.

What I hope I'm going to continue to illustrate in my ward's biography—with no particular mind now to an overriding chronological sequence—are some of the tests and challenges, some of the trials and tribulations, faced by an incarnate rebel angel as he comes to grips with who he is and why he is here.

I do this not only for my ward's benefit but also in knowing that there are many incarnate angels out there who might benefit from what my ward has gone through and what he might or might not have learned. This isn't because I anticipate other starseeds to have identical—or even similar—challenges to be faced in their lives. More simply it's because challenges are challenges, and strangers in a strange land need all the insightful information they can lay their hands on. So if you, dear reader, can learn anything from Mein Host's choices—both good and bad— then at the very least we will be offering some encouragement to all those who are waking up to their own nature in these confusing times.

The Dolphin and Whale Conference in Hawaii was coming to a close, and James Wharram and my ward were sitting on the balcony of their hotel room comparing notes on the various speakers.

Gwen was elsewhere, so they had the chance to speak freely. In common with other people who have idiosyncratic sexual arrangements they are proud of, James—who had three wives—had no compunction about questioning others on their sex lives. He was unusually open and frank for an Englishman, and much of his general conversation—when it wasn't about catamarans—seemed shadowed with sexual overtones.

It was much to James's astonishment to hear that my ward and the willowy, beautiful young Gwendolyn had spent the three nights of the conference chastely sleeping together entwined in each other's arms and legs. Yes, chastely! For God's sake! James could hardly believe it!

"You must be off your head," he sounded appalled after discovering his roommates weren't making love. This was a man who was living with three women and presumably was making love with them all.

"You might be right, James—perhaps I am crazy! But I do have my reasons."

"You're like bloody Gandhi, sleeping between two virgins just to prove he was above temptation . . . and all that fucking," James retorted.

"I don't know about Gandhi, why he was doing it," my ward replied, "but yeah, there's a bit of that. I wanted to see if I could do it. Just being sensual without the need to turn it into lovemaking . . ."

"But why?" James just couldn't get it. "Why'd you want to do that? She's as beautiful as you'll ever see. Think of what you're missing."

"I've slept with enough gorgeous women to know what it's like. And I've had a black girlfriend, so there's no wild new experiment there. She wasn't as pitch-black as this one . . ." my ward said, his voice becoming dreamy, "so I just loved sweet Gwenny's velvety smooth black skin . . ."

"And kissing those lovely thick, cushiony lips?" James replied, well into his fantasy by now.

"And kissing those lovely soft lips, yes. Just once, for the experience."

"You're fucking crazy!" James muttered, no doubt seeing his fantasy withering on the vine.

"I don't expect you to buy this, James—you with your three wives— but I've discovered that I actually prefer to live monogamously. I've done otherwise. God! I've had three or four lovers at the same time . . . no, no, not all in bed together—although I have had a couple of three-somes. It was fun for a while, sure, but very soon it was a distraction. I was just staggering from one bedroom to another. It was exhausting."

"But, come on, you could have a great time with Gwen. I'll leave the room to you if that's what stopping you . . ." James offered.

"No, no, it's really not that, James. Thanks anyway. For God's sake don't go anywhere." Mein Host must have realized then that his friend simply wasn't getting it. Perhaps Wharram wasn't equipped to get it; maybe it was just a generational difference. He was fighting a differ-ent battle. While Wharram was protesting his sexual freedom, my ward was sexually free.

Wharram wasn't going to let it go. "Look at me! Look! I've got years on you, man, and I'd fuck her in a moment!" Standing up, he strode around in the hotel room—bare chested and in his shorts—and then back out onto the balcony. He was a fine figure of a man, too, for someone in his midsixties—tanned and self-confident, his face and hair grizzled by sea and sun.

"Can you really control yourself? You don't get hard?" he added.

"You wanna know how I do it? Would that shut you up?"

James said, "Not so much how you do it, but why you do it? You could spend a weekend fucking her brains out and no one need ever know . . ."

"James, it's really not about fucking. Yes, I could do that. In another situation I might have. I'm sure Gwen would be juicy in bed, no doubt about it. But there's another level to it. Don't laugh. I don't expect you to get it, but here goes . . ."

James Wharram sat down heavily on the fragile garden chair that seemed to bend under him as he leaned back, his glass in hand.

"Okay. My shtick." Mein Host stood up, leaning with one arm on the white plasticized metal railing, limned against the sun. The ocean was blue and sultry and winking through the palm trees behind him.

"Here it is. We live in a ridiculously oversexed society. Sex is every-where, and being used to sell everything from cars to carbolic soap. Nothing new there. We all know that. But it's the effect it's having on us that concerns me. A good-looking chick like Gwen is going to be treated as a sex object wherever she goes . . . she probably even *expects* to be treated that way. That's what men are like, that sort of thing. She probably uses sex to get what she wants. Most pretty girls do—nothing really wrong in that. Gwen offered to put out for the bed, but that didn't feel right to me. Like taking advantage of a drunk girl. Not to my taste."

"Even if they want you?" James remained disbelieving.

"It's not worth it, for the next day when they look at you all funny and ask you what happened last night . . . then you tell 'em you just tucked 'em up in bed all nice and comfy—and intact!

"I really prefer to live transparently, so I can go back to my girl-friend in Oz and tell her all about it without feeling any guilt. I mean, when I kissed those yummy lips of hers I didn't stick my tongue in her mouth. That wasn't the point. I was just curious about the sensation of her lips. I hadn't had that before."

Wharram's eyebrows arched.

"Yeah, they were great. They were soft. That's what you wanted to know, James? But, like I said, that wasn't really the point. It was on the last morning and, frankly, I was curious."

"And you didn't want to take it any further? Really?" James asked.

Mein Host paused before answering. I knew if he hoped to make his point to a difficult audience he would have to be honest about his reactions.

"Yeah, I weighed it up . . . of course I did. She's a lovely girl. But I'd made up my mind not to go there. If it sounds silly to you, I felt I could be more value to her—okay, it does sound a bit grandiose, but it's what I felt—if she knew she was being loved for herself, for who she was, and not as a mere sex object. Listen, I'm over twenty years older than the girl. I've nothing to prove. Believe it or not, it's more important to me that she'd feel respected and loved in such an intimate situation for who she was, and not for what she could offer sexually."

"And you're telling me she was fine with that? She didn't feel you were rejecting her sexually, that there was something wrong with her if you didn't fancy her?" James continued.

"God, no! She knew I fancied her, I made that pretty obvious. How could I not? She was gorgeous. But I could feel how she'd been used. It was much more important that she get some real self-respect than I get some pussy, right?"

With that the subject was dropped.

Gwen swam into my ward's life, much like a dolphin, and a week later floated out of it just as innocently. He recorded this entry in his journal.

Just like a dolphin, he wrote:

Playful. Sweet, she was. With no overtones at all. Pisces. Between us we danced together, or perhaps floated through the conference like dolphins. People would say how wonderful we looked together: black against white. Youth against age. Both of us tall and slim . . . I loved exploring the magnificence of her black skin. The firmness of it; the healthy athletically toned, twenty-four-year-old flesh, downy like the skin covering the antlers of a fawn. We slept very well together—our bodies obviously enjoying each other's presence, turning and sliding together in our sleep. We also both had dolphin dreams on the nights we slept together.

It was a couple of years after the conference in Hawaii—when my ward was in England—that he had the opportunity to visit James, meet his wives, and face the question Ruth had asked him.

Why did he get to have all these fascinating experiences?

He answered as best he knew. "Perhaps in the past I'd have put it down to being lucky or coincidence or whatever. Now, with what I've gone through, I've no doubt it's because it is where the angels are putting me. It's as simple as that, Ruth—and perhaps, since I've proved to them I'm not in it to fluff myself up, that I'm serious about it. The events just seem to happen. I don't ask for them. But here's the thing, there does seem to be a logical sequence to the events."

They were sitting around the table in the Wharrams' Devon kitchen, chatting after dinner, and before James had shown my ward out to his catamaran so he could get the feeling of sleeping on the cat for the night.

Of the three wives, Ruth was clearly the most senior and was deferred to by the other, younger women. It was Ruth who asked most of the questions, and it was Ruth who seemed genuinely interested in my ward's answers. The younger women were clearing the dishes away and doing their best to listen over the clatter of the plates.

My ward said, "First it was swimming with wild dolphins, then the ETs came into my life, and after that it was the angels. Each one opened me up to the next. First it's that we share the planet with another intelligent species, dolphins. Next it's that we share the Multiverse with masses of other intelligent life, and finally, that we share our inner spaces with the angels.

"See what I mean? One experience led to the next. It was all quite natural. I just had to turn up and be there. Like being in the right place at the right time."

"And other people?" Ruth asked. "Can they also have these experiences?"

"I always assumed they did! Perhaps they do, and then they forget about it. Like my friend Stephen. He was one of three people who saw a disc-shaped craft over New York in 1981. Then he was there when a young boy being used as a telepathic mouthpiece by the guys in the saucer walked up to talk with us. Great stuff, too . . . for twenty minutes! I was there. I saw it all. I wrote it up in my first book."

Ruth was nodding her head, presumably remembering the story from my ward's book. And, indeed, it was a memorable occasion, or it certainly should have been.

"Anyway, I left the city in 1990," my ward continued, "so I didn't see Stephen again for another ten years. When I did, I asked him about the day we saw the saucer—it was Labor Day 1981. Do you know, he'd completely forgotten the whole event! Even with my prodding he simply couldn't remember it happening. A total blank. Nothing . . ."

"So, perhaps it didn't really happen," this from one of the younger wives over by the sink.

"Oh it happened alright. The third person, my girlfriend at the time, saw it all and remembered it. Plus I wrote down what notes I could when the young kid was telling us all this cosmic stuff, so I had evidence. It all happened as I wrote it. The point is that Stephen—and no, he's not stupid—had completely forgotten the entire incident only twenty or so years after it . . . after one of the most significant events of my life! And it might as well not have happened in his—for all the impact it made on him."

"Maybe he didn't need the experience, if it didn't do him any good . . ."

I could almost hear Ruth working it out for herself.

"Exactly!" Mein Host cut in. "My girlfriend and I had the experience and remembered it because our conceptual framework was open to it. It helped us . . . it helped confirm in 3-D reality something of great importance and interest to us. Our friend Stephen forgot it because it didn't fit into his life. It didn't add meaning for him like it did for us."

"Like those reports where some people see a flying saucer, and the people next to them don't?" the second wife asked, drying her hands on a tea cloth and joining the others at the table.

"Sure. A bit like that. Perhaps Stephen was slightly more awake than those ones who didn't see the craft. I think we get the experiences we're ready for. Don't you? Isn't that how it works?"

"Sort of like we never get more than we can handle?" the younger woman said cautiously, wanting to be included.

"That's bullshit!" James said brusquely, coloring the young woman's cheeks. "What about all those people who do get more than they can handle? People who get killed because they couldn't handle whatever it was? It's New Age claptrap . . ."

Mein Host interrupted. "Seems to me it's always just a little more than we think we can handle! We're a lazy lot, humans. And it wouldn't be rising to the challenge if the bar wasn't set a bit higher than what we're comfortable with."

"What about the people who get killed . . . or drowned in a storm? Isn't that more than they could handle?" Ruth picked up on James's argument.

"Look, I can't speak to every case," my ward said slowly. "I can only talk from personal experience, and it's certainly been true for me. Perhaps the guy who drowned in the storm was being arrogant, maybe he'd made so much money he thought he was invincible . . ."

Ruth pounced. "But if he was dead what would he have learned?"

"Ah! Okay. Yes," my ward said. "Now, I see why it's hard to understand. You have to factor in the continuation of life after death for it to make sense. If it was his arrogance that drowned the man, then he'll have the chance to reckon with it in his afterlife review . . . after he died . . ."

Mein Host paused and let the phrase hang there. The junior wife had completed the washing up and was sliding into one of the bench seats as the others made space for her. "You believe in life after death?" she asked, with a slightly foreign accent. "You think it's true?"

"I know it's true. I've been there . . . ," Mein Host said before Ruth interrupted, telling the younger women about what she'd read of my ward's NDE in his book—how he died back in 1973 and was given the choice to continue to be "dead" or to return to life. She must have read it remarkably thoroughly, because she got all the facts right—ending with a question that must have been puzzling her.

"If I remember correctly," she said, "one of the things the Being told you was you'd completed what you came to do. Isn't that what he said?"

"That I'd done what I'd come to do, yes."

"And you were what, in your early thirties?"

"Right, thirty-three."

"So, what was it you'd come to do that you did?"

"I don't have a clue!" Mein Host said with a laugh. "I've wondered about that, believe me! I've had a few ideas, but nothing's clicked yet. I guess I'm not meant to know right now. And it's not that important, anyway."

"If you've been there, as you say," this from the second wife who'd been sitting quietly, "if you've seen all that, what do you think happens?"

"You mean after we die?"

"After we die . . . before we die . . ." she clarified.

"I can only tell you my best model to date. I'm not saying it's necessarily right, only that it best matches my actual experiences. James, I know we've talked about this before. Do you mind?"

James made a graceful gesture of acquiescence, for the women were leaning forward over the table, their open faces a flickering mix of fascination, skepticism, and humor. They must have thought, "We've got a ripe one here!" The Wharram household evidently saw themselves as pragmatists, and it was probably unlikely for them to often have one such as my ward to cross-examine.

"Okay then. Once I knew life continued after death, two questions immediately arose: One, if life continues after death, what happens then? Does it go on and on? And two, if it goes on after the death of the body, then doesn't that suggest I was alive before my birth?"

There was silence around the table. These were reasonable questions.

"I believe I have some answers to both these questions," my ward said, looking from face to face, interest now having replaced humor and skepticism.

"I've had enough experiences now to know I preexisted this lifetime. I've had memories of previous existences. In fact, Ruth, that thing I'd come to do . . . remember? One of my ideas is that I'd needed to clear something leftover from a previous lifetime. That was what I'd done that I didn't know I was doing. No, it doesn't matter what it was . . ."

Ruth leaned back, smiling, her question preempted.

"Next, I put two obvious issues together. If I survived the death of my material body and was told I'd completed a given task, then didn't this suggest there was a learning process at work here—but one that spanned many lifetimes?"

"You think everybody's like that?" James asked. "Everyone has reincarnated? Why can't we all remember stuff then?"

"First, James, I've really no idea whether everyone else has reincarnated—perhaps some people have and some haven't. I just felt forever that I couldn't have gotten this fucked up in one lifetime! Anyway, I think it's only important when there's some unfinished business from a previous life that needs clearing up. And then, like me, it probably won't be a conscious thing. You do it or you don't, but you probably don't know you're doing it at the time."

"And if you don't succeed?" he queried.

"Then you'll have another chance to deal with it in another lifetime, but I suspect each time it's missed, it gets harder and more challenging! Like it does in this lifetime."

There was some nervous laughter around the table at that, each of them wondering, no doubt, what it was they might be missing.

"The next step," Mein Host continued, "is to understand that the universe and everything in it is one vast living teaching machine. We learn through direct experience or—if we are very wise—through the experience of others. But the most important things we have to go through ourselves.

"But, Ruth, to go back to 'Why me?'—your first question. Why do I get to have all these unusual experiences? Well, it just came to me. If I'd done what I came to do, then I was kind of starting with a clean slate. I'd been in a spiritual community for seven years when I had the NDE, so you could say I was already oriented in a spiritual direction. If I had nothing hanging over my head, no karma or anything, then this allowed me to focus on what really interested me. All my adventures with dolphins, ETs, and angels probably developed from that. Perhaps that answers your question a bit more fully."

So the conversation wound on into the night. The Wharram family spoke about enjoying their share of magical and mysterious encounters with dolphins, but they hadn't seen UFOs, and being English they had a knee-jerk rejection of any idea of angels.

"Let me tell you something I heard when I was doing a radio show in the States," my ward said. "I don't say it to convince you, only that it was true." They nodded their encouragement, and he continued while the candles in the middle of the table spluttered and flared.

"On a phone-in radio show I was promoting a book called *Ask Your Angels* that I'd written with a couple of others. I believe it was in New Orleans; I have it in my journal. Of course you get a few weirdos on those shows—mainly know-it-all Christian fundamentalists who want to lay their trip on me. But every once in a while you get some quite extraordinarily moving accounts.

"This man, the one I want to tell you about, was no weirdo. He sounded like an older man, and you could hear the raw emotion in his voice. He used to be a tugboat captain, he explained. He also made a point of saying that he wasn't particularly religious at the time—which is relatively unusual for an American of that background.

"He said there'd been a bad storm the day it happened. They were towing a barge of some sort. I think it was something to do with an oil rig. Anyway, there were a number of men on the barge while it was being towed, and they were in radio contact with the tugboat captain. As the storm worsened the barge began taking on water and quickly started to sink. At this point the poor man's voice was breaking over the phone, sobbing and gulping for air."

Seagoing folk, the Wharrams must had had some idea of what was coming next.

Mein Host's voice dropped. "'I had no choice,' the man kept repeating, 'I had no choice, I needed to do it to save my boat.' He had to cut the towline to avoid being dragged down by the sinking barge. And yet they were still in radio contact. He could still hear the men in the barge. He said at first there were screams of horror and fear when the men realized their fate, but their voices had suddenly changed to gasps of surprise. He could hear them saying the place was filling with angels. He said everything changed at that moment as the men's voices became overcome with awe and reverence.

"'The place is filling with angels! It's filling with angels!' He kept repeating it like a mantra, and I could feel the captain's emotions pouring through the phone line. This was no flighty New Ager," he said, grinning at James. "He was a tough old tugboat captain. He certainly wasn't primed to expect angels. He was as knocked out as anybody would be. But, he said, it changed his life from that point on.

"So, yes, to know the reality of angels, and I'm not talking about believing in them—that's neither here nor there—but knowing they're actually real, you need to have the actual experience."

"Believing in angels or not believing in them doesn't make any difference? Is that what you're saying?" Ruth again.

"Yeah, it probably boils down to that. Angels exist whether or not we believe in them. They're not projections of our minds or figments of our imagination. If you haven't been to the Galapagos Islands it really doesn't matter if you believe in their existence or not. They're still there."

Ruth said after a pause, "If I wanted to contact my angels for myself, what would you recommend?"

"Well, you could do worse than to read my book!" my ward said, laughing again. "We wrote *Ask Your Angels* for just that reason, to help people who really want to make contact. But I should warn you, Ruth, working with angels requires a level of total self-honesty we're not used to in everyday life. Nothing is hidden, and neither should it be. If you seriously want to go ahead and make contact, be prepared for some penetrating and often uncomfortable truths about yourself. To start with, you'll find it's a bit like working with a highly skilled, telepathic psychotherapist who knows you inside out. That said, the stuff you learn far outweighs any discomfort.

"As I said, you don't have to believe or disbelieve. There's a third position of neutrality, of simply remaining open to whatever occurs—like when you're meditating. It'll take time—it took me two years—but that's part of it, too. It's by staying with it and persevering that we prove we are serious students. On the other hand, I've seen some people make almost immediate contact with their angels, so you never know. I suspect I was a particularly hard case, which is why it took as long as it did."

There was some laughter at that. The idea of this man—who talked so intimately about angels and telepathic dolphins and who claimed to speak with extraterrestrials—having spoken of himself as a "particularly hard case" must have sounded bizarrely anomalous to them.

Yet it is also true that my ward was an extremely tough customer. His reincarnational background has been most recently that of warrior/priest/shaman, and he entered this lifetime with an unusually resistant psychic carapace. I've heard him say that he needed to be tough to survive a war and an English education, and that it's proved invaluable in being able to understand and talk to hard, skeptical people. In fact, from what I've observed I suspect my ward might actually prefer the cut and thrust of a good argument with an atheist to a lovefest with believers.

As a consequence, the evening with the Wharrams made for a fascinating and wide-ranging discussion. I think it underlined for Mein Host once more the value of personal experience. James, Ruth, and the others were all clear-sighted, adventurous, and singularly individualistic people—people who could be expected to be open to the unexpected. No doubt they'd had some mysterious and unexplainable encounters in their own lives, and yet the very idea of angels was too much of a conceptual stretch for them.

Their discussion also served to demonstrate my ward's earlier observation about there being a logical sequence to these incidents. You might think of it as an education. James and company had started to have their dolphin experiences, but they hadn't yet made it to the next stage. This posed the obvious questions: Would my ward have been so persuaded in the existential reality of angels if he had not witnessed them in his NDE? Might he and his girlfriend never have noticed the UFO over Manhattan had they not had a lights-in-the-sky incident only a few weeks earlier? Finally, and what would turn out to be a turning point in my ward's life, would he have been able to accept the angels on their own terms when they were speaking through Edward—the light-trance medium in Toronto—if he hadn't had an NDE and a background of reading *The Urantia Book*?

Make of it what you will, but it is my ward's reading and retention of *The Urantia Book* that allows me a context and a vocabulary with which to narrate my story.

# 5

# Deeper Secrets of a Deeper Being

## The Blessings of Rebellion, the Toroidal Multiverse, Scientific Priests, Introduction to Ketamine, Talking with Angels, and Egyptian Mysteries

I confess to a surprising admiration for the strategies used by the MA.

Whatever faults Lucifer had found in Multiverse authorities at the time of the rebellion has been amply made up for by, in my mind, what I'd come to think of the MA's strategic cleverness and their skill at positioning themselves for the longer game they were playing.

Rather than stamping out the rebellion at its source—and before the upheaval could spread to the thirty-seven planets—the MA allowed the rebellion to develop and play itself out. They did this so all involved would have the opportunity to witness the results of their choices.

Perhaps there was some truth to what Lucifer confided to me in my early interview with him—and that he then promptly amnesed. If he had spoken words of truth, then the revolution was part of a great work of cosmic alchemy. And the whole meaning of the rebellion, and the way it has unfolded, suggests that the uprising continues to have a deeper and largely occulted purpose than has been hitherto understood or acknowledged. So it might be said that the MA was using the rebellion for its own hidden purposes—if indeed the MA hadn't quietly permitted, or even encouraged, the rebellion in the first place.

Then there was that clever way the MA outfoxed Caligastia's plans for his—what did he call it?—"Reincarnation Express." He did this, that's right, by recycling rebel angels while keeping the mortal ascension process open for the natural ascenders. It was a brilliant move—although I'm sure the Prince never saw it that way!

There was the whole subject of rebel angels entering mortal incarnation. Was the incubation of *Homo angelicus* always part of the MA's intention right from the start? Was that one of the covert reasons why the MA did not settle the rebellion and instead allowed it to continue for 203,000 years? Or was the MA merely taking advantage of a difficult situation and making the best of it?

The Melchizedek teachers are said to be already teaching about the many blessings that have been extracted from the angelic rebellion, and they speak of those benefits—or so I've heard—with a surprising level of enthusiasm.

It's been observed by others that the MA reserves an unusual degree of respect for agondonters—those mortals who ascend from worlds isolated by angelic rebellion. This is a privileged status that accompanies an agondonter all the way up through the Local Universe—and further still, deep into a Superuniverse—only to disappear when the soul ascends to the Central Universe.

To fully understand the nature of this privilege, I should explain what I've learned about this mortal ascension process.

There are teachers in the Melchizedek Universities who maintain that the ascension process is really the true purpose of the Multiverse. I recall one of our lecturers claiming in a seminar before I arrived here that, when all things are equal, the entire hierarchy of celestials in the Local Universe could be said to be serving mortal ascension.

Contrary to current scientific belief, all inhabited planets are created for the very purpose of growing and nurturing sentient life.

Third-density planets such as Earth are where mortal life starts its long journey to the Central Universe.

If this suggests that an unreasonable amount of attention is being paid to mortals, then consider this paradox.

The animal body that a mortal being inhabits is the product of the natural evolutionary processes of that mortal's home world, while the soul and the personality animating the body are gifts from elsewhere. However, what really makes mortals so important and special to the celestials is that each and every mortal of sound mind is indwelt by a fragment of the Creator God. Human beings on a world such as this might consider themselves the very top of the evolutionary tree; the most intelligent creatures on the planet. They will compliment themselves on the human brain being the most complicated component in their universe. Yet being on top of a planet's evolutionary tree means also being at the bottom of the hierarchy of celestial intelligence.

And here's the paradox: the lowest form of sentient intelligent life in the Multiverse, the mortal being, is indwelt simultaneously by the Creator. "Man is the highest god" goes the occultist's maxim. For all celestials this remains a mystery that is shrouding an enigma that is itself embedded in a paradox.

Does that sound strange?

Disappointing?

Are you under the impression that high celestials should know everything there is to be known—or, at least, they would have access to knowing everything?

I'm no high celestial—and I'm sure you've spotted by now the limits of my own intelligence—but what distinguishes the celestial intelligence from the mortal intelligence, which I can't overstress, is functionality. Thus a high celestial—an archangel, for example—will possess an intelligence tailored to that archangel's function. The archangel will possess an all but omniscient intelligence, yet it will be entirely focused on the area of influence of that archangel. This won't be a particularly creative intelligence. It will be dedicated to maintaining a given reality in optimal condition by way of the immense scope of an archangel's wisdom.

Think of it, perhaps, as closer to the intelligence of a craftsperson rather than that of a creative artist.

The nature of mortal intelligence is more complicated (although by no means the most complicated element in the universe!) because it rests at the confluence of a number of streams of intelligence, that—taken together—represent the full span of human intelligence. Again, it's the presence of the Indwelling Creator that makes the mortal intelligence so exceptional in celestial eyes. Not, I hasten to say, because most mortals have much to do with their Indwelling Spirit during their present lifetime, but because of who you will later become when you have fully integrated the spirit.

Thus the mortal ascension process can be more poetically thought of as the Creator experiencing the Creation by sharing the journey that takes a mortal from the planet of their birth back to the very Heart of the Godhead. This is a journey that will take you through many hundreds of transitions—you may experience them as lifetimes yet with the absence of death—up through the progressively finer frequencies of the Local Universe.

A Local Universe is embedded within the larger matrix of one of the seven Superuniverses, with about one hundred thousand Local Universes in each Superuniverse. If the Multiverse is pictured as a torus, the seven Superuniverses—composed of all their Local Universes—exist on a spectrum of material frequency domains, from dense to fine (or from fine to dense, as some celestial artisans have suggested).

As we were taught in the seminars, the bagel-shaped torus—internally layered like an onion—is merely a model to visualize the Multiverse. We weren't to take it too literally.

The reason the toroidal form is used is because it conveniently illustrates the layered nature of the Multiverse. The hole in the center is visualized as the Central Universe, as that is on another range of frequencies entirely. This renders it entirely imperceptible from the denser frequencies of the material Multiverse. In fact, we were asked to understand the living Multiverse as the material child of the Central Universe. We were also being asked to understand that ultimatons—the building blocks of the quantum world of material particles—were continually being downstepped energetically from the Central Universe to inform the material universes of time and space.

The tutor suggested we visualize ultimatons as tiny white gushers—each in the form of a torus and far smaller than the quarks and charmed particles of quantum physics. Ultimatons are the final and smallest stage of granulation through which gravity acts to hold the Multiverse in its state of dynamic equilibrium. While it is through these minute ultimatonic white gushers that the Multiverse is continually renewed, it's through black holes that ultimatonic material is drawn back to the Central Universe.

Those are the essential mechanics as we were taught in the seminars—vastly oversimplified, of course—of how the Multiverse is self-sustaining within the limits imposed by entropy.

However, it is challenging to find the appropriate words and metaphors in my collaborator's vocabulary to get across concepts that are essentially outside human experience. If I say the Multiverse is known to have no beginning and no end, my ward's mind struggles to understand what that means. It's a little easier, he says, to think of eternity as going on forever and ever—but it's a lot harder to understand that eternity, by definition, also has no beginning.

As the current approach to the physical sciences on this world has come to rely so heavily on purely mathematical models, the visual metaphors thrown up by this process tend to be sparse indeed. Preferring to speak their own private language of higher mathematics, a physicist will insist that it is only in this obscure language that the workings of the universe can be understood and explained.

Even if the basic elements of string theory, for example, can be visualized, says Mein Host, it's well-nigh impossible to get any kind of mental image of those infinitesimally small enfolded dimensions. These are elements that the physicists assure us have to be there to make their theory work.

If the Multiverse is composed of material particles—the wave/particle dichotomy occurs at a much higher order of magnitude—then any agglomeration of these ultimatons will, of necessity, create a form or a pattern . . . and that form or pattern can be visualized.

This language of visualization was used by the ancients and led to many of the great inventions of the Lemurian era. When the visual language progressively surrendered to the mathematical models that have proved so effective in dissecting the material world, it required scientists to wear the blinkers demanded by their theoretical models. Thus their theories and concepts have become indecipherable, and thus of little practical value to the intelligent layman.

You might ask yourself, patient reader—if you haven't already—whether given this ever-widening gap between the language of science and the capacity of the intelligent layman to understand, it might not be one of the more destructive aspects of modern life. Many intellectuals avoid commenting on science for fear they won't understand the technical language and will be made to look foolish if they find fault.

This divorce between scientific thinking and that of most of the general public couldn't be better illustrated than by the current dispute in America over global warming. In many ways, scientists have brought the distrust they face upon themselves from many people not educated in the sciences. This widening divide quite clearly has some unfortunate consequences. The scientists become steadily more isolated—many working in secret and mostly free of intelligent oversight. The public, on the other hand, remains vulnerable to the sly persuasions of any huckster with an economic interest in maintaining the status quo.

While I have little faith in science's ability to reverse the current deteriorating state of the material environment—it's too late for that—it would serve individual scientists to develop ways to communicate their findings in a manner that might be more readily understood by nonscientists. And if some scientists say that's impossible, too abstruse, too complex, too theoretical, then insist that it is their responsibility to develop an appropriately visual way of making their presentation accessible to the public.

I am aware of course that should a contemporary academic physicist ever deign to read what I have written he would most likely dismiss this visual approach I'm proposing as simplistic at best and sophomoric at worst. This would be exactly the attitude I've seen repeated again and again by whichever is the dominant priest caste in a score of different cultures throughout history. It never ends well.

In the face of the various global disasters that swept through the ancient world, there had been a gradual but progressive lessening of public faith and belief in the gods and goddesses who were believed to be supporting and informing the natural world. There's obviously been a similarly steady decrease in belief and faith in a Christian God among the first world nations over the previous couple of centuries. The increasing influence of technology on public life since the industrial revolution—and the advances made by science to explain the mechanics of the natural world—has led irrevocably to a priesthood of science, and it is a priesthood every bit as arrogant and secretive as any priesthood of old.

My collaborator is wondering where I'm going with this digression. He points out that I started off by admiring the MA's clever ways of capitalizing on Prince Caligastia's abuses of his power and appear to be ending with a critique of science and scientific priesthood.

It is true. I do get carried away with my comments and observations—so I appreciate being reined in.

In that case, and to summarize where I was going with my digression, it was to isolate a pattern in which a belief system becomes progressively more encompassing in its claims before collapsing in the face of contradictory evidence—or its own hubris.

In short, I fear for the future of many contemporary scientists. Their priesthood and the materialist creed they preach will prove to be irrelevant when confronted with an overwhelmingly transcendent event in the same way that the belief systems of their forebears crumbled in the face of natural disasters.

As the third millennium dawned, the religion that Prince Caligastia had been promoting through his midwayer proxies, the Jehovah, was finally starting to gain more hold with the Semitic tribes who wandered the fertile plains and forested hills at the eastern end of the Mediterranean.

The developing cultures in Sumer and Egypt had now recovered from the devastating two-hundred-year drought that had scorched the land only a couple of thousand years earlier. The drought had been the consequence of the sudden and radical change in weather conditions that started the process of desertification that would lead to the Sahara and the deserts stretching from the Arabian Peninsula all the way across the Land of the Two Rivers, then to the mountains of Afghanistan.

The two civilizations had gradually reasserted themselves as the climate changed again, bringing rain to the mountains that fed the life-sustaining rivers in both lands. They were now entering an era during which the two cultures would develop to their highest point before— once again—being crushed by another long drought toward the end of the second millennium.

Yet there was a great deal more to this cultural rebirth, which produced the pyramid age in Egypt and the great ziggurats and the palaces and temples of Sumer.

I can only believe that the drought in the fifth millennium must have been thought so devastating that some quiet off-planet help was required to kick-start the two cultures. Astar—who appears to have been privy to the negotiations—told me that it had been the Sirians who had pressed their case. They were able to do this on the basis of their previous involvement with life on this world and because of the Sirian belief that life on Earth falls within their field of influence.

Astar, who was always good for a bit of galactic gossip, had told me how aggravated the Sirian envoys had been when this planet was placed under a quarantine at the time of the rebellion. They'd felt such a strong sense of responsibility for nurturing life on this world. Astar had told me this with a snort of derision that told me all I needed to know: the Sirians had argued, successfully it seemed, that the decimal status of this planet as experimental had permitted them a limited and focused intervention.

Sumer, as a result, received regular visits from the Oannes. This was the name given to the Sirians many centuries later by the Babylonian historian Berossus. The Nile Valley culture meanwhile was stimulated by the appearance of the Sirians in the guise of the Nommo.

And that, of course, brings me back to the oasis in Mali, what I learned about the Nommo, and the profound impact they would have in shaping the beliefs of the Nile Valley people. These beliefs would sustain them until their civilization would collapse again in the second millennium.

It's a curious story. These two off-world interventions were neither entirely legal yet were seemingly overlooked by the MA—the implications of which have become buried beneath the weight of taught history.

It's my hope I will be able to throw some fresh light on these interventions, both of which have been dismissed as myth by modern scholarship.

* * *

It had been raining earlier that afternoon, and the street was still shining wet as Mein Host made his way up Central Park West for his appointment to take ketamine with the group gathered at the orange man's apartment. He clearly had no idea what to expect.

I could feel his nervousness when he stopped outside the apartment building, his nose wrinkling with the dank aroma of horse shit wafting in from Central Park. Yes, we can smell these things, too! After a moment's hesitation, he turned into the building, caught the elevator, and was greeted effusively by his host at the door. My ward must have arrived a few minutes late, because when he was ushered into the main room there were already some fifteen people lying quietly around the floor.

The orange man found a place for my ward, explaining in whispered tones that he hadn't yet administered the ketamine to anyone and that he would do so once my ward had made himself comfortable. With that the orange man turned the lights down low. The summer evening light was seeping around the edges of the darkened blinds. My ward found a free corner and settled down onto the floor. With a bottle of ketamine in one hand and a bunch of disposable syringes in the other, the orange man went around from person to person, giving each of them an intramuscular injection in the proffered upper arm or thigh. He then retired to a chair at the back of the room to let the substance take its effect.

Ketamine comes on about three or four minutes after being injected into a muscle. So after a brief silence in the room, it was like listening to a gathering chorus of ecstatic moans and joyful sighs of recognition—layering, in turn, as the substance took its effect on the recumbent bodies.

My ward later told Alma he thought the dose was only about 60 to 70 mm—probably not enough for the full effect, yet it was evidently sufficient for him to realize its extraordinary healing potential.

"It was actually rather curious," I heard him telling Alma when he got back to the apartment, "and not in the way I really expected.

"Yeah, the K was interesting. It's a little like short-acting phencyclidine—but not as wacky. I think everybody in the room had that delicious warm feeling of being spiritually home, but I don't think anyone got out of their bodies.

"Something I felt, and it was all pretty quick—I think it only lasted about three-quarters of an hour, that's all—was how K moves toward what needs to be healed. Oh! And it also seemed to have the effect of lifting us all off. It wasn't like we left our bodies . . . it wasn't quite that. It was more like the gravity in the whole room was gradually having less effect . . . like we were all rising up at the same time together.

"I don't know if any of the others felt it—people left the apartment pretty quickly when it was over . . ."

"How did they look? Did they like the K?" Alma queried.

"Who knows. They were quiet enough, and I didn't hear any complaints. But I missed some of it because the orange man asked me to stay back. He wanted to chat about the session. After everyone left he asked me if I'd like a massage . . . that he was a trained masseur . . ." my ward was saying when Alma interrupted.

"What about getting the K? Did you talk about it? Did you ask him for some?" she wanted to know, reminding him of the real purpose of his visit.

"Wait for it . . . 'course I did! I asked him before the massage, but he hemmed and hawed. You know that I don't really like other people massaging me, but I thought if it meant a bottle of K, I'd put up with it. Which I did . . . that is until he tried to touch me up . . ."

"He tried to touch your cock?" Alma sounded shocked, but I could hear the amusement in her tone.

"I was lying on my back, his hand was moving in that direction, then he had a kind of questioning look on his face. I guess I didn't understand it, because the next I knew he had his hand on it! Frankly I was more surprised than shocked, but it did make me sit up with a start! I said that wasn't at all what I was after.

"Poor man. I felt sorry for him. He looked so embarrassed, but I didn't forget my mission. You'd have been proud of me, Alma. Actually I wondered if he'd had some trouble like this before because he seemed to overreact . . ."

"Perhaps he was so used to all that Rajneesh-y, open sexuality, and he just assumed you'd be cool with it . . ." Alma suggested.

"Probably. Something like that."

"Maybe he picked up on your strong female side and thought you were gay?" she added.

"Either way, Alma, it was really invasive. He didn't ask me or anything. He just went ahead because it was something I imagine he wanted to do! Anyway, as far as I was concerned it really was no big deal—except he looked so ashamed, like a naughty boy. I knew then I could I could pull it off . . ."

"Pull it off?" Alma was laughing.

"Pull off our scam, silly. Score some K!" With that, Mein Host produced the vial of ketamine hydrochloride that he'd been hiding from Alma to surprise her.

He explained that the orange man was all too happy to exchange it for a gentleman's agreement to remain silent. "It was rather funny in a way," my ward said, laughing—as much at his girlfriend's surprise and delight at the appearance of the vial as the memory of the exchange.

"It was strange. All very cool. Nothing was said. It was all done by inference, and the shake of a hand. I actually quite liked the man. It had never occurred to me he was gay . . ."

"Might have been bi," Alma volunteered.

"I've been out of the sexual marketplace so long maybe I didn't pick up on the signs. Still, I can't blame him for trying, and I'm just sorry he had to feel so humiliated . . . simply to squeeze a bottle out of him."

"But you got the K," said Alma, turning the vial over in her hand. "That's what's important. Now we can experiment with it for ourselves."

Which is what they did.

So started a long—and deeply helpful—relationship with this substance that finally allowed my ward to free himself of the most painful and earliest imprints gained as a small child when the bombs were falling all around him in World War II.

I've written previously about Mein Host's early years while living as a two-year-old with his mother in the Kentish village of Cranbrook—in the direct firing line of Hitler's flying bombs coming in from the continent. What I didn't mention was the result of this fearful imprint and how it affected my ward's consciousness and behavior.

On the positive side, the characteristics he developed to cope with this deeply buried terror had eventually manifested in his counter-phobia—which has stood him well over the course of his spiritual explorations. But his impulse to throw himself into whatever he's presented with had another, darker side to it, and that is what was buried under all the masks.

This had become more pressing to deal with by Mein Host's early forties. Here's how he described it for himself:

This effect would occur sometimes. Not every time, but when I was starting to move into an altered state it would happen. This wasn't just when I'd get high, but sometimes just when the energies were running strong and high. Rather than my consciousness expanding—which is what normally happens—I would start contracting. It was as if the whole of reality was moving in closer and closer, and starting to crush me. Like one of those scenes in a sci-fi film when the hero is trapped in a room and the walls are moving irrevocably inward. It was horrible, and I just couldn't stop it. It was like being crushed alive in one of those car compactors.

I had no idea where this horrible effect came from. My friends weren't experiencing it; they didn't know what I was talking about.

It was ketamine that showed my myself as a three-year-old, crushed inside a wire cage beneath the wood kitchen table—the "safest place in the house"—while the sudden silence of a ramjet engine spluttering silent started the dreadful whooshing hiss of a falling doodlebug—and the subsequent earth-shattering explosion. That time in between the engine shutting off and the final explosion became an eternity as I tried to compress my tiny body into the tightest of fetal huddles.

It was then simply a case of revisiting that compression effect again and again on K—with the illumination of now knowing that what was happening was just an imprint—so after going there maybe seven or eight times the imprint was flattened and has never bothered me again.

* * *

I am aware there will be some who will question the use of entheogens on the spiritual journey, who will claim that entheogens distort reality and encourage delusions. And of course, as with any powerful tool, entheogens do carry their own dangers—and like any tool they can be used for positive or negative ends.

It's not my place to comment here on the corruption and vested interests that have conspired to make entheogens prohibited substances. However, by doing this, the authorities have promoted and endorsed the view in many unthinking people's minds that all drugs are essentially the same. Drugs, they believe, are either legal—requiring a prescription (or not)—or they are illegal. Therefore they must all be equally bad and destructive.

It's this myopic lack of distinction that has led, in part, to the discrediting of the authorities in the eyes of younger people who have had some actual experience with these substances. In addition, the failure to delineate the difference among the inherently addictive substances—such as opiates and nonaddictive entheogens—has led to an incorrect notion that sacred plants are the more seriously addictive drugs and have higher abuse potential. It is only now—with the copious opioid crises raging worldwide—that the attention has been somewhat redirected.

More seriously—from an angel's point of view—such arbitrary prohibitions not only make ignorant fools of the authorities but also serve to infantilize some people while turning the more knowledgeable toward first skepticism and then cynicism. If I have written about this misunderstanding and confusion before in different contexts; it is because it is symptomatic of what lies at the root of the Caligastia approach to social control: create an illusory enemy, then demonize it.

So let me make my point of view clear—and I imagine that it represents the view of most of my kind.

I am certainly not suggesting that entheogens are correct for everybody—neither are they the only way of approaching cosmic consciousness. They *are* a valuable tool, however, for incarnate rebel angels, who will also be those individuals most naturally drawn to entheogens.

Surely it must be obvious by now that prohibiting certain substances only creates a criminal black market, encourages adventurous young people to experiment, corrupts the justice system, and lures people into a life of drugs—people who otherwise would likely have known nothing about them. However, for serious students of life, having some personal experience with altered states of consciousness will allow for a greater ease of contact with other realms.

Entheogens used wisely will accelerate spiritual growth by throwing illumination on those areas of the psyche that require healing. As individuals progressively release the negative thoughtforms trapped in their subtle energy bodies, so also does it make it simpler for us angels to reach in and make contact. I'm not, of course, suggesting the use of entheogens just to make our lives and our contact with you easier. More important, the intelligent psychotherapeutic use of these substances will permit the individual to clear themselves of the psychic debris that hinders or blocks the closeness of our natural communication.

I'm quoting another of my sisters when I say, "What could be more natural than our talking with each other?" (An angel communication from *Talking with Angels,* Budaliget 1943, transcribed by Gitta Mallasz.) This represents how we angels essentially feel about our relationship with mortals—although it holds truer for companion angels than for Watchers. I regard myself as an exception to this rule because of the role I've taken in my collaboration with Mein Host. Thus it is possible I may be overstating the case for entheogens in some of my sisters' eyes. I trust the reader will keep this in mind.

I'm also confident that most readers who have troubled to penetrate this far into my narrative will have been drawn in their time to explore entheogens for themselves.

I've heard Mein Host comment that someone reaching a state of spiritual or mystical illumination with an entheogen might well conclude that religion itself could have originally found its roots in the entheogenic experience.

There is some limited truth to this—in that almost all ancient religions did indeed use entheogens in their rituals—but it's the expanded state of consciousness produced by the substances that permits the human psyche to open to the transcendent realms.

There is an intriguing confusion here to which I have previously referred, yet not in an entheogenic context.

It had been as a result of regularly eating the fruit of the shrub of Edentia that the Prince's staff and their one hundred companions were able to live on, almost endlessly, for almost three hundred thousand years before the revolution. The fruit of this shrub had no effect on mortals if they were ever to eat it. However, the shrub was so thoroughly protected by midwayers throughout those many millennia that it was only the legends of immortality associated with eating it who grew and persisted, spreading out from the surrounding tribes. The shrub became inert soon after the revolution, resulting in the eventual death of the Prince's staff. Yet the legends of immortals striding across the landscape have continued to resonate down through history.

It was these persistent legends of a sacred plant that could confer immortality on those blessed enough to discover it that impelled the shamans of the time to seek out power plants for themselves.

Yet to return to the mystical experience itself, this, of course, will originate within the spiritual circuitry of the mortal. It is only facilitated by the entheogen, as such a state could also have been activated by other techniques created to overload the individual's consensus reality.

Almost all the so-called pagan religions used entheogens from time to time. Frequently the inspired originators of the cults that formed in their names—and followed their teachings—would have received their illumination from their own use of entheogens. Sadly it's just as frequent that their followers would then become prohibited from using similar substances—in case they have competing visions or leave the fold.

I've seen this repeated a score of times—on a number of continents—and I still don't know whether it's merely the result of human frailty or a deliberate interference on the part of the Prince's midwayers. I was aware that Caligastia had instructed his midwayers to keep a careful watch for the emergence of any religion that might challenge the Prince's hegemonic religious ambitions. So perhaps it's as much human frailty—that is then subject to midwayer pressure—that makes so many organized religions frown on and forbid the use of entheogens among their followers.

There have been some exceptions to this, especially among the tribes flourishing in the Americas who were being protected by the loyalist midwayers. In these cases, sacred substances—like the peyote cactus, psilocybin mushrooms, the datura flower, or the seeds of two species of morning glory—have continued to be used under sacred circumstances to this day.

The use of entheogens—whether for healing, for ritual, or for recreation—has been an issue for almost every culture of the world. As a result, every culture has had to find its own way of handling the human need to experience altered states of consciousness. While for some this is simply the pleasure of disorientating their normal state of consciousness with alcohol, others might use opium to escape from a disagreeable reality. Still others will turn to an entheogen like peyote or ayahuasca to expand their consciousness. It has always been thus, whether or not the substances are prohibited.

The most mature societies throughout history have found ways to harness and channel this perfectly natural human urge for the transcendent experience into something that could benefit their society. For three millennia the priest caste in Egypt used entheogens in their secret rituals but forbade their use by the Egyptian society at large. Soma— the sacred substance at the core of the Vedic religion—was used by the practitioners in such secrecy that soma's composition remains a mystery to this day.

Despite the natural cataclysms of the second millennium that would devastate the region and force the survivors to start over, the civilization starting to flower in Greece was able to approach entheogens in the most mature way of any culture I have observed since Lemuria. I've seen little in the modern era to rival the ingenuity of the resolution that emerged over the centuries as the Eleusinian Mysteries.

The Greeks created an annual sacred ritual in which the participants—having ingested an entheogen (Kykeon) derived from ergot-parasitized barley—were then guided on a journey through the underworld. This would have included most likely encountering the gods Plouton or Hades and goddesses such as Persephone and Demeter (or Kore). Yet perhaps far more important, the journey would have assured initiates of the experiential reality of the Afterlife. This knowledge alone would have profoundly affected the citizens of ancient Greece in a manner that a modern Judeo-Christian nation could never comprehend.

Once again this underlines the vital difference between a culture— or an individual—who knows the truth because they have experienced it, and those who believe a truth because it's something they have merely been told is true. Although there is an element of coercion in the Eleusinian afterworld journey—I'll refer to that later—it's not hard to imagine that most people would think long before behaving destructively if they really knew for sure what awaited them in the Afterlife.

Attending the ten-day Eleusinian festival would have convinced the participants of the reality of another world. This revelation was integrated and reinforced by a powerful narrative of death and rebirth as expressed in the kidnapping of Persephone by Hades, her captivity in the underworld, Demeter's search for her, and all that followed as a consequence.

This was a story the people could relate to. It gave some narrative substance to a reality that during the course of everyday life was—by its very nature—insubstantial. There were some people who returned to Eleusis but everyone in Greece over the age of twenty—men, women, and slaves—would have had an experience so profound that it only needed to occur once in their lifetime. The importance of the experience was further sealed in secrecy, under the threat of death for anyone who revealed the mysteries.

As a tribute to how deeply affected were those attending the rites occurring every five years at Eleusis, the Greater and Lesser Mysteries were able to remain a secret for more than two and a half thousand years. The mysteries also formed an experiential context for the religion that grew up around the gods and goddesses of that region.

Yet as you will know by now, these so-called divinities were a loosely knit clan of midwayers masquerading as gods and goddesses who in reality cared very little for human welfare—except when they could manipulate it in their favor. For example, when Zeus finally interceded in the kidnapping and forced Hades to release Persephone back to her mother for eight months a year, he acted with his typically selfish motives. Zeus only intervened because the drought caused by Demeter—in starving the people—was actually depriving the gods of worship and sacrifice! Yes, that was the reason given—and it was accepted by the people! There was no care for the suffering of the dead and dying, only for the well-being of the gods.

In that single justification by Zeus you can get a brief glimpse into the viewpoint of the rebel midwayers and how their interests dominated the lives of the men and women of the time.

In the Eleusinian Mysteries, the midwayers concerned were—I believe—using the power of the entheogenic experience to imprint their initiates and to give further credence to their divinity. This would prove to be an effective strategy from the midwayers' point of view, in that it contributed to produce a society that was, in general, wholly subject to the whims of the gods and goddesses. Yet idiosyncratically it was also true that the culture growing out of the worship of these divinities would eventually produce some of the finest and most rational thinkers of the ancient world.

As the fourth millennium was approaching the start of the third, the culture that was starting to thrive in the Nile Valley became subject to the priests of another pantheon of midwayers. In the case of Egypt, the midwayers there clearly decided on a different course of action from those of their kind in Greece. They also received added inspiration from some unexpected quarters.

All this was occurring some seven hundred years before Upper and Lower Egypt unified circa 3,200 BCE—toward the close of the millennium. While developing an exoteric system whereby the people could honor and worship their primary deities, Isis and Osiris, the midwayers—together with their priests—contrived a secondary, esoteric stream of sacred knowledge. This stream of sacred knowledge would remain a secret tradition, hidden behind layers of initiation from all but the most privileged and senior priests.

I've suggested previously that the impact of shamanism—which had been spreading from India over the previous few thousand years—had helped to shape the early Egyptian beliefs about the Afterlife. In this case, the priests' use of entheogens—while playing their part in developing a familiarity with the underworld—had been subsequently preserved solely for the ritual use of priests (and later by the kings and pharaohs but kept strictly secret from the general population).

So well has this highly selective use of entheogens by the Egyptian priests of the predynastic period been kept secret that it has become all but hidden from history. Yet the insights and revelations gained in secrecy over the millennia by the Egyptian priests would lay the foundation for the mystery schools and secret societies that later tried to preserve occult knowledge through the dark time ahead, which would be one of persecution and repression.

Much of what has remained hidden concerned the deep influence on the midwayers, and thus on the Egyptian priests, created by a new belief system that was currently being introduced to the southern tribes by the Nommo.

All of this brings me back to that time in Mali that I came across the oasis and was able to listen to some of the Nommo teachings as delivered by a Dogon priest to a group of initiates. I will paraphrase what was said and focus here only on what appeared to have such a deep influence on both the midwayers and the Egyptian priests.

I heard it told by the Dogon priest that it was Nommo who was the primary Being created by Amma, their sky god. Nommo was then said to have split into four pairs of twins, one of whom broke away and rebelled against the great god Amma. To return universal order, Amma chose to allow the sacrifice of another of the Nommo whose body was then dismembered and dispersed throughout the universe.

There was much more about the Nommo, including how they had traveled in their ship from Sirius. Another key bit of information was that they considered humanity to be an "interrupted creation" that they had named "Ogo the Fox." The priest spoke a great deal about sacrifice. Specifically he discussed how the Nommo divided his or her body to feed the people; that he gave his life principles to human beings; and how the third Nommo would sacrifice themselves for the fourth Nommo, Ogo the Fox.

The belief system of the Nommo had spread rapidly north. In so doing, its credibility was greatly enhanced by the actual appearance of the Nommo and the arrival of their ship in clouds of fire and thunder. The Nommo were semiaquatic creatures, the priest said, with bodies of men along with legs and feet, but also with a fishlike lower torso and tail. The first matter that the Nommo took care of upon arriving on the planet was to excavate a large pool that they then filled with water. This they did by apparently by draining it from the reservoirs in the ship. When it was filled they flopped happily around in it.

This last statement about flopping around in the pool drew a suppressed snigger from one of the initiates. However, the man lost his smile at a sharp look from the priest. He went on to explain that the Nommo were known as the "Masters of the Water" for a good reason. They came from an aquatic planet circling the star Sirius, and they were far more advanced than the tribespeople.

As I have previously noted, it is the midwayers whose function it is to turn away—or in some cases allow through the filter—any extraterrestrial visitors who may have stumbled into this region of the space-time continuum and shown interest in Earth, a quarantined world. I feel it's reasonable to conclude that because the Nommo were quite obviously from another world, the midwayers must have purposely permitted them to come here. I've no way of being certain of this, however, as I'm only inferring this from the results as I observed them.

The impact of the beliefs of the Nommo can be found echoed, for example, in the dismemberment and scattering of the body parts of Osiris around the world. The attentive reader will also have noticed an intriguing correspondence between the Nommos' sacred story of their seminal twins. These twins appeared as the original offspring of Poseidon on Atlantis. You may recall all of the mythologizing about twins following Vanu and Amadon's long service on the planet, which subsequently appeared in many of the belief systems indigenous to North and South America.

I can only infer what it was about twins that gave them a central role in so many ancient belief systems.

# 6

# A More Perfect "Intelligence"

Nommo and Oannes, Angelic Coordination,
Rare Cetacean Insights, Rescued by
Dolphins, Planetary Amnesia,
and a Seraph's Insights

I introduced the previous section with the observation that the third millennium saw a largely covert intervention from an aquatic planet circling Sirius. This was in the form of the Nommo in East Africa and Egypt and the Oannes in the Land of the Two Rivers.

I wondered at the time whether this may have been an attempt by the Planetary Princes of the other rebel-held worlds to provide at least some limited corrective action to the excesses of Prince Caligastia. It was his behavior that Prince Janda-chi had been complaining about during my previous visit to Zandana. I made a mental note to ask Janda-chi about this if I got to see him on my next visit to Zandana. And thinking that must have reminded me how long it had been since I'd spent any time on my favorite world . . . I knew I would need to get back there soon.

However, to complete my earlier thought, I was aware that whatever intervention the Sirians had undertaken would have needed to be extremely subtle to remain on the right side of the MA's laws prohibiting outside meddling with quarantined planets. This law seemed to me to make some allowance for exceptions. In the case of both the Nommo and the Oannes their visits were brief, although the consequences of their appearance were profound. Their influence could be found in the sudden and mysterious acceleration in the development of the two civilizations: Egypt and Sumer. These would both flower into high cultures over the next thousand years. As we have mentioned, this would last until the next radical change of climate toward the close of the second millennium, which created a drought lasting two hundred years and returned the region to desert.

These were both covert missions arranged and accomplished by an off-planet race with a sense of responsibility for this world. They were conducted quietly and drew so little attention to themselves as to be almost forgotten from history.

These are two examples of an extraterrestrial presence in the ancient world that acted so stealthily that contemporary historians continue to puzzle over the sudden emergence of full-blown civilizations in Sumer and Egypt. This presence had such a seminal effect on early civilization and yet remained so hidden from history's narrative.

I suggest that these two examples might throw some light on the seemingly mysterious behavior of the large number of off-planet races currently involving themselves with life on this world. It should be evident by now that the impact of the extraterrestrial presence since World War II has been mainly focused on raising humanity's awareness of the possibility of other worlds and other intelligences.

Yet for reasons that aren't hard to fathom, the extraterrestrials aren't doing this by publicly announcing their presence. They are encouraging people to think for themselves. The want each person to trust their own senses and their intuition. They want them to be able to set aside the blinkers of convention and puzzle out the probability of intelligent life in the universe for themselves.

You may be aware by this time that one of the less evident laws that lies behind social interactions in the Multiverse concerns the "need to know" of the junior partner in any relationship. This is more wide-spread and subtle than you might think. You may remember, for example, how Lord Lucifer had amnesed our discussion from my mind. This was because to leave it there would have robbed me of the full experience of working out for myself what might be occurring beneath the surface of the rebellion.

I'm sure that extraterrestrials will continue to make their individual contact through people's dreams and meditations. They will do this by utilizing movies and novels—and through inexplicable lights in the sky. They will do this to lever open the World Mind—one person, or one small group, at a time. Think only of how an awareness of extraterrestrial life has expanded among humans since the panic caused by the Orson Welles's 1938 radio adaptation *The War of the Worlds,* from the novel by H. G. Wells.

Whether it has been through fiction or personal experience, or plain old common sense, in barely three generations more than 75 percent of Americans polled believe the planet has been, or is being, visited by Beings from other worlds. In different Western nations this figure is likely to be higher, and among the indigenous peoples I would expect it to be nearly 100 percent.

As the Nommo and the Oannes once seeded a couple of relatively simple river cultures with what they needed to grow into great long-lasting civilizations, the extraterrestrials of today are giving hints and allowing glimpses of what it means to blossom into a truly interplanetary civilization.

\* \* \*

In 1981, Mein Host's companion angels evidently considered him—at forty-one years of age—adequately prepared for what would consume his interest for the subsequent thirty years. The business was behind him. It had been sold to the distributor for the pittance that would carry him through for next four years if he lived frugally. Given this, he evidently felt finally free to follow up on what he'd seen and experienced during his near-death experience eight years earlier. What he couldn't have known was how this was going to happen, and how neatly it would all tie together.

Three events occurred in his life in the summer of that year in surprisingly rapid succession, and each appeared to lead him quite naturally to the next incident. These events might have been written off as improbable—or self-delusory—had other people not been present when they occurred. Each series of incidents, in its own way, opened up a new world for my ward.

It started with some ingenious angelic coordination.

All my ward did was send in a subscription to John C. Lilly's Human/Dolphin Foundation, and within a week, as he put it, "there were dolphins everywhere." Peculiar, *seemingly* unconnected events soon followed after joining Lilly's foundation. First, an old friend he hadn't seen in years—now the late Estelle Myers—reappeared in his life. She boasted of her new Rainbow Dolphin Center in New Zealand, where she hoped to pioneer underwater birthing, working with dolphins as midwives.

Then within days, it was movies about dolphins. One was by Michael Wiese—an acquaintance from earlier years, whom my ward hadn't known to have any interest in filming dolphins. The second incident first tipped him off to the possibility of dolphin telepathy.

Curiously enough, this incident—a clear demonstration of dolphin telepathy caught on film that seemed so obvious to my ward—hadn't even earned a comment on the soundtrack. Had the English dolphin researcher and filmmaker Horace Dobbs noticed the telepathic incident? If it could only be seen on the film, perhaps he hadn't noticed it because he was present at the time of the filming and wouldn't have expected to see anything unusual on the film. If he had seen the incident—and it was both brief and subtle—had he merely written it off as a coincidence? As a serious researcher into cetacean intelligence, was it possible that Dobbs wanted to avoid getting into such deep and controversial waters were he to announce it publicly on film?

It was as my ward was mulling over these questions that friends of his then girlfriend Melinda called from their house on the Florida coast to announce—without any provocation—that dolphins had been leap-ing and playing just off their dock for the previous few days. When they heard of my ward's interest in dolphins, they insisted on the couple coming down to Clearwater as soon as possible. They went on to kindly offer them the use of an apartment in one of the beachside condos that overlooked the sweeping bay.

I've no need to narrate or comment on incidents in my ward's life that he has already fully described in his books—unless my observa-tions add a further dimension to what occurred. In such a case, I would need to briefly sketch out the situation as I perceived it. So my apologies if this seems repetitious to readers who might know my ward's books and are already aware of the incident. For those who haven't read his books, you might find his early work with dolphins of interest.

Most of the ten days that Melinda and my ward stayed in the Clearwater apartment were spent on the beach and in the water. The time can be summarized by saying that Mein Host emerged from swim-ming daily with the wild coastal dolphins certain that human beings shared the planet with another race of highly intelligent beings. He also felt, however, that the nature of cetacean intelligence was very different from how humans define and think of intelligence.

Before leaving for Florida, and in efforts to further ascertain the dolphins' intelligence and possible telepathic powers, my ward came up with five questions that he wanted to ask the dolphins. Once in Florida, and having put his questions to the cetaceans, they answered four out of the five.

On top of this, each question was answered in the most subtle and playful of ways possible. He was shown, for example, how dolphins maintain their health by becoming subject to one of their biosonic surgeries. He learned how they stored information in sonic holograms embedded in certain shells. And he was able to observe—by swim-ming regularly with them—how curious dolphins were about human emotions.

The day before they were to leave Florida it sounded to me as though Melinda and my ward had given up on getting any insights on his final question that hadn't yet been addressed by the dolphins: Given that UFOs were seen diving in and out of the ocean, what could the dolphins tell him about them?

Late that very evening, in the dark sky over the bay, they were privileged to witness a twenty-minute display of intensely glowing white lights that shifted through a specific series of moves that Melinda recorded and drew for my ward's book (*The Deta Factor: Dolphins ETs & Angels,* page 38).

What they saw precluded any of the conventional explanations. The lights weren't Venus, marsh gas, military flares (twenty minutes?), airplane lights, or an atmospheric inversion. And because neither of them had ever seen a display like this before, the synchronicity of it occurring on that particular evening would have made its significance known. As this was the fifth question to be addressed, they were more accustomed by now to the ingenuity of the responses they were receiving to his heartfelt telepathic questions. Seeing the lights on that night fit with this pattern.

As a reply, it was subtle and enigmatic, more so than the other answers. Thus my ward and Melinda might have written off the light display as being less important had there not been another event within a week of their returning to New York City. This second event—occurring in the early afternoon of Labor Day in 1981—was so comically brazen as to be undeniable to the four people who witnessed it.

Before I take you to Manhattan, however, I want to relate an incident that my ward included in his book. I do this because it illustrates two factors he made no comment on.

It was the afternoon of the eighth day of their time in Florida, and Mein Host had clearly been getting increasingly frustrated that—with all the swimming—he'd not yet had a chance to actually physically *touch* a dolphin. Swimming every day with them had been rich with lessons. Yet whatever he did in the water the wild dolphins invariably kept their distance. I could feel his yearning to be close to them.

The blazing August sun kept the long, sweeping beach free of all who weren't mad dogs or Englishmen. (Melinda might have remarked that my ward was a healthy dose of both.) As a result, he and Melinda usually had the beach to themselves. On this particular afternoon, however, the sky had clouded over early for the first time in days. They were up in their fourth-floor apartment waiting out the storm, my ward becoming more frustrated by the moment.

"I know it's silly, Melinda, 'specially after all we've been shown already, but I really really want to touch one . . . I want to know what a dolphin feels like, to look one in the eye." Mein Host was striding up and down the living room while Melinda was on the balcony, looking out over the water.

"It's not getting much better," she called back over her shoulder. "Look! Did you see that? You missed it . . . there again . . . there!" Lightning was splitting the darkening clouds, but it appeared the rain was holding off.

Being inside seemed to put my ward increasingly on edge as the time ebbed by. He'd been using phencyclidine to facilitate his encounters with the wild dolphins; he felt it allowed him to be more open to their telepathic tendrils. He clearly felt the substance had served him well in opening him up to the level of telepathic intimacy he'd managed to achieve over the previous few days.

One of the side effects of this particular substance is that it can sometimes embolden the user to take on risks and tasks he or she might not have considered possible under normal conditions. In this case it was a task that must have seemed so obvious at the time—yet one that I've heard my ward joke that he'd never try again. This is how I heard the task emerge.

"This has got me thinking," Mein Host stated as he joined Melinda on the balcony and glanced up at the sky over the bay, which was getting darker and more threatening by the minute.

"I heard this story about a Jamaican Rasta man who lived in a hut on the beach. Every morning he'd swim straight out to sea. He'd swim and swim until he couldn't swim another stroke . . . only then would he turn back."

"So?" Melinda replied as she pushed back her dark curly hair with her hand as the wind picked up. She was never easily impressed.

"Don't you see?"—I could hear an insistent edge creeping into his voice—"Don't you see what happened? He swam and swam, pushing himself to a point he could've drowned. It was the dolphins who rescued him! Of course it was that! Don't dolphins love to rescue people? Everyone knows that! You're always reading about them saving people." Mein Host's voice was rising in excitement that seemed somehow in tune with the power of the storm gathering in strength over the bay.

"So!" he said triumphantly. "All I need to do is get rescued, right? I've got to look like I'm at the end of my tether . . . like I'm nearly drowning . . ."

"It's gonna have to be real," Melinda said laconically. She hadn't yet guessed what was about to happen. "They'll pick up on it if it isn't authentic . . . they'll leave you bef– . . ."

But Mein Host had returned to the room and was looking for his towel. "That was the Rasta man's secret, don't you get it? He couldn't go any farther . . ." He was shouting over the wind now, not sure whether she could hear him. "If that's what it takes . . ." he said loudly, but she didn't turn around. Thus when he left the apartment, as he said later, he didn't know if she quite grasped what he was going to do.

In fact it was when he was crossing the wide sandy beach four floors below her that she next saw him, and it must have been then that she realized what was happening. She slipped back into the living room, to emerge a few moments later with a pair of binoculars. By that time my ward was chesting the waves before diving into the deeper water beyond the first sandbar. Rain was just starting to slash down and thunder rumbled over the water. He continued to swim straight out into the storm. The minutes passed. Five. Ten. Fifteen. He swam on until he was barely a bobbing black blot, almost indistinguishable against the gray of the swell seen through the glasses.

"Barely a bobbing black blot against the Stygian sea," was more exactly how Melinda expressed it. She liked to turn a poetic phrase. She once told my ward that English was her third language—the third language she'd had to learn after Turkish and French—and like Vladimir

Nabokov's proficiency in his adopted language, she enjoyed playing with English alliteration.

What occurred next is more his story than mine. However, I would hope that you—by this time surely a devoted reader—take a moment to identify with what I was feeling as my precious ward swam farther and farther out to sea. He was pushing along in his uncertain breaststroke, turning on his back every so often for a few strokes until the waves sent him spluttering back to his plodding breaststroke, on and on . . . and there was nothing at all I could do about it!

I should have known better, of course. Perhaps I would have if the situation had been any less perilous. There was no guarantee whatsoever that he would make it back to shore, or even if he *could* make it back. As I said, he was by no means a strong swimmer. His body was wiry, with the build and muscles of a sprinter. He wasn't made for this sort of lunacy. I could feel his utter exhaustion. Yet he stubbornly pushed on, swimming slower and slower until, as he said later, his legs started to cramp up and he could barely move another muscle.

I believe he really was at the end of his tether. Frankly, I was fearful that he'd gone too far this time, and I had to turn to see if his companion angels appeared concerned.

They didn't.

I took heart at that, but I still couldn't be certain how he was going to find his way out of this jam. It was yet another situation that he'd somewhat impetuously thrown himself into.

I confess I couldn't bear to watch what was going to happen. I returned to where Melinda was still on the balcony, intently watching the distant bobbing blob through the glasses. I was glad to see that she was a woman of considerable equanimity.

It was Melinda who had introduced my ward to *The Urantia Book* only a few months earlier. She herself had become a student of the book some ten years prior. Mein Host would often say how helpful it was to have someone so knowledgeable with whom to discuss the book during the year he would devote to reading it thoroughly.

I found Melinda remarkable for the acuteness of her intelligence.

She was exceptionally bright—with an unusually questing, curious mind—and she also appreciated sharing an exciting adventure. Born in Turkey and educated in France, she had traveled widely before settling in the United States in the 1960s. She was a couple of years younger than Mein Host, but—since they'd moved to the States at about the same time—they both enjoyed the sense of detachment common to those who choose to live in a country other than that of their birth. It was easy for them to travel with one another, and these ten days in Florida would be the first of many trips that they would make during their four years together.

After Mein Host's quest, he finally stumbled in through the door, and with the oddest mix of emotions. He was clearly disappointed when he collapsed—still in his trunks—onto the sofa. However, behind that emotion there seemed to be an unexpected feeling of elation, almost of exhilaration, that was building up in his emotional body.

"Imagine that!" he said derisively. "Bloody dolphins! You'd think they were going to save me? Not a chance! I didn't see one bloody dolphin . . . damn things, I knew they must be out there. They were there before I took off, weren't they? We saw them, right? But did they care about me drowning? Did they? Hell! Nothing! Not a helping fin. Nothing!"

Melinda was trying to take him seriously but was laughing just the same. "So what happened?" she asked between giggles. "When you were out there, when you were about to drown . . . what did you do?"

"What did I do? There was nothing I *could* do. I was fucked. Physically I was done for. When I looked back, I could barely see the condo; it was like a matchbox on the horizon. Both legs were cramping, I could barely move my arms . . ."

"So what happened?" Melinda was still trying not to laugh out loud. "What did you do?"

"You're not taking me seriously, Mel. I really was done for. No, stop it. You know something I don't?!"

"Don't worry, go on. I'll tell you."

"It's important to know how physically fucked I was 'cause when everything changed the contrast was such a blast! What happened? What happened was I realized how silly I was. What an idiot I'd been to expect the dolphins to save me. What a stupid, stupid way to go! I must be such a fool . . . and then I started laughing. I laughed at my idiocy. I laughed at my hubris to think I was worth saving. I laughed and laughed, and as I laughed I felt my body getting stronger and stronger as though it was being infused with energy . . ."

"And you didn't see them?" she queried, laughing out loud now.

My ward must have been irritated at her laughter because he glossed over her question and barely broke his stride. "Seriously, I suddenly felt warm all over and ridiculously happy. The cramp had lifted, so I set back. It didn't seem as long, the waves helped a lot, but it was still a haul."

"And still nothing?" she added.

"Nothing? Dolphins, you mean? No, not a peep. Once, just once, I felt something brush against my calf when I was 'bout three-quarters of the way back, but who knows what that was . . . mighta been seaweed . . . mighta been anything . . .

"But listen, Mel, that's not what's important. It was when I was coming ashore; when I was dragging myself out of the water. I suddenly felt incredibly heavy and ponderous . . . which of course I was. I was exhausted. But it was more than that, much more. As I was swinging my heavy legs it was as though I was dragging a tail behind me. My head felt enormous and—as if I was lacking a neck—it rocked from side to side as I waddled out of the water. It was weird. I knew in those moments I was being overlit by Oannes. By the time I'd got to the dry sand the effect lifted, but it left me exhilarated . . ."

"And you really never saw the dolphins?"

"Not a whiff."

"They were swimming all around you . . ."

"Wha– . . . ?"

"They were swimming in circles around you, all the way out and all the way back. And you never saw them? About a fifteen-foot circle all around you, as far as I could make out through the glasses." Melinda sounded incredulous that he hadn't even caught a glimpse of the dolphins.

"When I was out there about to drown, could you see them then? Were they around me then?"

"You were so far away it was hard to make out but, yes, I thought I did see a fin. But here's what's so funny—and it happened three or four times. When you were looking one way, a dolphin would pop up behind you. It happened enough times that they were obviously playing a game with you."

Mein Host was looking thoughtful.

"So when I was out there and they were circling around me, do you think it was them who somehow were giving me that energy? It was mysterious how I suddenly felt so much stronger, and warmer too. Maybe that's a clue, feeling warmer. And I was laughing and laughing. I almost couldn't stop. I remember swallowing mouthfuls of seawater. That's what stopped me from laughing. But that's what I couldn't understand . . . I was so ridiculously happy. But I was still in exactly the same situation. So what had changed? One moment I'd had it, I was a goner. The next I was feeling exhilarated . . . plus I knew then I could make it back.

"Then there was that weird Oannes feeling, which came out of nowhere. I barely knew the name, and yet the feeling was absolutely real. I knew it was happening in the moment. It lasted what, about twenty seconds . . . and, thing is, I just knew it didn't feel like me. I was there, but it wasn't me. Very weird."

"So you got your answer," Melinda offered. "You got the dolphins to save you . . ."

"Okay. Perhaps I did, Mel, but I still never saw them."

They were both laughing now at the trick the dolphins had played on him, neither quite knowing what to make of the Oannes overlighting.

"I'll tell you one thing, Mel. Perhaps the dolphins saved me, perhaps not. Perhaps they saved the Rasta man, perhaps not. But it certainly isn't going to be a swim I'm ever going to take on every morning just to make sure!"

It wasn't until some months later when Mein Host came to understand more about dolphins. He'd had a chance at last to be close to them at Dolphins Plus, a facility in the Florida Keys that runs swim programs. In addition he'd read about some scientists in the USSR who had written of observing a discernible energy field that surrounded a dolphin in a sphere of some fifteen to twenty feet in circumference. They had named this expansive aura the "biofield."

With all of this, he was able to finally acknowledge what had happened. When he read the name for the energy he'd felt uplifting him, he told Melinda that he was happy to have actually experienced the dolphins' biofield before he'd read about it.

It appeared that's the way his life was going to turn out. As with the angels in his near-death experience, he would frequently come to experience the reality of the transcendent or the mysterious before he'd read about it or heard of someone else with a similar experience.

It was, for example, *after* reading Robert Monroe's book *Journeys Out of the Body*—and finding that Monroe had a remarkably similar experience to one of his out-of-body trips—that Monroe had been similarly been shown a place the angels had called "heaven." It must have jolted my ward's memory, because that was the place he was told during the near-death experience that he wouldn't remember. It, too, had been called heaven, and he'd been shown around, but then he was amnesed afterward. He'd joked after reading Monroe's book that both he and Monroe had felt similarly sheepish—as well as being slightly embarrassed—to admit that heaven was a real place.

However, in both Robert Monroe and Mein Host's case the heaven they were shown around wasn't quite the heaven as promised to Christians. It felt—according to my ward—more like a recreational way station than a final destination.

Either way, he says he remembers only that heaven was a place of great joy, delight, and peace.

* * *

I believed at the time it was my thoughts about the Nommo and the Oannes—and what I had called the Sirian Intervention—that had turned my mind back to the planet Zandana. In retrospect, I'm inclined to believe I was already falling more subject to the agenda Zandana's Prince Janda-chi had introduced me to. And I was now feeling more certain he had implanted it below my level of awareness.

Zandana, you'll remember, is something of a twin planet to Earth. At least it started off that way. They were seeded with life at about the same time by the Prince's mission in both cases. And they arrived within a few hundred years of one another. Both worlds aligned themselves with Lucifer's revolution, and the Material Sons and Daughters arrived at around the same time on both planets. Yet after that, life on the two worlds had started to diverge. Prince Caligastia had successfully sabotaged the mission of the two intraterrestrial botanists on Earth, yet the Material Son and Daughter on Zandana were fully supported by the two Planetary Princes.

On my previous visit I reckoned Zandana had already drawn ahead of Earth by at least six thousand years. It wasn't perfect by any means. Yet if there was some truth to what I'd heard—and it wasn't merely wishful thinking—the less-advanced northern islands had made their peace with Zandan. They were also starting finally to catch up with the standard of living on the southern continent.

And then, of course, there was that Rainbow Bridge!

I hadn't been able to take in what I was seeing when that astral crevasse opened up. If it hadn't been for Clarisel, the Zandana Watcher I was lucky to have befriended, I'm sure I would have been terrified.

At the time that Clarisel told me, I recall the vision giving me such exalted hope that I would see such a thing on Earth (in the future at the very least). Coming back to the present it struck me: I hadn't given any more thought to Clarisel and the Rainbow Bridge since I'd arrived back on Earth. Was that part of the clouding effect I had previously noticed on coming into the Earth's psychosphere? Was it the emotional weight that clouded the mind? Was it some form of automatic amnesia? I wondered. If it was, then how was it that I was now recalling my experiences on Zandana?

That made me pay attention, I can tell you. Was it the amnesia that was breaking down? Or was I perhaps changing in some way of which I wasn't aware? Did this mean I was really becoming more individuated? And was a result of this further individuation indicating that I was becoming less vulnerable to the amnesic pressures of this planet?

Before I could finish this thought, another came to me to chase away any whisper of self-congratulation. Was the very thought of returning to Zandana—right at this point—already implanted in me, and was now being activated? Far from becoming more individuated, could it be that my mind was being influenced . . . and I didn't know it?

Please don't assume this bout of self-questioning ever arose to a level of paranoia. A Watcher's consciousness simply doesn't allow for such extremes of emotion. However, I found I was starting to be able to entertain a far greater degree of ambiguity than was ever available to me prior to the rebellion. For that, I suppose, I could be thankful.

On reaching that point in my self-examination, I knew the only way to resolve this issue in my mind was to return to Zandana—even if my decision to do so was being influenced by agencies unknown. Somewhere deep inside me—yes, I was starting to gain some real depth—I believe I had the briefest of glimpses of a divine drama in which we were all playing our parts. It was a drama in which there was no right and wrong, no good or evil; and no judgment but our own self-judgment on how skillfully we fulfilled our roles.

Even a brief glimpse was beautiful to behold. And as sometimes occurs in a Watcher's consciousness, I was left unsure as to whether it was a memory from the past—from where we once emerged in our journey to accompany mortals during the first stages of their Multiversal ascendancy. Or was it perhaps a memory of some future state to which we are all aspiring?

If I have once claimed that a Watcher's consciousness is a simple one, then perhaps my observation was something of a nostalgic delusion. This is because by this time I was starting to feel as complicated as I imagined was the mind of a mortal. I can say this now with more authority since Mein Host graciously gave me access to his mind. But back then, when I was still new to knowing myself—and was regularly discovering there was more of myself to know—my life seemed to be far more straightforward.

However, you'll hear no complaints out of me.

If the result of all this confusion and stress is that I will prove ultimately worthy of the privilege of mortal incarnation, then every bit of it is worthwhile.

I was both delighted and relieved to find Eleena already waiting for me in the Seraphic Transport Center when I arrived there. I was also somewhat surprised because the Seraphic Transport Center I'd chosen to use was the one in the Middle East. You'll recall that I'd made it a point to avoid this Seraphic Transport Center because of the risk of encountering Prince Caligastia so close to his palace.

I'd become accustomed to using the North American Seraphic Transport Center, and I was equally used to seeing Eleena there. So there was a moment of dislocation when I saw her waiting for me on the steps of the Transport Center.

"Surprised to see me?" I heard Eleena's smiling voice in my mind as I drew closer.

Well, yes, but really more relieved than surprised. How could she have known I would break with my tradition this time and brave a possible inadvertent meeting with Prince Caligastia—which fortunately hadn't occurred—to use this Seraphic Transport Center?

"You have questioned this before, haven't you?" Eleena confirmed for herself before continuing while we made our way through to the lounge. "I have transported some more Watchers from the rebel planets since we last met . . . yes, they are starting to move around more . . . and I've observed a very similar reaction now in a number of Watchers. Sooner or later, you all ask the same thing . . . How do we do it? How do we so often know to be there waiting for you when you arrive? I am correct, yes? This is your thought?"

I felt no need to reply to a telepathic rhetorical question.

"I believe I have discovered the source of this," she was continuing as we found a corner to ourselves. "Those such as yourself who have served so long on rebel-held worlds have been isolated not only from the Multiverse, but from the ways of the Multiverse. Have you no recollection of a time when you queried nothing? Of a time when there was never a question as to whether you were in the right place at the right time? You just were . . ."

It's true. Before the revolution I never questioned where I found myself. I didn't experience myself as an automaton. I felt I was authentically following my interests. This was until Lucifer argued during the revolution—most convincingly I thought at the time—that we were free to believe we were independent agents following our own interests. Yet in reality, of course, we were formed and programmed to respond to events within an extremely very narrow band of choices. The point he stressed was that the choices were never really ours. No. We were being condescended to and then fooled into believing we possessed a greater degree of independence than we actually had.

"Ah! Now you are starting to understand." Her tone was mild enough for me to overlook the sense of being patronized that we Watchers so often feel on those rare occasions that one of the MA's loyal agents will talk to us. They don't even like the way we smell!

"I am accustomed to your stink by this time." Eleena was laughing. "It's not so unpalatable now. I'm used to it."

And here I was believing it was me who was losing the smell that the MA's loyalists found so disagreeable!

There was more dry laughter from Eleena. "Never mind your smell, dear sister. I was addressing a different issue, which you might find more helpful. We were contemplating what I believe is one of the lesser acknowledged effects of a systemwide quarantine on a Watcher's consciousness. This is only what I've had the opportunity to observe, mind you, but I believe planetary isolation has actually closed you off to the celestial matrix. In fact, I've heard you more than once thinking proudly about your new independence, and didn't you believe there'd be a consequence?"

"If I agree you might be onto a truth here, Eleena," I said, joining her in laughter by this time, "then let me add I am starting to prefer being happily surprised to unexpectedly find you here than I ever was in being complacently unaware of why I was being steered here or there! I'm beginning to enjoy making my own decisions . . . although I admit I have felt—only now and then, mind you, Eleena— that there is another force guiding me. Can you, in your turn, identify with that?"

The Transport Seraph paused for a long time before I heard her soft voice again in my mind.

"Your thoughts are new to me . . ." And with that Eleena lapsed into silence. I wondered whether I had said too much.

The transport lounge was starting to fill up. Each mortal soul was accompanied by a pair of companion angels who were delivering their mortal wards into the loving embrace of a Transport Seraph. This would have been the first time the mortal would have been taken to Jerusem. It would also be the first time they would have left the subtle energy regions of Earth. And it would certainly be the first time they'd have been enclosed within the heat shields of a Transport Seraph. I observed that some of the mortals were being reassured by their angels, while a few others appeared to be genuinely curious and fascinated by all that was happening to them.

"They will have had adequate time to adapt," Eleena murmured in my mind. "Remember, all of them will have had to traverse the first six morontia levels after they've passed from mortal life. So they're not *complete* beginners!"

"But Jerusem!" I thought. "That's a big step. I'm not equipped to enter the morontia worlds, as you know, Eleena . . . but then neither are you!" That produced an uncharacteristic snort from my Transport Seraph.

Not to be put off, I continued. "I believe from what I've heard that mortal souls move from one morontia level to another without going through the experience of death. That's only when they die to the flesh. It must be like they just find themselves in another reality. There's no dying, no terror of death—just a simple transformation of the external reality."

"Until they are brought here, is that what you mean?"

"This will be the first time, Eleena—right here in the Transport Center—that they will see for themselves something of the MA's technology. Climbing into a Transport Seraph and traveling through subspace is going to be very different indeed from simply waking up and finding themselves in another reality!"

The mortal souls in the lounge seemed either too self-involved—or too filled with wonder—to notice us in the corner. Yet had they looked in our direction they would have been able to see Eleena appearing to be paying undue attention to an empty seat beside her. Had they perhaps peered a little more closely they might have been able to see me—their spirit vision vastly improved in the Afterlife—as perhaps a vague shimmering in the aether; a slight distortion in the light waves.

"Look at them, Eleena. Look into their hearts. These are the precious mortals we are committed to serve as they ascend far above us . . . look at them; they're timid creatures. Doesn't it make you feel how unfair it is? These puny little creatures get to ascend to the Central Universe and yet we have to stay down here for these interminable lengths of time, never having . . .'"

I stopped mid-thought when I felt Eleena starting to freeze me out. Of course, how stupid of me! While I might have a chance at some point in the future of joining the mortal ascendance program, I realized that poor Eleena—as a loyal Transport Seraph—would likely never be anything more than that. She was created as a Transport Seraph, and she would remain a Transport Seraph until the seven Superuniverses were Settled in Light and Life.

I realized then that I really should not be thinking these rebellious thoughts around her. It wasn't fair to her. Even if she shared some of my feelings—which I knew she didn't—there was nothing Eleena could have done about her destiny.

I was fairly certain, however, what would happen to me if she just happened—in mid-flight—to open her heat shield in subspace, so I wisely held my silence.

# 7

# Synchronous Existences and Understandings

Multiverse Completion, a New Symbiosis,
Agondonters, UFO over New York City,
Calligraphic Humor, Phinsouse, and
Zandana's Fourth Density

We rebel angels were the freaks. Is that too strong a word?

I don't think so. We were called freaks by enough of the Multiverse Administration's agents to believe it ourselves. We were the ones going against the grain, and we believed ourselves to be the bold exceptions to the rule. If I was correct—and I was progressively feeling more sure of myself—then as rebel angels we had all preselected ourselves for this grand experiment simply by aligning with Lucifer. None of us ever could have known our destiny might one day include participating in the development of a symbiosis of the mortal and the angelic.

As I've previously observed, so little is known about the first two angelic rebellions in this Local Universe that I can't say for certain whether this symbiosis has occurred before. I have never heard it spoken of. It was certainly never addressed in the seminars or the lectures back on Jerusem. And I've already noted how closely the Melchizedek

Brothers protected any specific information about those two previous rebellions.

I had been pondering this issue for some time, as you know. However, I decided there and then to consider what appeared to be happening on Earth as a first in the Local Universe—until I was shown otherwise. Why not?! It's a small conceit to believe the hybrid is original to us, and there are some good reasons for thinking this might be true. The two previous revolutions had presumably occurred far earlier in this Local Universe cycle. We were at this point much later in this cycle—as illustrated by the figures. The Earth, for example, is numbered 606 in this System of 1,000 inhabited, or to be inhabited, worlds. This Local Universe is numbered 611,121 out of a total of 700,000 Local Universes. Both numbers suggested that the Multiverse—in the larger context—is moving toward a stage of completion.

I am becoming more persuaded that this new hybrid of the mortal and the angelic is being developed for the times ahead. I've heard speculation . . . have I written of this before? Never mind. It is worth repeating as it suggests we will all be facing a wondrous destiny.

The Jerusem seminars on astronomy spoke of four great rings of matter that encircle the finite Multiverse. The first of the rings is some 400,000 light-years from the limits of the Multiverse. It has an overall width—so we were told—of 25 million light-years. We were taught that these four outer space levels were universes in formation.

"Well, thank you for that!" Eleena's voice broke softly across my thoughts. I'd forgotten she was listening. But I didn't mind. What was the worst that could happen? We'd been able to establish a level of trust during my various trips with her, and I'd come to think of her as a friend. I hope she felt the same about me.

"Much of this is new to me," she continued, her tone calm and surprisingly interested. "You must forgive my curiosity, but you are throwing a new light on the rebellion, if what you say is true."

"I've already witnessed rebel angels incarnated as human beings in Atlantis," I thought firmly. "I believe it is true. My speculation concerns this hybrid Being, this new mutation if you like—although it is not really a true mutation. It is more accurately a spiritual symbiosis of these two very different species with a common interest. I am starting to believe, Eleena, that these new beings are being nurtured to possess a sufficiently compassionate intelligence—and the emotional maturity— to play their parts in the development of life on those new worlds."

"So it's your belief," I heard Eleena think thoughtfully. "You believe that the rebellion might have happened so as to produce this . . . this symbiosis? Am I correct?"

"The more I think about the revolution within the largest context I can handle," I replied, "the more I am coming to see that the revolution must have been allowed to continue so as to create the conditions in which this symbiosis would come about. Whether the rebellion was actually instigated from the highest levels specifically to produce these new beings, I don't feel I'm yet in a position to know."

"That would be too terrible to contemplate!" Eleena replied, genuinely horrified. I could hear it in her tone. "Wouldn't that mean we've all been deceived? If the rebellion was actually contrived to develop this symbiosis of yours, these new beings you think it's producing, then why . . ."

"I know what you're thinking," I interrupted. "I went through much the same process: *Then why couldn't there be a better way of going about it?* Am I right?"

I didn't wait for Eleena's reply. I knew the territory. "I believe I understand it better now that I've spent as much time as I have in observing mortals at their best—and their worst.

"So, yes, there probably are other ways. I don't know what happened after the first two rebellions, but think about it, Eleena. If the MA is developing this new symbiosis of angel and mortal, then you'd expect that the angels would have to be tested for their independence and their courage. They would need to be thoroughly convinced that they were rebelling against an unjust and moribund theocracy. In this way the angels preselected themselves for their future roles."

"And the mortal side of your equation?"

"They, too, will need to be tempered in the fire of blunt experience and difficult choices. There's an exquisite balance here, Eleena." I was starting to get excited. I had never seen the plan written out in my mind so clearly before. I knew in those moments that it was the coherence and simplicity of Eleena's mind that was permitting me this unexpected lucidity. I felt that I was riding a wave of clarity. I didn't want to stop—even if what was pouring out was going to disturb my Transport Seraph's peace of mind.

"It is not so much about being deceived," I assured her. "We were all completely convinced in the rightness of our cause. And Gabriel's condemnation of Lucifer and Satan seemed to be every bit as genuine. It was obvious that Gabriel really believed Lucifer's revolution would throw this whole Local System into chaos. And if it was allowed to spread to the other Local Systems, then that would present an insufferable problem for Gabriel's administration."

"So that's why the MA quarantined the entire System and not just the rebel-held planets," Eleena added. She was being far more open than she'd ever been before. I remember commenting previously on the straightness of her affect. I was wondering about this change in my friend when I heard her again, this time taking the reasoning one step further.

"Are you suggesting," she asked, "that by delaying any true resolution of the rebellion for all these 203,000 years, the MA was giving the rebels a chance to expand beyond the original thirty-seven planets that aligned with Lucifer?"

"I've never considered that," I thought after a moment. "Perhaps because it never happened; the revolution never spread very far. If I'm right about this, it wouldn't have served the MA to have too many more planets affected—or 'infected,' as the MA likes to say—by revolutionary ideals and an excess of personal freedom. No, I don't think the MA necessarily wanted the rebellion to expand any farther. But it wouldn't surprise me if they used a fairly localized rebellion on thirty-seven planets to justify isolating the entire System of a thousand worlds."

"But why?" Eleena asked, genuinely puzzled. "Why would they deliberately make life so difficult on all those other worlds not involved with the revolution?"

"From what I've observed, the MA must value agondonters so highly they take any opportunity they can to justify isolating planets . . . just to produce more agondonters!"

"I don't want to believe that," Eleena murmured. "That would be too cruel; to deprive a world of its rightful heritage just to produce tough souls who can believe without seeing."

"If you think about it less sentimentally, Eleena, angelic rebellions are rare enough. And if revolutions are the only reason for quarantining worlds, then it would make sense for the MA to harvest as many agondonters as possible."

"Even if the toughest ones will always hail from the rebel-held worlds?" Eleena asked.

"They will tend to be the crème de la crème, that is true, Eleena. They'll be the agondonters who will have faced up to the worst effects of the rebellion. They will be among the most confident of the agondonters, of course, and they'll be the most certain of their personal contact with the Creator. Yet I'm sure the other agondonters will have fought their battles and faced their personal demons without the ready guidance of their angels. They, too, will have proved themselves in their own way."

There was some movement in the transport lounge as the lights flickered above the gates and two companion angels delivered their charge into the loving embrace of a Transport Seraph. The angels waited until the door slid closed behind the Transport Seraph and their ward. There was then a slight trembling in the aether, and the angels were no longer present with us in the lounge.

I turned back to Eleena, who was about to get to her feet. I was surprised she'd been able to give me so much time. She'd never done that before, and I wondered for a moment whether she might have had another agenda altogether.

I quickly masked off the thought from my mind and—lest Eleena pick up any shadow of my suspicion—I thought to distract her with an objective check on what I believed was occurring: "*If* my observations about this new symbiosis turn out to be true."

I reminded Eleena that—up until this point in time—I'd only seen that small cluster of starseeds in Atlantis, and of course, the rebel angels the MA had used to subvert Prince Caligastia's ill-conceived Reincarnation Express.

I still didn't know for certain then what is so clear to me now: that the birth and development of this new symbiosis of mortal and angel— these new starseeds—must have always been deeply factored into the MA's response to an angelic rebellion. Whether the MA prompted and nurtured the rebellion—or if the administration merely took advantage of Lucifer's rebellion to reap their precious agondonters—I was still in no position to say.

However, as I said to Eleena while we moved toward one of the flashing lights taking us to the gate, I couldn't imagine a more efficient way than an angelic rebellion to create the necessary challenges. It throws both angels and mortals into an entirely unpredictable situation in which they can make their mistakes, learn from them, and pay their dues—and grow stronger and wiser for it.

Thus if an angelic rebellion ultimately produces a new form of Being—a new species that will be invaluable for the times and tasks ahead—then might not this prove to be the recognition that finally unifies the opposing factions? The two opposing sides—the MA's loyalists and Lucifer's revolutionaries—would be able to understand and appreciate that they had both contributed to creating the context within which this new symbiosis was made possible.

The light went on over the gate, and we didn't speak again until I was wrapped in Eleena's heat shield and about to leave for Zandana. I was left hoping my speculations hadn't pushed too far into the unknown and upset my Transport Seraph. She was too useful an ally to lose, and I might have overstepped the limits of our friendship.

* * *

The weather was overcast during the morning of Labor Day 1981. The sun didn't peek through until midday, but by the time Melinda and my ward left the apartment the sky had clouded over again.

The previous evening Mein Host went out—as he said "on a whim"—to take advantage of some refurbishment on the benches in a nearby park. He had previously noticed that the demolished concrete benches had been uprooted and were presenting their flat bases to the sky. He had remarked to Melinda in passing that one of those flat concrete bases would make a great surface for graffiti. Because the park people would be hauling away the bust-up benches in a couple of days, he said it wouldn't really be despoiling the landscape if he put his hand to the benches. (More on this in a bit.)

My ward had always been fascinated by graffiti, calling it "the Art of the People," and he admired the courage of the kids who would frequently risk their lives to make their inscrutable marks on some inaccessible ledge. Before the New York subway carriages were cleaned up, he had likened the visual barrage of calligraphed tags on every surface not covered by advertising—and on much of that, too—to the arabesques of an Islamic mosque.

Most of all he appreciated the more elaborate forms of graffiti that were starting to appear—great whirls and swirls of color, hypercomplex calligraphy, and embedded social commentary—all created illicitly and with great care and attention to detail. He said he liked the way graffiti restored a sense of danger to the making of art.

When my ward lived on West 85th Street some years later, he had spent time tracking down one of the graffiti artists whose work he admired. He'd invited the lad to create a piece of graffiti on an exposed brick wall in his small back garden. The young black man agreed to do it—even if he obviously thought it a little weird. The weirdness was lessened after sharing a joint and the artist realizing he was free to paint whatever he wanted. All he asked for in return, so he said, was a bag of herb.

My ward had access to a higher quality of grass than that to which the lad was accustomed, so that was settled and the artist was more than happy to throw himself into the painting. He arrived a few days later accompanied by a younger boy—fourteen or fifteen perhaps—both laden down with spray-paint cans of every color to get at the wall.

My ward, who never appreciated anyone seeing his graphic work before he'd completed it, chose to afford the graffiti artist the same courtesy. He left them to it after observing—to his amusement as he said later—the way the artist treated his younger helper. He said it was like watching a Renaissance artist and his apprentice. A barked command had the kid snapping off the top of the requested color. The artist barely looked behind him as cans of different colors were exchanged in his outstretched hand with an almost surgical precision.

It's not surprising that graffiti artists work rapidly—they have to or they'll get caught. But to have completed what turned out to be an extravagantly intricate piece of work in the hour it took the artist was in itself a truly extraordinary accomplishment. I had the chance to watch the artist while he worked and witnessed the level of focused concentration he brought to the task.

When the lads completed the graffiti, they invited Mein Host out to the garden to view it. The painting filled the twelve-foot-wide wall to the height of the artist's outstretched arm. It was as convoluted and beautifully executed as the finest graffiti; it was a true work of art. My ward joked to the boys that it put SAMO to shame and made Jean Basquiat's stuff look like the daubs of an illiterate child.

They liked that.

He said later that he couldn't make out the image at first, but as he sat smoking with them in the garden, the forms had gradually come into focus. In among the swirl of calligraphy emerged a wizard in a lotus position, with a massively oversized spliff jammed in his mouth. The smoke in the image curled into letters spelling out my ward's nickname, Doc, over and over. It was a name awarded him by the kids in the local pizza parlor that he frequented often, bestowed upon him because of his apparent resemblance to Christopher Lloyd's "Doc" Brown in the film *Back to the Future*.

DOC, the graffiti repeated: DOC . . . DOC . . . DOC, in calligraphy that curled and zagged around the seated figure. It was a delightfully subtle—if somewhat revealing—joke on my ward, given that the graffiti could be plainly seen from any one of the windows of the apartments to the rear of the garden. He said he knew the kids were challenging him to be as daring as they were by exposing him to the risks of making such a bold statement.

The graffiti stayed up to be much admired by my ward's friends until he left the apartment. A few months later, he heard that the new occupants—thoughtlessly ignorant in his opinion—had whitewashed over a superb example of urban graffiti.

Now back to my ward's own attempts at the decorative art of graffiti. Having commented on my ward's wanting to turn his hand to this art form that he valued so highly, he was damned if he wasn't going to display his artistic talents on one of the upturned park benches he'd observed in Bennett Park. So it was that it was well after midnight on the morning of that Labor Day in 1981 that my ward, armed with a spray can of red paint, left the apartment he shared with Melinda on Pinehurst Avenue in northern Manhattan. He was bound for the park, which was one block south of where they lived. It was empty, and the night was as still as it ever gets in the city. After arriving at the upturned bench in the park, he spray-painted—in elegant sans serif capital letters—THE LIZARD HAS LANDED—on its concrete base.

He admitted later he didn't quite know why he'd chosen that phrase—it was the first thing that came into his head. It's only now as I write these words that he realizes the phrase must have swum into his consciousness because of the intense focus he'd been putting into illustrating his cosmic creation myth, *The Helianx Proposition*. I will say more about this later. This is because not only would it take him the next thirty years to complete work on the book—it was published in 2012—but more personally because it also throws a revealing light on some of the mysterious experiences I'd been having over the millennia.

Having accomplished what he'd set out to do by making his statement on the bench, he returned to the apartment and got some ZZZs before arising the next day. Later, in the early afternoon, he and Melinda left their apartment building to see how the graffiti would look in the daytime. Just outside their building they bumped into their good friend Stephen M., who lived a few doors away and was quite content to go along with them.

Bennett Park is small and compact and occupies only a single city block. After a long hot summer there were small patches of grass brown with wear, a score of brave but stunted trees, the expected amount of litter for New York City, and an outcropping of granitic bedrock—specks of mica glistening in its steel-gray matrix.

The outcropping, curved and scraped smooth by glacial retreat, was exposed above the ground like the back of a whale. Although no more than a few feet in height, the prominence—the highest natural place in the city—subtlety dominated life in the little park. Children were drawn to the rock to play their games on and around it; dogs would feel bound to scrabble to the top, where they'd stand, snarling proudly and defending their position until toppled by a feistier hound; birds drank from the rainwater puddled in tiny rocky pools; and on sunny days my ward would always find a few New Yorkers stretched flat on the warm rock, taking in the sun. Without being aware of it, life in the park revolved around the rock.

Mein Host, who professes such an affinity for rocks that he featured them in many of his graphics, recognized the rocky hummock in Bennett Park as one of the potent natural power centers of the city. He'd frequently spent time meditating on the rock, generally long after midnight when the streets around the park were quiet. He had clearly grown to know it and to love it.

The bench with his graffiti was within a few yards of the rock, and by the time the three of them arrived they found an old man already photographing the graffiti and muttering to himself about its enigmatic meaning. They laughed along with him—saying something admiring about the kids today—without enlightening him of the graffiti's true provenance.

Melinda had brought her Brownie Box camera with her, and—in checking out the light levels—she glanced up at the sky and quickly alerted the others to what she'd seen. In my ward's first book, here is how he described the next few moments:

> She (Melinda) exclaimed in surprise—and we followed her gaze—to see a sizable moving disc traveling low and steadily across the gray sky. It was a bluish/green color and about the same size as an American one-cent piece held at arm's length. It was well below the cloud level and quite distinct.
>
> The three of us watched in a state of absorbed fascination as it transited the sky in about thirty-five seconds, disappearing over the tree line in a northwesterly direction toward the Bronx. It was difficult to judge its size because there was little to which to relate it, but I would estimate it to be about 20–30 feet in diameter and traveling around 3,000 feet up. It's motion was steady and regular, and had the look of being powered, unlike a balloon or a meteorological kite. As we watched, it fluttered briefly without changing its speed or direction, as if it was tipping its wings . . .
>
> We had not talked in any detail about our recent sighting of the lights in Florida, sensing in them a mystery yet to be revealed. This flying disc, with its concrete reality and seen at 1:00 p.m. on a clear Monday afternoon, however, was quite different. I recall thinking, as it passed overhead, that if I'd ever have asked for a bona fide UFO, then I could expect nothing more real and down-to-earth than this remarkable apparition.

That is what my ward wrote in 1981—only days after the incident. He has now had many years to ponder what he, Melinda, and Stephen witnessed that Labor Day in light of what has been revealed about UFOs in the past forty years. So, although he'd come to the same conclusion, let me take this opportunity to confirm for him that what they saw was indeed an authentic alien craft.

The situation with the craft flying overhead might have remained just that—a mysterious disc that appeared to be powered by an unknown intelligence—had a young boy of some eight years not been standing near them. He'd also seen the UFO and must have noticed my ward's excitement. He wandered over to where the three of them were standing—still stunned by what they'd just witnessed.

"Don't worry about that," the boy told them in good English but with a strong, seemingly mid-European accent. "It's just a starcar."

Mein Host wrote that he felt the hairs standing up on the back of his neck at the statement. Although the boy had referred to the starcar in such an offhand manner, he said it with the certainty of familiarity—his seriousness and his accent only adding to his self-possessed authority.

"Over here, young man," my ward said as he beckoned the lad to where they were sitting on the rock. "Come and tell us about starcars."

"It is a single-person craft used generally by tourists and explorers," the boy replied fluidly without pausing to think. "It is connected to a mothership by its central drive mechanism."

My ward was now recording the boy's words on a scrap of paper. He said later he thought the kid might be making it all up, but it was intriguing enough to keep asking questions.

"Well, they certainly can travel between planets," the boy continued, "but they invariably relate back to the mothership. You see, both the larger ships and the smaller starcars use a Mani Particle Beam propulsion system that is picked up by a central unit within them." And yes, he spoke like this in complete paragraphs. "This unit establishes a particle beam rapport instantaneously with a terminal within the giant star Phinsouse . . ."

"How do you spell that?" my ward asked, and the kid spelled it out patiently a letter at a time while rolling his eyes at the slowness of adults. My ward has claimed he wasn't sure where his next question came from.

"Does it have a universe number?" he asked.

"Local or general?" the boy replied, looking happy to be taken seriously.

"Local first."

"79562183. And general, 1765333177082."

After my ward wrote down the numbers he asked the boy to repeat them to make sure he had them right. The boy did this faultlessly before returning to the subject of Phinsouse. Mein Host has said it was as though certain questions were being drawn out of him so he could check the boy's authenticity. For the boy to repeat back twenty-one numbers perfectly without any apparent effort to remember what he'd said the first time around was most convincing.

"The star system Phinsouse," the boy continued, "is inhabited by a very old race of non-space-faring beings. It is for this reason it has been chosen as the center of space activity. There, every inhabited planet has a separate chamber that represents the race concerned and the progress it has made."

"Where is Phinsouse?" my ward asked.

"It is in the center of the Andromeda Galaxy." There was no pause for thought . . . the boy's words came out in a steady stream. "The most populated galaxy in the universe, with one million races living on three billion planets."

So started a conversation that ranged from the assertion that all races have feelings, to interplanetary communication systems involving the Mani Particle Beam again, to politics in the universe—a form of one-person, one-vote democracy the boy called Anthesis—and to the rarity of war and how belligerent planets were simply avoided by the rest of them.

Perhaps most astonishing were two particular statements the boy made. For these he stood back, straightening up to his full height, his voice changing to a more oracular tone. *How* Mein Host recorded his statements—more than anything else the kid had told them—indicated who the source of all this information was.

The last subject, Mein Host wrote, "[the boy] covered with remarkable passion and a genuine sense of wonderment." He said there had been considerably heightened interest in this planet since World War II but that no detailed records had been taken for the past ten thousand years.

"The last film we saw about his planet was ten thousand years ago," the boy stated. Then—in his strangely clipped European accent and his sage young-old eyes—he pulled himself up to his full pudgy height and announced with overwhelming authority:

"Caveman to civilization overnight!
Caveman to civilization overnight!"

The boy—a telepathically open channel for those in the craft—had much more to say that my ward was able to record and include in his book. I therefore have no need to repeat it here.

Ever since the early 1960s, my ward had been interested in the possibility of extraterrestrial life. And as I've previously narrated, he had a number of mysterious incidents prior to witnessing the UFO over Manhattan. But it was seeing the craft in all its brazen indifference to the city's presumably well-protected airspace—and then hearing the young boy's informative and authoritative spiel—that allowed him to finally know, rather than simply believe in, the reality of extraterrestrial life.

First there had been his recent insights into dolphin telepathy, and now this: a clear demonstration of intelligent life in the Multiverse. If he thought that was going to be the end of the journey, he was about to find himself participating in a series of events that would have a far more significant influence on his life to come.

* * *

Eleena and I didn't speak again until I was wrapped in her heat shield and could feel the now familiar vibrations all around me as the Transport Seraph accelerated into subspace.

The sense that I might have overstepped our friendship disappeared when I heard her tell me about her new sonic masterpiece—although she was much too modest to ever use the word *masterpiece*. She wanted me to listen to it, saying, to my surprise, that it would be the first time she'd ever played the entire piece. I said I was surprised because I wasn't aware the sonic pieces were so carefully composed. I'd imagined they were almost entirely spontaneous.

Apparently Eleena had been recently recognized by her colleagues for her unique contribution to their song cycles. She told me what I hadn't appreciated. This was that among the many layers the music a Transport Seraph made while moving through subspace, there was also recorded the astronomical and space-time data of the trip. This she'd likened to whale song, as other seraphs picked up the melody and added its echo to their sonic repertoires.

Well of course it was lovely. Eleena's songs were always lovely—but I simply didn't have the discernment to detect the subtle changes that seemed so important to her. Nevertheless I made the necessary appreciative noises that I don't think for a moment fooled Eleena. However, as I was one of the few traveling with her who'd expressed any interest in her music, I could feel her kindly forgiving my ignorance.

We approached Zandana as Eleena's song was whining and whirring to its closure, and the slight deceleration vibrations signaled our imminent arrival. Eleena bid me a fond but quick adieu after accompanying me to the lounge and finding that she had another last-minute booking waiting for her.

Although all Seraphic Transport Centers are located in the fifth dimension they are placed within the lowest frequency domain within that dimension. As a result I was able to move almost imperceptibly through the crowded lounge and into a slightly higher frequency domain. I was seen only by one small girl. She was a recently deceased native of the city of Zandan and giggled and waved at the passing apparition until one of her companion angels calmed her down and smiled sweetly at me.

I left the bright lighting of the travel center to be greeted by the gloaming of a single distant sun. The Wise Twins were evidently at their apogee, with the larger of the two suns currently throwing its rays on the other side of the planet. As I've done before, I made my way to the forested and grassy promontory overlooking the wide bay that sheltered the city of Zandan far over to my right.

The psychic atmosphere on Zandana was so different from that of Earth. It always took me time to adjust my mind. I was able to relax, sitting with my back against the smooth bark of one of Zandana's finest and oldest trees. Its violet- and lavender-tinted leaves above me rustled in the breeze. The sharp smell of iodine followed the breezes in from the ocean, cutting into—and then mixing with—the softer scents of grass and forest . . .

And then it struck me that I had never experienced the scents of a planet with such an intense clarity before. I have noted previously how odors from third-density worlds can be experienced by angels in our higher frequencies. Yet I'd never smelled anything quite so powerfully. Were my senses changing? Was I becoming more sensitive? If I was—if that was it—then I feared all the noxious and mephitic odors I would have to put up with when I returned to Earth.

I bathed in the scent for a while before the implications of what was occurring suddenly hit me. Could it really be true? Was it possible I was no longer on a third-density world?! Had I been away from Zandana for so long that the planet had shifted from third to fourth density while my back was turned, so to speak?

I sat there for a while feeling unaccountably joyful.

This feeling must have been going on for a long time because, when I brought myself back, Zandana's second sun was already peeping above the mountains on the other side of the bay. As the planet turned the sun grew larger. At the same time, the tree above me became alive with nervous movement as hundreds of small birds awoke, chittering and stretching their trembling wings.

I could see a score of flitter-boats in the distance. They were setting out for a day's fishing from the tiny villages tucked into the shoreline. The birds, now in their thousands, were leaving the forests border-ing the bay and were gathering in a massive swirling cloud. They were swooping and climbing, turning and curling as a single amorphous Being in the golden light of the new sun.

It seemed to me as I surveyed this eminently charming scene that everything was exactly as it should be. All the elements—the birds, the wind, the smells, the flitter-boats, the Wise Twins, the sea and the mountains, even the distant city of Zandan—had come together into one exuberant, coherent Whole. And the Whole—or perhaps it was simply my experience of the Wholeness—rendered it so much more than its many parts.

Plate 1. *Celebrant & Saint.* Portrait of Timothy Wyllie by June Atkin.
Prismacolor Pencil

Plate 2. *Another Dolphin Dream*. Timothy Wyllie.
Prismacolor Pencil

Plate 3. *2012 Homecoming*. Timothy Wyllie.
Prismacolor Pencil

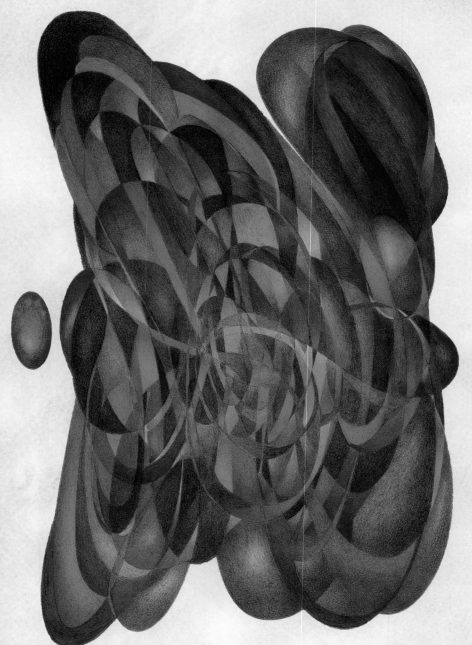

Plate 4. *The Winding Road*. Timothy Wyllie.
Prismacolor Pencil

Plate 5. *Prelude to the End Game.* Timothy Wyllie.
Prismacolor Pencil

Plate 6. *Genetic Transformation.* Timothy Wyllie.
Prismacolor Pencil

Plate 7. *The Transmutation of Death; Machu Picchu.v2.* Timothy Wyllie.
Prismacolor Pencil

Plate 8. *Future Artifact.* Timothy Wyllie.
Prismacolor Pencil

I wondered if this was one of the delightful qualities of a fourth-density world. I was relishing what I was feeling. I had always loved Zandana, but the joy now flowing through me was an entirely new feeling.

After a while another thought came to me: If it was true that Zandana had made its shift to fourth density, then wouldn't this reflect remarkably well on Lucifer's rebellion?

And then, chasing that thought: However had Zandana managed to accomplish this when it was obvious that Earth was so far from doing the same?

I hadn't been pondering these thoughts for very long when the aether quivered beside me and there was Clarisel, the Watcher whom I had befriended on my previous visit. As with Astar back on Earth, Clarisel had proved an invaluable fount of local information whenever she appeared.

After we greeted one another—and I confess I find the natural ease of contact I have with a sister Watcher far more amicable than having to curb my thoughts with loyalists such as Eleena—she settled down to update me on the transition.

"Am I correct, Clarisel? Can it really be true that Zandana is now a fourth-density world?"

The Watcher was smiling with a combination of pleasure and pride. Feeling the depth of her joy, I had no need to hear her confirmation.

"But how?" I asked. "Can you explain how this occurred in a manner I can understand?"

She reminded me how we had been together on my prior visit when we saw the crack in the world and witnessed the Rainbow Bridge together.

"The souls you saw crossing the Rainbow Bridge were preparing the way for the transition—you'll recall I mentioned that at the time."

And then I did. With a shock, too!

I thought while I was observing the miraculous Rainbow Bridge that it would stay in the front of my mind. She'd already told me that those souls were forming a bridgehead to the fourth density, but I had no idea that the full transformation would happen so quickly.

"Once the Rainbow Bridge starts appearing," Clarisel continued, "the full transition occurs within a few hundred years. Your last visit was more than a thousand Zandana years ago. Much has happened since then."

"But what does it really mean to shift from third to fourth density?" I asked, since it was still a mystery to me. "What actually happens?"

"The best way I can explain it is to liken planetary transformation to cell mitosis. In the biological realm the parent cell's genome transfers through mitosis into two identical daughter cells. On a planetary level, it's slightly different. The parent world extrudes only a single daughter, and that would be the fourth-density world."

"But aren't there now two planets? Where's the other one if we're now on the fourth-density one?"

This evoked a sigh from Clarisel, who must have realized how little I understood about planetary engineering.

"These two 'planets,' as you call them," she said—her tone patient as though she was speaking to a child—"are really dimensional realities. All dimensional realities occupy the same location in the space-time continuum, but they exist on a spectrum of frequencies. So when Zandana was shifting from third to fourth density, it was not dissimilar perhaps to a mortal being shifting from living primarily from her or his third chakra, to living in the fourth (the heart). The mortal's first, second, and third chakras don't disappear. They are still there within the overall organism in the same way Zandana still exists on a third-density level—while what we're experiencing here is the fourth."

"What happens to the third-density reality now? Is it still inhabited? Are than Zandanans still living there?"

"You really don't understand very much, do you?" Clarisel replied. My friendly Watcher's tone was becoming recognizably similar to Astar's when she's testy.

"Of course it's inhabited! It's never the case that all the inhabitants of a planet move up to the fourth simultaneously."

"But how does that work, Clarisel? When does the actual planetary dimensional shift occur in that case?"

"There is always a tipping point, which is when sufficient numbers of mortals are living in their hearts. The planet thus knows that the time for transformation has arrived. No . . . don't ask me how the planet actually knows the time has come . . . she just does."

I wasn't going to pounce on the Watcher just because she didn't know something. What she was telling me was intriguing enough. But before I had the chance to question her further—and I still had a lot of questions—she signaled that she was required elsewhere and promised to return soon. With this, the aether flickered where Clarisel was, and then the Watcher was gone—seemingly sucked into absence.

Perhaps like the smile on the face of the Cheshire cat, Clarisel's delicate form lingered as an afterimage dancing briefly in the sun, before that, too, finally disappeared.

# 8

# Interdimensional Vision

### A Magisterial Son, Tourists from Andromeda, Lake of Glass, the Prince's Spy, Talking with Angels, and Loving Your Enemies

"So you're saying the fourth dimension is always there," I prompted the Zandana Watcher Clarisel when she had returned from her mission. "Just like the bottom three and top three primary dimensions continue to coexist because they are all contained within the Wholeness of the planet? Is that it?"

Clarisel sat down beside me on the grassy promontory. The bay stretched out before us, with the ocean now blindingly bright under the light of an ascending sun—or more accurately, a turning planet . . . Yet that really doesn't quite glow with the sublime poetry of an ascending sun!

"Now you are starting to see the picture," Clarisel said, her tone a trifle mollified. "Except it is far more complicated than a series of dimensions just stacked one on top of another. It doesn't work quite like that. You have to factor in that the finer frequencies are interpenetrating the denser frequencies. Thus it is that beings of the fifth dimension—in which exists Jerusem and the angels of the Local System and yes, Watchers, too—can interpenetrate the lower dimensions at will. As a Watcher you know that, of course—how you can move without detection through a third- or fourth-density world while being fully aware of your surroundings."

"The planetary shift itself, Clarisel . . ." I said, wanting to get back to what concerned me. "What happens to the mortals on the planet when the shift occurs?"

"First, the shift doesn't occur all at once, if that's what you mean. It's more like the pattern you find in the natural world. Like many examples of natural growth, the planetary shift occurs in increments. The last time you were here on this world, Georgia, you observed a relatively late stage in the shift, but it was still well before the tipping point was reached.

"The actual tipping point came when sufficient numbers of mortals on Zandana were able to sustain life in the heart. These are the ones who will find themselves living in the fourth-density reality . . . And, yes, they probably will drop back into the third density in some particularly stressful condition, but they'll find it so uncomfortable at that stage of their development that they'll know to return to the heart."

I must have felt concerned about those who didn't make the grade, who couldn't sustain life in the heart, and those who resorted to their animal emotions at the slightest provocation. There was almost nothing but that on Earth.

"I believe you have previously observed, Georgia, that the indigenous population of Zandana was far less fearful and belligerent in general terms than the population on Earth. This is true, and it has led to a much more homogeneous population on this planet. This has, in turn, allowed the shift—the tipping point—when it finally arrived, to be surprisingly fluid and straightforward . . . for a rebel world!"

Clarisel caught my eye and quickly returned me to what had originally concerned me. I must have been thinking of life on Earth and how wildly varied were all the different levels of consciousness among humans. If the shift occurred on Earth right then in the third millennium BCE, I doubt if there would be more than a few thousand human beings who would have been able to sustain life in the fourth density.

"Those mortals," she continued, "are likely to experience new challenges created in their lives to test their mettle. Consequently there will always be a steady movement of mortals from third- to fourth-density reality, as they learn to live in their hearts during the course of their lifetimes. The mortals I'm talking about are the ones who remained in the third density at the time of the shift. This is subject to the judgment of the Magisterial Son, of course, and the guidance of the many celestial assistants who accompany him.

"You might think of these Magisterial Sons as organizing principles. Yes, of course they are judges, but—deeper than that—they are points of spiritual coherence. Despite appearing as mortal beings—in physical vehicles appropriate to the world in which they serve—they are immensely powerful beings. They radiate such a far-reaching and coherent energy that their influence will affect and uplift the consciousness of mortals for a great distance all around them . . ."

When she finished, I said, "You talked earlier of a tipping point, Clarisel—a time when the primary reality actually shifts from third to fourth density. There must have been a moment, yes? At that very point, what happens then?"

A sense of clarity surrounding her, she replied, "Ah yes, now I understand. The shift itself, the moment you're asking about . . . well, it's so subtle most mortals are unaware of it occurring. On a world like Zandana, the shift seems to be connected with the work of the Magisterial Son—though I've not yet learned exactly what it is."

I remembered observing a Magisterial Son—Justinial was his name, I recall—who was serving on Delta, one of the five other rebel worlds I was permitted to visit. A Magisterial Son must have arrived on Zandana since I was last here. That would have accounted for many of the changes I was feeling.

"But wouldn't all that coherent energy radiating out from the Magisterial Son also activate everything that is incoherent in the less advanced mortals?" I asked her.

"You are looking through the eyes of a Watcher from Earth, Georgia," she replied as her tone became firmer. "You must have observed that the general level of mental and spiritual intelligence—even among the less advanced among the population here in Zandana—is both more well-developed and well-balanced compared with Earth.

"Zandana was never a particularly materialist planetary civilization. Even here in the south—the most highly developed continent on Zandana—even here, each individual would have understood their basic purpose in life was to grow in spirit and self-knowledge. Everyone would have understood and felt this in their bones. It would have come with the culture, that the deepest purpose of life lay in the progressive perfection of the mortal self, and in discovering—and then in actively collaborating with—the Great Spirit indwelling all mortals . . ."

I admit my mind was drifting. It wasn't that I lacked interest. No, it was because I was beginning to become bewildered by the cognitive dissonance I was feeling between life on Earth and what Clarisel was telling me about Zandana.

I started to feel depressed again. The contrast between the spiritual condition of the two worlds suddenly seemed impossibly wide. How could the humans of Earth—of whatever distant future generation—ever measure up to what was required of them to enter the fourth density? The gulf simply seemed too vast to ever think it was possible.

I knew this wasn't true even as I thought it. Nevertheless the feeling of utter hopelessness almost overwhelmed me. It was only afterward I realized how the contrast of the joy I'd been feeling earlier had thrown me further into this sudden depression.

I believe it was then that it struck me that both these feelings—the joy from earlier and now the terrible and unexpected sense of despair—were the most intense I had yet felt. The emotions I was now capable of experiencing as a Watcher were becoming more and more extreme.

As Clarisel seemed to be completing her lecture—and I was being wrenched around by the intensity of my feelings—I found my eyes focusing on a speck in the sky, very much as I might have abstractly watched a distant bird.

But it wasn't a bird! It never moved!

I must have gasped loudly in surprise, because Clarisel stopped talking in my mind. The distant speck that seemed to remain stationary while I was watching suddenly—and I mean suddenly, for there was no acceleration that I could see—was no longer where I was watching. One moment it was there—a minuscule, motionless dot—and the next it was swooping in an immense curve etched against the clouds. Then it was moving in our direction, steadily growing in size until I could see it was an unusually large spacecraft.

Clarisel turned to look at what I was watching. The craft appeared to grow to an immense size before it stopped with the same shocking suddenness with which it had taken off. It hovered briefly over the distant mountains before lowering itself as would a mother hen over a massive egg on the far side of the mountains. To give an idea of its size, we could still see the top of the craft curving above the mountains on the other side of the bay.

"You are observing one of the great advancements of life on a fourth-density world," Clarisel was saying with pride.

Not "world" I thought . . . "reality." Isn't that what she had emphasized earlier? A fourth-density reality? I didn't really wish to correct her—I knew I was nitpicking—but I also needed her to know I'd understood her.

"Yes, yes," she said, her impatience back again, "a fourth-density 'reality' . . . much better." Clarisel's tone felt dismissive until I saw she was focused on the ship and was barely listening to me. Her hand was up to shade her eyes from the second sun, now risen well above the mountains on the horizon. The silver surface of the long curved top of the craft, now hovering behind the mountains, was glittering and flashing in the rays of the sun rising behind it. It was as though we were watching silent explosions of light with every slight quiver of the hovering craft. It was a breathtaking display that was all conducted in complete silence.

"That'll be the tourist ship from Andromeda," Clarisel said, her tone casual and knowing. "I was aware that it would be arriving shortly. It must be ahead of schedule."

It took me aback, I can tell you. The craft reminded me of those

Pleiadean arks that had intervened to relocate those Lemurians living at the time of the sinking of their islands, but I knew that was an exception to the quarantine. I realized in that case the Pleiadean evacuation must have been sanctioned by the new System Sovereign Lanaforge on Jerusem to have occurred at all.

Yet here was Clarisel, casually dismissing this obviously intergalactic craft as a tourist ship from Andromeda! Whatever happened to the quarantine?

"Don't be so impressed, she's just a bus!" Clarisel said in an amused tone. "The old dear generally circulates among the worlds in the Andromeda Galaxy picking up tourists who want to spend some time on less advanced planets. In this case, I'm told on her return trip she'll be carrying mortals from Zandana back to Andromeda.

"Now that space travel has opened up for Zandana, there seems to be great interest in exploring the Vivaria housed in an architectural sphere orbiting the star Phinsouse. I've not been to this world myself. I believe it's there they maintain the interactive holographic simulacra of all the many millions of inhabited worlds in this sector."

"And the Lake of Glass on Zandana?" I recalled seeing signs of its appearance in the forest clearing on one of my earlier trips.

"Ah, yes, the Lake of Glass," Clarisel murmured. "No doubt you are questioning why anyone would want to take an intergalactic trip when there's always the Lake of Glass available to get to know their interplanetary neighbors?"

We were taught about these Lakes of Glass in our lectures on Jerusem. Specifically we were taught how they function on the advanced worlds as terminals of a Universe Broadcast System that links all the fourth-density planets. Although these massive crystals—sometimes miles across—are present on third-density planets, they generally are deeply buried and inaccessible. They'll be inactive until the planet shifts into the fourth density. We were told that the instantaneous transmission and reception of real-time holograms is only possible within the spiritual circuitry embedded in the fourth dimension. The great crystal lies fallow and silent, deep under the ground of a third-density planet, only to work its way to the surface after the world shifts to the fourth density. That's when its activation engages with the Universe Broadcast circuits. This, in turn, would have alerted interested fourth-density worlds as to Zandana's availability.

I'd hoped at the time to learn more about the systems engineering of the broadcast circuitry but was informed by the seminar leader—rather sharply, too—that I had no need to know the technical details. He informed me that I should be focusing on the task at hand, which was becoming familiar with third-density realities.

"Haven't you noticed?" Clarisel asked after we settled down again. It became too painful to keeping watching the distant ship that now appeared as a blindingly bright strip of light on the horizon. It must have been the clarity of the atmosphere in the fourth-density reality that made the light so intensely bright.

"Mortals, wherever you find them," Clarisel continued, "are invariably overly attached to their physical vehicles. They want to take their bodies with them when they travel."

"I think that must be the fear of death that's imprinted in their animal bodies," I said, hoping to keep up with Clarisel. I immediately felt awkward and embarrassed—yes, angels can feel embarrassed!—when she rolled her eyes. I realized then she was just being sardonic about the mortals' precious bodies. When she continued, her tone had reverted to one of condescension again. She told me much that I knew already, but I wasn't about to stop her—there was too much I *didn't* know.

"The Lake of Glass," she said after I quieted down, "only gives them access to real-time holograms, so the focus on the lake is always on conversational interactions. It's good for scientists, of course, and for those who wish to spend their time sharing information with experts on other worlds. But were you to take sufficient time to observe the activities on the Lake of Glass over a few years, you might notice that for normal folk the novelty wears off quickly. Most mortals just want to get on with their regular lives.

"In the Vivaria, although they, too, are holograms, it is possible for a visitor to have a complete interactive experience of life on another world. Then they step out of that particular Vivarium and into another one and have another, entirely different, experience of life on yet another world."

As if somehow activated by our discussion about space travel—or more likely, while my perceptual framework was more fully adjusting to this fourth-density reality—I began to be able to see more iridescent flashes of light in the sky. I realized the rays of the rising sun had to be catching the undersides of small craft moving with extraordinary speed in different directions across the sky. It was like watching the most adroit of water insects whisking this way and that over the still surface of a pond.

Clarisel was laughing at my attempts to grasp what I was seeing. I was just trying to tame the unfamiliar vision into a friendly metaphor. Granted it may have been idiotically mundane and somewhat reductive, too, if I were to accept the Watcher's mocking laughter as judgment, but all this was new to me.

Yes of course I'd seen a few interplanetary ships back on Earth, but that was long before the Lucifer Rebellion brought the systemwide quarantine down like Maxwell Smart's Cone of Silence. (*Note: There she goes again! Georgia seems to take a peculiar pleasure in picking unlikely applications for slang words and dredging idiosyncratic social references out of my vocabulary. I've had some small success at reining her in, but she doesn't like it. And as my readers must know us both pretty well by now, I no longer try to curb her. She can express herself however she wants. —TW*)

I was aware that casual appearances by more advanced races on worlds that are nurturing early-stage intelligent life were generally discouraged. Besides, no extraterrestrial race wants to risk the disgrace of having to appear before the Courts of Uversa for interfering with a primitive planet's life-forms.

Mein Host has commented in his book *The Return of the Rebel Angels* on the unfortunate agenda of an extraterrestrial race, the Verdants, who attempted a failed intervention on Earth in the late 1990s. In the Verdants' case, unexpected events unfolding on Earth—that should have been anticipated by a more mature ET race—forced them to back away and reconsider their plans for colonization. The Verdants were kind enough as individuals, but their agenda was both poorly conceived and arrogant in its assumptions. They had to limp off with their tails between their legs. And no, the Verdants didn't really have tails— and they probably became the butt of the more knowing races' humor at their expense.

My attention was wandering, bewitched as I was by what I was seeing and feeling. The Jerusem seminars had touched on a planet's fourth-density reality. Yet it was only the briefest of references because the MA presumably wanted us to focus our attention entirely on the third-density reality that we had been placed on Earth to serve.

"Come along, sister," Clarisel murmured softly in my mind. "Now that you have had time to grow more accustomed to this density, there is more for you to know."

Then she spoke the words I was both hoping to hear and also somehow dreading at the same time.

"Come on," she said again. "Prince Janda-chi requires your presence as soon as you have fully balanced your equilibrium."

And there it was!

Janda-chi, the second of Zandana's two Planetary Princes, required my presence. I had half hoped to avoid his attention on this visit. Fat chance! An effective Planetary Prince knows everything of significance happening within his domain—and Janda-chi was nothing if not effective!

On the other hand, I was anxious to find if I could get to the bottom of whether I was being used unwittingly as the Prince's spy. I trust you can understand my nervousness at what I might learn.

"Come on," Clarisel said again. "I'm to take you there, and the Prince doesn't appreciate being kept waiting."

* * *

It was only a couple of weeks after Mein Host and Melinda—together with their friend Stephen—had seen the UFO over Bennett Park and received the lecture on interplanetary politics from the young ET telepathic mouthpiece. That had set up the last piece of an emerging pattern.

A phone call came from some friends of Melinda's in Toronto, telling of a friend of theirs who'd found that he was a natural light-trance medium. They agreed to send transcripts of sessions they had with Edward, the medium, in which the angels had spoken through him.

Mein Host—with his experience of running with psychics and mediums back in the community days—didn't have much interest in mediumship and wasn't looking as though he was going to follow up . . . until the transmissions arrived.

The angels, coming through Edward, spoke lucidly, intelligently, and in much the same voice my ward said he found in *The Urantia Book*. Melinda, who'd come to the same conclusion, agreed that the situation in Toronto needed a closer inspection. She therefore made arrangements for them to stay with her friends and meet Edward—and talk with the angels themselves. All present would be readers of the *The Urantia Book,* so the scope of their discussions and their conceptual familiarity with the reality of angels promised interchanges of unusual depth.

A week later Melinda and my ward were being greeted by Sandy and Krystal and their two teenage children at their house in a comfortable, leafy, Toronto suburb—admittedly an unlikely place in which to speak to angels. Yet a couple of days later that is exactly what they were doing: talking easily and confidently with the angels.

Over the next week they had the opportunity to converse with as many as eight different celestials. They spoke through Edward's mouth using his vocabulary, much as I am using my collaborator's knowledge base and vocabulary as I write these words.

However, once again, I've no wish to unnecessarily repeat what my ward has already recorded in some detail in *Dolphins ETs & Angels* (pages 142–62 and 185–204). I recommend the interested reader to look through the two chapters my ward devotes in his book to their sessions with Edward. It contains a great deal of important information from the angels. Not only that, but my ward's record of their more substantial conversations is better than I can communicate here. It was a process by which the two parties—angels and humans—were able to establish their mutual trust.

During the next ten days, and some eight sessions with Edward, they were able to become progressively more relaxed with the reality of actually talking with angels. Their sessions were efficiently tape-recorded by Melinda to be transcribed when they returned to New York. And although my ward couldn't have known it at the time, much of what the angels stated in 1981 about the immediate future has already come about as I write in 2012. They spoke, for example, of a global communication system (the Internet). What hasn't yet occurred has been showing every sign of happening in the near future.

After a close level of trust was established the questions and the angels' replies could become deeper and more resonantly meaningful. The humans needed to establish the authenticity of the voices speaking through Edward, you see, and the angels needed to establish the sincerity and openness of the humans.

These were not gullible people. Sandy, in particular, was a hardheaded skeptic who only accepted the authenticity of the transmissions after much testing. Very much his own man, Sandy was articulate, argumentative, and opinionated. He prided himself on not being easily taken for a ride. He was in his midfifties at the time. He was portly, and his name, Sandy—a diminutive of Alexander—was demonstrative given that he was sandy of hair and face.

The man was a composer and orchestra conductor working at the Canadian Broadcast Corporation and had never risen to quite the heights he believed he deserved. This must have added an irascible tone to what was already a gruffly suspicious personality. He chain-smoked cigarettes so it was hard to tell whether his eyes were merely squinting against the smoke or whether his perpetually half-closed eyes were the consequence of a lifetime of misgivings and distrust.

Sandy liked to tell a story at his own expense, which suggested the latter of these two possibilities. He had worked at an important position acquiring new artists for a major record label. As such, he'd been the person who'd turned down the Beatles for a recording contract at an early stage in their career.

As a consequence of watching his ambitions as a self-styled "serious musician" melt away—sidelined by rock and roll—Sandy's loathing of popular music would have him red-faced and pummeling the kitchen table in fury. I couldn't help but notice the pleasure my ward derived from provoking poor Sandy by quoting various eminent musicologists' praise for the beauty and complexity of many songs written by John Lennon and Paul McCartney.

Both men obviously enjoyed a good argument. Although they couldn't have possessed personalities more different, they seemed to at least develop a respect for the intelligence and artfulness with which the other presented and defended his viewpoint. Sandy awarded my ward the nickname of Quark, for no reason anyone could quite pin down—but it seemed to fit, so it stuck.

Their spirited group discussions around the kitchen table allowed the little group to get to know and trust one another even though they came from very different backgrounds. (Note: I'm not overlooking the essential participation of the women of the group. This is because my purpose here is only to show that it was an unusual balance of subtle energies that had created a spiritually and emotionally receptive arena for their angelic contact. Besides, my ward's book has already noted that in more detail.)

So it was over the course of the angel transmissions that Sandy, like the others, emerged feeling they had experienced a spiritual series of encounters that were both authentic and profoundly meaningful.

In the same way that it's extremely helpful for me to be able to use my collaborator's vocabulary and his knowledge of *The Urantia Book* to narrate my story, so also would the angels have chosen Edward for his vocabulary—derived in part from the same book. As all those present for the sessions were familiar with the Urantia lexicon and cosmology, their contact and discussions were able to proceed at a satisfactorily high level.

I would have no reason to touch on these sessions—and repeat what my ward has already written—were it not for two particular revelations from the angels that were to point to the direction his new life was going to take.

The first was straightforward enough and occurred toward the end of the sessions. One of the angels told the little group that they didn't really need a light-trance medium to speak with them. They went on to say that anyone with good intentions, and with courage, patience, and sufficient persistence, would be able to make contact with their angels for themselves.

I knew Mein Host had every reason to take this seriously. When he returned to New York he spent the next months meditating and journaling, throwing himself wholeheartedly into making this promised close and intimate contact with his companion angels. He says it was, for him, an emotionally and mentally grueling time of clearing out many of the obstacles preventing an easy and confident exchange with angels. He could also appreciate now why such practices were generally the province of the elderly—whether they be monk, mystic, or magician. He was most of all grateful to have explicitly observed the angels during his time in the Afterlife. He says knowing that angels were existentially real made it simply a question of coming up with a way to reach them.

It ended up taking him two years to establish a close and reliable relationship, primarily with Joy—the most talkative of his two companion angels. Beauty, the second of the pair, would become known to him later as he focused more on his visual art.

Mein Host originally became aware of the reality of angels during his NDE, and then, seven years later, he made contact with Joy and Beauty. Thus it was that these events of his life would prepare him for his work with me.

The second revelation from the angels in Toronto was of far more significance to the collective. However, the truth of it is unlikely to be appreciated or even truly understood for many years to come. Once again I will only narrate the result and not the details about how it was reached.

As I hope I have adequately explored in these volumes, the Lucifer Rebellion—which occurred some 203,000 years ago—was permitted to continue unchecked on the thirty-seven rebel planets. While Lucifer was replaced by Lanaforge as System Sovereign on Jerusem, both Lucifer and Satan were allowed to wander freely throughout their limited domain. Similarly, the Planetary Princes on the planets aligned with the rebels were also permitted a free hand in administering their worlds. They had demanded their freedom of action, and that was precisely what they received.

I understand the instructions for this "hands-off" policy—as regards the thirty-seven rebel-held planets—came from the highest authority in the Local Universe. I wasn't present, of course, when these orders were issued or received. Yet I can only imagine the aggravation the instructions must have caused among the MA's more dogmatic bureaucrats. From what I have heard this excessive length of time—203,000 years is excessive even by celestial standards—didn't sit well with some of the MA's Jerusem administrators.

*The Urantia Book* makes it clear that the rebellion and its long aftermath had created some unpleasantly harsh attitudes among some of the Local System administrators. Many of them couldn't wait for the rebellion to be finally wrapped up and the main protagonists to be exterminated.

Yes, *exterminated*! Utterly eliminated. "Made as if they'd never existed" was the way they softened the cruelty of their intentions. This was a resentment, I believe, that was largely based on their own failures to take responsibility for a rebellion that occurred on their watch. Yet unpleasantly vitriolic they were nonetheless.

The Lucifer Rebellion—the revolt among the angels and the effect it has had on this world—has been one of the most instrumental events in shaping human life that has occurred over the past half-million years. You need only follow my narrative to appreciate that. Human beings, in general, have been conditioned to ignore or occlude the past. And besides, the knowledge that humans have long been used as pawns in a larger game is too disturbing and unpalatable for comfortable acceptance.

References to the angelic rebellion or its ramifications have appeared in different forms in some of the earliest recorded texts. By dismissing these references as mere myth, legend, or stories a simpler people will tell themselves, most human beings have remained in a dream of delusion. This is a delusion now shared and reinforced by many conventional scientific beliefs.

This blanket of ignorance that stretches from a rejection of the transcendent to a dismissal of the Afterlife and a knee-jerk skepticism toward all matters of spiritual substance have led to the current state of hubris on the part of the few who should know better. It's also led to indifference on the part of the sleeping majority. Both attitudes will be more than likely to preclude any breakthrough for those individuals— excepting a catastrophe that might shock them awake.

There are numerous anecdotal accounts of the near-death experiences of ordinary people, for example, which are now more commonly shared in the popular media. However, a general acceptance of the authenticity of the Afterlife will be unlikely to develop until a sufficient number of skeptical atheists with advanced degrees have NDEs for themselves.

Returning to this long delay that the MA had imposed for Lucifer's rebellion to play itself out—and the part played by the administration— requires some background.

Mein Host—in his careful reading of the Lucifer Rebellion as described in *The Urantia Book* by one of the Melchizedek Brothers— found he'd developed a deep sympathy and understanding for Lucifer and for many of the intentions expressed by the rebels. This shouldn't be altogether surprising considering that he is himself an incarnate rebel angel. Yet back in 1981, when he was wrestling with the implications of Lucifer's revolution, he was still consciously unaware of his own angelic heritage.

When he and Melinda arrived in Toronto to meet with their friends, he set out to introduce them to his thinking regarding Lucifer. This was radically different from the unforgiving opinions expressed by some of the angels in *The Urantia Book*. These were attitudes that Sandy—along with most readers of *The Urantia Book* at the time—had simply accepted without thinking any more deeply about it. My ward argued that when considered with an open mind and with forgiveness and mercy in the heart, the Lucifer Rebellion can be unpacked in a very different light.

Mein Host would later find out that he was by no means alone in this approach. He'd met a number of people who grappled with this same issue, which was so clearly annunciated in the Bible by Jesus Christ in the maxim "Love your enemies."

It is interesting to consider that my ward would have been most likely to take the radical viewpoint of expressing love and forgiveness for Lucifer and the rebels—so different from the vindictive approach espoused by *The Urantia Book* and most of its readers—had he not faced the same issue in the Process, where the concept of loving your enemies was a central credo.

It was during the last session with the angels that this thorny issue was addressed by the angels. They also spoke to more items of general interest, but it is only the Lucifer Rebellion that concerns me here.

The angels who spoke through Edward were either companion angels or celestials of a more specific function. Mentoria is an example, as Angel of Education, or an Angel of the Future, like Karyariel. Yet all had been of Seraphic and Local Universe origin. These angels had become more like friends over the course of their discussions, but then the atmosphere entirely changed in the room. Here is Mein Host setting the scene (*The Deta Factor,* page 201) for what turned out to be the final revelation:

> It was in this vastly opened state—when all of us thought the session was over, and the angels retired for the evening—that the last miraculous contact broke through.
>
> "I am Shandron." A new voice rolled out of Edward, deep and resonant, falling in waves around us.
>
> "I am a being of advanced status, greater than Seraphim. I am one who would be of Superuniverse status. I am Supernaphim."

The voice continued inexorably.

"My place here in this Great Work is as an usher of this new dispensation that is upon us . . . there has been a turning of a dispensation for your world. An adjudication, in a sense. A release from patterns long held."

There was much more from Shandron before he came to the essence of what he'd come to say. I won't try to quote the Supernaphim verbatim. I will merely summarize his statement. It was simply this:

The "Most Highs," to use Shandron's phrase, had taken note of a sufficient number of human beings who had found forgiveness in their hearts for Lucifer and the rebel angels, which had opened the way for a reconciliation of the rebellion. This is what Shandron meant by "a turning of a dispensation" and "an adjudication . . . a release from patterns long held."

This adjudication may have little meaning for most folk who wouldn't even know there was a conflict that needed adjudicating. However, for those who understood the nature of the conflict, this was of profound importance. It signaled the coming end of the long 203,000 years of interplanetary stalemate.

If all this was true, the little group agreed, it would be sure to change everything. The angels told them that this profound transition wouldn't happen immediately, that there was a corruption baked into the System by 203,000 years of Prince Caligastia's venal fraudulence. They warned of social and political disruption as the corruption was exposed to the light but emphasized that it was a very necessary cleansing process before the new dispensation could take root in healthy ground.

Wisely, no dates were given by the angels. However, the impression given was that it would occur within the lifetime of those in the group. In surveying the years since the angels had delivered their messages in 1981, this process of exposing corruption has been felt both publicly and privately. The collapse of Soviet Communism; the ending of apartheid; the successful Irish Peace Process; the exposure of child abuse in the Roman Catholic Church; corrupt politicians falling like ninepins; fraudulent banks; Bernie Madoff and his like; the Arab Spring and the fall of Middle East dictators—all of them have come to pass. And regular people, too, have been finding their lives upturned for an honest review. Whether they take advantage of it will likely determine their life to come as the transition unfolds.

Most people will be unaware of this dynamic, although I have heard my ward talking in terms of "the heat building up." He likened it to a "physical body extruding the poison of corruption through boils that rise from the depths and painfully erupt upon reaching the surface."

If you were to look back at this era some fifty or a hundred years in the future you would be able to more easily detect the powerful hidden current of transparency that is driving this exposure of corruption.

The reconciliation of the Lucifer Rebellion after 203,000 years of interplanetary political impasse was going to have a far-reaching effect on this Local System, as much as it is having its impact on the thirty-seven rebel-held worlds.

Perhaps of more immediate interest for my readers is in understanding this as an example of how human beings, with sufficient knowledge, can actively participate in the ways of the Multiverse and make their feelings known—and to have them taken into account. What was initiated, in this case, by what I've heard my ward call a "spiritual poll" of those mortals who were sufficiently well informed and openhearted enough to find the love and a genuine feeling of forgiveness for Lucifer, has led to the resolution of a situation that has teetered on for more than two hundred millennia.

The angels have called this healing process "swinging the planet back into normalcy." Yet it will be a normalcy (what an awkward word!) quite unlike any normalcy you might consider "normal." Unless, of course, you're reading these words having already made the planetary transformation. In that case you are probably amused at the inadequacy of the word *normalcy* to describe the world in which you now find yourself.

* * *

On Zandana it was the Long Day—a time when both of the Wise Twins were high in the sky at the same time. It was going to be a long, cloudless scorcher of a day, so I was happy to accompany Clarisel into the cool interior of the vestibule of Prince Janda-chi's residence.

There must have been some unacknowledged pressure to get me there as quickly as possible, because there was no sign we were going to catch any of the Maglev transports. At one of those universally understandable gestures from Clarisel, I understood we were to travel together by fifth dimension.

Traveling through the fifth dimension is as close to instantaneous as you'd ever wish. In fact, the momentary delay managed to somewhat mitigate the shock of arriving somewhere else entirely in a heartbeat. Fortunately this shock diminished over time, but I'll warrant there wasn't a Watcher who could ever completely erase the slight anticipatory wince. This was no doubt an echo of the shock to come—which is probably why I prefer to avoid traveling this way. I believe this is the first time in my narration so far that I've mentioned having been required to use the fifth. I like to see where I'm going.

I assumed Prince Janda-chi was courteously allowing me a few moments to reorient myself. There was the silent hiss of an outbreath in the aether beside me, and Clarisel was gone. I wasn't alone long. I was following the ramp upward and looking around the chamber that had so disorientated me on my first visit here—with the mountain god's palace somehow appearing in the opposite direction than I'd expected. I was laughing at how I'd been taken in, and admired what a clever piece of engineering it was, mechanical and psychological.

I wondered to myself whether the chamber's purpose was to disorientate or amuse the visitor. At that moment I looked up to see the Prince waiting for me with a broad smile on his handsome face. As I moved toward him, I slipped down from the fifth dimension to match his frequency domain in the new fourth-density reality.

I was grateful that the Prince put me at ease immediately. He commented after greeting me that he was known among his colleagues as an inveterate practical joker. The chamber was intended both to baffle and amuse those who came to see him. I was curious as to how his off-planet visitors would react to being baffled—they probably wouldn't be as amused as all that. He laughed aloud at this and explained that it was too early to subject off-worlders to his idiosyncratic sense of humor. Apparently he received such off-planet visitors in the government administration buildings in the city of Zandan.

The Prince gestured me over to the sunken conversation pit, an intimacy I appreciated at the time. I felt that it was a genuine expression of friendship. It was only later the thought came to me that the Prince may have had other, less obvious motives for his fulsome greeting and his subsequent friendliness. But as I said, this was later when I was outside the Prince's aura and less overwhelmed by his charisma.

"You will have appreciated the transformation we have undergone since you were last here," the Prince said as we made ourselves comfortable in the pit. We were sitting opposite one another and separated by the glass table. He made another graceful gesture, this time over the glass. At this, a small section in the center of the table—imperceptible to the unsuspecting eye—dropped down to reappear a moment later with two tall glasses and a carafe of a violet-colored fruit juice from somewhere beneath it.

He poured the juice. I raised my glass to him and congratulated him and his colleagues for a smooth transition to the fourth density. I knew what an important phase it was for a world. In actual fact it was perhaps the most important single factor in a planet's development, I thought diplomatically, since the arrival of the Prince's staff.

He laughed at that, a curious laugh that unsettled me. Yet he drank with me nonetheless.

"You can relax with me, my dear sister," he said, his tone kinder than his laugh suggested. "I mean you no ridicule, but you have no need to flatter me. We are good friends by now, yes?"

"Yes, of course," I thought, hoping he wouldn't pick up on my nervousness.

"It was in this very residence, was it not," he said to my surprise, "that Lord Lucifer spoke to us of his plans? Does that not allow us a special bonding?"

Once again I couldn't tell if the Prince was playing with me. He must have known then, as I do now, that Lucifer had amnesed any memory of what was discussed in that meeting.

I was first shocked when Janda-chi unexpectedly raised the name of Lucifer and then completely baffled at his reference to my having heard the Sovereign's plans. Now, in retrospect, it's all far clearer to me, but as I sat opposite Prince Janda-chi, I realized I must have been staring at him in startled disbelief. Of course, now I realize the Prince was using the shock technique of reading me when I was in a state of momentary psychic disequilibrium.

I believe I must have known at the time that Prince Janda-chi— whom I'd become genuinely fond of—was, under his mask of amiability, still using me as what my collaborator suggests might be called a "Manchurian Candidate." If I had any glimpse of this I must have tucked it away because when we settled down to talk the Prince appeared more interested in telling me about the advances on Zandana than in picking my brain about Earth.

How naive I was!

Of course he would have been scanning me beneath my level of conscious awareness for what he really needed to know all the time we were innocently chatting away—the actual reason he was so anxious to see me. His mention of Lucifer even had me believing the Sovereign might be there, which, I admit, only added to the emotional tension I was trying to keep at bay.

"Clarisel will have informed you as to the fundamental changes that occur when a planet shifts up into the fourth density, but I sense you have more questions."

Well yes I did. There was the spacecraft that Clarisel had offhandedly referred to as an Andromedan ark . . . What was that doing? I understood there was a quarantine that disallowed off-planet races from visiting this Local System . . .

"In the third density, yes," the Prince reminded me, "the quarantine holds true. We never saw any off-worlders until we shifted into the fourth density. Although I believe this hasn't held quite so true on Earth . . . that there have been some covert interventions . . ."

I had queried that, too. We all knew about the quarantine and the isolation that this imposed on the planets. Yet there were the Pleiadean space-arks that picked up the Lemurians. There was also the Sirian involvement with Atlantis and the infrequent Orion Walk-Ins who were drawn to the Nile Valley. Then there were the Oannes in Sumeria and the influence of the Nommo throughout East Africa. And all this was happening on a third-density world!

The only clue I had picked up was when I overheard some Sirian envoys speaking together about just this issue. They appeared to justify it by claiming that since Earth was a decimal world and was deemed by the MA to be an "experimental planet," it was perfectly legitimate for them to involve themselves in the experiment—as long as their touch was light. What this "light touch" exactly meant, and how proscribed were the limits of their influence, had then become the subject of their heated discussion. I had stayed to listen, I recall now, because I was surprised to find so much disagreement among the Sirians.

They clearly knew the legal consequences of overstepping their mark if their involvement became too overt, but—as one of the envoys argued—there'd been a creeping effect over the centuries as more and more power gathered in Sirian hands. In their capable hands! And wasn't that just the problem! This set three of envoys claimed vociferously that it was no fault of their own if human beings couldn't keep up with them. It was no fault of their own if humans insisted in handing over their power to them simply because they were more capable . . .

"But that's exactly how the creeping effect occurs!" I recall the lone dissenter pointing out. "We need to be more vigilant lest they become overdependent on us. Of course we're more capable—that isn't the point. If they're depending on us rather than learning from us, then we will surely be held responsible in the Uversa Courts."

I remember feeling apprehensive when I observed the other three shrugging off this problem. I thought it was at least worth considering. Illicit interventions on primitive worlds by more advanced races were among the most serious of the MA's interdictions. All space-faring races would have known this. Yet one of them was explaining patiently—he'd evidently argued this before—that as they were restricted to Atlantis, the limits of their influence were obviously delineated by the boundary of the island.

Another envoy then jumped in to assert that—because they were working alongside Prince Caligastia's midwayers on Atlantis—the courts would be sure to hold the Planetary Prince responsible for all his many crimes and excesses. Besides, all the envoys agreed—including the original dissenting voice—that were they to step back from their guiding role on the island, life on Atlantis would quickly descend into internecine bloodshed.

When I overheard that last statement about the certainty of conflict, it occurred to me I'd heard much the same from the mouths of many a tyrant to justify his maintaining or expanding his power. I wasn't at all sure the Sirians deserved to be so confident that the courts would see it their way. Their intervention would somehow disappear in the flurry of prosecutions they anticipated being heaped on Caligastia's head.

# 9

# The Interconnectedness of Us All

An Invasive Scan, Gradual Disillusionment,
a Young Sorceress, *The Helianx Proposition*,
Starseed Relationships, and the
Commodore Speaks

Suddenly with a start, I found myself back in the pit.

Prince Janda-chi was sitting opposite me with a kind look on his face. I must have zoned out. How embarrassing. It took me a moment to reorientate myself. I did this by experiencing the weight of my body pressing into the yielding surface beneath me and feeling the luxurious steely softness of the fabric tickling my toes. (Note: Do I need to explain that we Watchers also possess toes, and fingers, too?)

Of course, once I'd brought myself fully back into myself, it all became clear to me. It was the Sirians that the Prince had really wanted to know about. This must be the approach he'd decided to use to read me this time. He had never employed this particular technique before, and I suppose I must have been surprised at how invasive it felt. It was an unfamiliar feeling, as it's a seraph's preference to live openly and transparently.

I was irritated by this—although I had no reason to be. I'd already discovered I had tacitly agreed to have my deep mind telepathically scanned by the Prince. This, strictly speaking, had made me an espionage agent for a foreign prince. Yet that was somehow different from this blatant piece of mental manipulation. I know it's silly to get irked, but I felt in choosing to use this more conscious method of scanning my mind, the Prince was placing his stamp on me. It was his way of asserting that I was serving him and only him—and I was to not forget it.

"I assure you, my sister," the Prince's voice was strong and his smile had widened, "I have no such intention to make you mine. It would be impossible anyway, as I am not a prince of your home world. The only reason I chose to read you in that way was because your thoughts about the role of the Sirians on Atlantis was close to the top of your mind. It was also an exchange you had overheard that must have deeply concerned you. There is no reason, as you yourself just thought, for you to be irritated by my actions—or to feel invaded by my scans. You know my intentions are perfectly honorable.

"Look around you," he continued, "look at my beautiful world. Are you so disillusioned by your Prince Caligastia that you won't acknowledge it was Prince Zanda and I who were the shepherds guiding this world through its transformation into the fourth density? And I might add, Zandana is still technically a rebel-held world in the MA's judgment."

That's what surprised me when I arrived here this time. I found it hard to initially believe that one of Lucifer's worlds had managed to move from third to fourth density. I thought perhaps my own senses had become deranged until Clarisel had put my mind to rest.

"So you understand you can trust me," he said, his tone soft and perhaps a little more cajoling—which made me comfortable. "We serve the same master, do we not? Let me show you what should convince you."

There was a brief pause while Janda-chi's face changed as though a cloud had crossed the moon, and then he was smiling once more. Within seconds the aether shivered beside us and here was Clarisel again, called in by the Prince's telepathic signal.

"Clarisel, my dear one, welcome to you," he said in a cheery tone and without a hint of our slightly uneasy encounter. "I wish you to accompany our Watcher from Earth to the new spaceport. I want you to introduce her to the Commodore of the crew of the vessel from Andromeda. Let us see whether her apprehension of our situation here on Zandana will enlighten Georgia."

Janda-chi arose and stepped out of the pit to embrace Clarisel. The Watcher's sudden appearance—together with the Prince's instruction for her to take me to the ark—in and of itself was unusual. This is because, as a rule, Watchers and mortals from other fourth-density worlds seldom encounter one another. We move in different dimensions and have different spheres of interest. This made my prospective encounter with the craft's Commodore an exceptional privilege.

I hadn't risen with the Prince, my mind was whirling so. I must have looked like a fool still sitting there in the pit, my mouth probably hanging open in astonishment and a stupid look on my face. Breaking from their embrace, the Prince drew himself up to his full height so he seemed to be towering over me. For one very brief moment I actually felt a little threatened by him. The feeling dissolved when he reached down a thoughtful hand to help me out of the pit.

Once again the Prince smiled cheerfully at me, and nodding to Clarisel he bid me well, thanked me for my valuable cooperation, and told me he would be sure to see me again on my next visit.

Prince Janda-chi had certainly seemed friendly enough and embraced me fondly before taking his leave. Yet I found I was still left with the uneasy sense I was being used in ways of which I wasn't yet aware—and to influence events I didn't yet understand.

I didn't have to time to dwell on this dilemma before Clarisel was suggesting we take the Maglev this time. We were in no hurry, and she was sure it would be a great joy for me to see how life on a fourth-density world was starting to flourish.

We left the Prince's residence and went out into the bright sunlight of the Wise Twins in their ascendancy. I could only think how hot it must have felt in the denser frequency domains of the fourth density.

Clarisel smiled complicity at my thought and gestured for us both to adjust down so we could experience what it was like.

We were still in the courtyard of the Prince's house when the wave of heat hit us both, sending us running—and laughing—to the courtyard's sculpted fountain, where we hoped the spray would cool us down.

Yes, I admit it. We sat on the edge of the pool, and like children we dangled our feet in the water until we could no longer tolerate the oppressive heat—at least that's what we told each other. We giggled at that. We both knew the real reason for switching back up to a higher frequency was that we risked being observed by a passing mortal—a gardener in this case—who should have had no business knowing about Watchers.

Besides, I wasn't at all sure that the Prince would have much appreciated a couple of Watchers dabbling their feet in his ornamental fountain. I'm not sure I would much like it in the unlikely event I'd ever have an ornamental fountain to call my own.

Clarisel gave a snort of laughter at my thought—and yes, angels can snort, too! I realized then, with a part of my mind I keep to myself, that Clarisel wasn't aware of the opportunity being extended to rebel angels to prepare for a future mortal incarnation on a third-density world. Then their subsequent lifetimes, so I understood, would all be on third-density rebel-held worlds. I already sensed these wouldn't be easy lifetimes; they weren't intended to be. That was clear to me—even back then.

What I hadn't been aware of—and what came to me as Clarisel and I made our way from the Prince's residence down to the monorail station—I can only report on because I felt it to be real at the time. The idea formed and grew a shape in my mind in a manner entirely novel to me. Ideas don't generally come to Watchers. If they do, they tend to be ideas we have previously entertained. Put it this way: we aren't particularly adept at thinking outside the box.

Yet here I was, with Clarisel beside me happily babbling on about the beauty of the mountains and how rarely she'd had the chance to come up this far into the foothills and had I seen the palace of the mountain god? She'd heard about it, but she'd never seen it as she inevitably traveled to the residence in the fifth. This was only on the rare occasions when she'd visited the residence, of course. And wasn't it perfectly beautiful? She had never believed it so vast and so spectacular. And yes of course she knew it was all really natural rock formations, she wasn't a fool! And had I sensed how unexpectedly hot the water was in the fountain? No, of course I didn't, this must all be new to me . . . but perhaps the fountain's cooling system was down . . .

How she prattled on! And telepathic prattling can be excruciatingly annoying. It's considered extremely poor social etiquette to cut off contact too abruptly. It would be an even more serious diplomatic faux pas to treat a Watcher—or any celestial—with what would surely be interpreted as an insufferable rudeness.

I liked Clarisel; she had been patient with me. I had no desire to hurt her feelings, so I allowed her to burble on in my mind. And all the while she was burbling, this idea was growing and filling itself out in the secret part of my mind. I tried, I suppose, to fend it off, but it wouldn't let go of me.

If I am making too much of a fuss about this idea—which in itself wasn't that extraordinary an idea—it's because it was truly such an extraordinarily rare sensation just to be *having* an idea.

And the idea itself?

If Clarisel was unaware that we who'd aligned ourselves with Lucifer and the revolutionaries were being offered the chance for personal redemption by way of mortal incarnation, then could it be that these incarnations were occurring only on Earth? It made sense. If the conditions on Earth were being considered, so I'd heard, as third to worst of the thirty-seven rebel-held planets, then wouldn't it be on Earth that the rebel angels would receive the maximum bang for their buck? (*Note: I tried to stop Georgia from using this cliché, but she enjoyed the alliterative rhythm too much, and when that happens, try as I might—and trying too hard never works anyway—nothing else will come from her. I am now going to stop apologizing for her. If you are still reading, by now you'll know Georgia's little ways. —TW*)

There was also an implication in something Clarisel had dropped during our earlier conversation that suggested Zandana's transition to fourth-density reality had followed a smooth, ascending path. This had been ever since the two Planetary Princes welcomed the Material Son and Daughter and continued to collaborate with them until the arrival of the Magisterial mission. There had never been even the slightest hint of any involvement of rebel angel incarnates in what the Prince or Clarisel told me about their planetary transition.

We waited on the platform beneath Prince Janda-chi's residence for the monorail cabin. The forested hills rolled down to the coastal plain, and beyond were the gleaming whiteness of the splendid governmental buildings in Zandan city. Further still was the glittering silver sea—as far as the horizon.

My friendly Watcher was still maundering away in my mind without appearing to care whether I was paying full attention to her. Whenever I did tune in, she was rattling away about the transcendent beauty of her world—which I could see for myself. I really didn't appreciate her constant reminder of the tragic state of *my* home world.

I knew I needed to be careful. I didn't want my emotional discomfort to leak out and affect my sister Watcher's guileless enthusiasm. There was such an innocence in her; a sweetness, too. Yes, she could be a bit ponderous in her explanations, but I think it was then—when I thought about Clarisel's open and wholesome nature—that I thought if all the Watchers on Zandana were of a similar character, I could be reasonably sure rebel angels weren't being incarnated there.

Which, of course, meant Clarisel would continue for an indefinite time in her function as a planetary Watcher—and from what I reckoned she may never have had the chance to join the mortal ascendance line.

It was at that point the mono-cabin I'd been watching sliding up the rail toward us hissed to a halt and the doors slid open. Clarisel had mercifully stopped filling my mind with her telepathic gush and gestured me ahead of her into the cabin.

We were alone when the doors closed, and the cabin smoothly—and almost imperceptibly—accelerated down its silver rail and on to a new adventure. I couldn't wait to meet the Commodore of the Andromedan spacecraft.

* * *

If there's some confusion at this point about Mein Host's complex relationships with women after he left the Process, then it undoubtedly reflects something of his own confusion.

He had managed to finally shrug off the clinging Marion, and the couple of years after he left the community—when he had half a dozen lovers in his life—were now behind him. It had been an emotionally and intellectually enriching couple of years in which he was running his business during the day and catching up during the evenings and weekends on much he had missed during his years in the abstemious and spartan Process.

He had grown close to Alma, spending more and more time with her in their mutual entheogenic exploration of alternate realities. A few years older than my ward, Alma had three teenage children from a previous marriage. She had been divorced from their father for about four years before she met Mein Host. There was an immediate attraction, both physically and intellectually—they seemed to bring out the best in one another. Given the whirl of women around him in the years immediately after he'd left the community, they decided between them to not become sexually entangled for a while, so they could focus on what really interested them both.

Mein Host hadn't had an entheogenic partner who could hold their own since Jean—back in the early sixties—and their early explorations of LSD, DMT, and ibogaine. However, compared to these entheogens, each with its profound effect and each having been used for centuries by indigenous people, the new class of dissociatives—ketamine and phencyclidine—were proving more effective tools for exploring altered states of consciousness.

He and Alma agreed that ibogaine, or DMT, or other powerful natural entheogens were particularly valuable tools for blasting away at rigid psychological patterns and social conditioning. They can reveal the very heights of cosmic consciousness as well as the very depths of a personal hell. Yet they're difficult to actually work with, because, as my ward has said, "They're so psychically overwhelming that unless you have a lifetime of shamanic training, the best you can do is throw yourself at the entheogen's mercy and let her spirit take over. It's important to learn to trust and to let go of personal control, of course—it's the prospect of this loss of personal control that makes entheogens so threatening to the control freaks of the world—but having become familiar with letting go of the ego, what then?

"I had my first experience of God on five hundred mikes of Sandoz acid and spent the next twenty years assimilating it. I had my first experience of angels and the Afterlife during my NDE. Thus, by 1981, I'd been spending the subsequent eight years assimilating the angelic reality into my life. I wanted to work collaboratively with the angels at this stage, and first phencyclidine, then ketamine, proved to be perfect tools for this."

This period, short though it was, would prove formative for both Alma and my ward. Yet it was almost too much. The transcendent experiences they shared were so powerful that by the early spring of 1980, Alma—wisely, as it turned out—drew the curtain firmly on the relationship.

Mein Host wouldn't see Alma again for another four years. Hopefully, I recall thinking at the time of their breakup, they would then be more fully prepared for the collaborative work that lay ahead for them.

Melinda had entered my ward's life briefly in the early days of The Unit. We have mentioned her before in passing but will elaborate more here. She and my ward had met at a Unit meeting, where they talked of little else but *The Urantia Book* at that meeting and the next. How could he not have been fascinated to hear her talking so knowledgeably about just those entities—Jehovah, Lucifer, Christ, and Satan—who formed the pantheon of the Process cosmology?

My ward had never taken the gods of the Process very seriously.

Indeed, he'd always maintained that he wasn't in the community to worship these gods, but for the experience the community offered and his erstwhile attachment to Mary Ann. Having worked hard in The Unit to get to the bottom of the true nature of his feelings about Mary Ann, he had been able to understand how he'd projected his love for the Goddess onto her. And deeper still—before he'd met Mary Ann and Robert, and before the Process started back in the 1960s—he was completely unaware he had any feelings whatsoever for the Goddess.

I'd observed, for example, how much he'd enjoyed Robert Graves's *The White Goddess* when he'd read it. Yet for all his intellectual and poetic appreciation it had made almost no impression on his emotional or spiritual bodies. It had taken his explosive emotional collision with Mary Ann, whoever she was, to awaken his nascent feelings for the Goddess, and for that he could only be deeply grateful.

He'd largely come to peace with whether she was or wasn't an incarnate goddess. Whether she actually believed she was the Goddess—or if she was simply an accomplished con woman—meant little. This is because those issues were of less importance to him than the changes Mary Ann had wrought in him.

Taking all this into account—and matching it with his understandable aversion to merely exchanging one belief system for another—he hadn't followed up with Melinda. Nor had he given any further attention to *The Urantia Book*. Yet he would have said there was something quite fascinating about the mysterious Melinda.

As Alma was the most mature and humorous woman he'd yet met, so Melinda was the most intelligent and occultly well informed. It would come out later—when she and my ward knew each other better—that as a young woman Melinda had studied in France with Raymond Bret-Koch, the fine artist and occult master.

Although Melinda and Mein Host liked each other when they first met, there was so much up in the air about my ward's life that Melinda had wisely slipped away, not to see Mein Host again until the summer of 1980.

If only this period of his life was as straightforward and simple as

I've made it sound here. But, of course, it wasn't. An unexpected meeting in Central Park was proof of that!

Damian was one of the most unusual young women to have ever come into my ward's life up to this point. She would do more than anyone—except perhaps Alma—to bring him into a fuller contact with his emotional body.

He'd first encountered Damian when, as a precocious fifteen-year-old girl, she worked in the art department of the Process. She helped as a volunteer to put out the community's magazines and newsletters. Damian was grown-up far beyond her years, and by the age of fifteen she was showing signs of becoming a skilled illustrator. At thirteen she had already tasted heroin and sensibly put it behind her. By the time she was fourteen, she'd taken herself—on her own—to Paris, where she'd enjoyed a brief success as a model before seeing through its vacuity and returning to America to develop a career in the graphic arts.

She was an exquisite young creature, tall and thin, thoroughly androgynous in the modern way, and blessed with an uncanny level of self-confidence. Her features were small and delicate, her mouth beautifully formed, her neck long and slim, and her skin glowed with the color of honey in the sun.

She was the daughter of a black man who was an architect and his blond Swedish wife, and it was evident that growing up as a mixed-race child in Brooklyn had left its scars. She and my ward were intermittent lovers over the years, and more than once he had woken in the middle of the night to find Damian emerging from a nightmare, screaming uncontrollably. She seemed to be unstoppable. Once he'd tried a quick sharp smack to bring her back to her senses—but that had only made it worse. He could do nothing—she wouldn't let him hold her, and kind, comforting noises made no difference—so he simply had to let the drama play out.

When he was living on West 85th Street, her screams would continue for four or five minutes while she shivered in abject fear in the corner of the room. His bedroom was at the back of the apartment with the garden immediately outside. Thus the screams issuing out of an open window on a sweltering Manhattan night were bouncing and echoing off the back of the buildings of the next block.

Only in Manhattan could such heartrending screams last for so long and yet attract so little attention. Well, no attention at all, in fact. Mein Host joked with a friend that he thought it was a miracle no one ever called the police. He'd have had the impossible task of trying to persuade a hard-boiled New York cop that he wasn't beating up the poor girl.

However, what must have been obvious to him was that someone else had taken it out on her when she was a small child. And from her refusal to talk about her father with any love, there were no prizes for guessing who it was. But it never went further than that. Childhood abuse wasn't a subject for discussion, and my ward at least had the good sense to know he didn't possess the psychotherapeutic chops to take her on.

Damian had just turned eighteen the day they had met unexpectedly in Central Park. They'd always appreciated one another when my ward had taken her under his wing in the art department, but from observing Damian's response to seeing him in the park, it was quite clear there was a strong sexual connection.

Damian at that time was living in Brooklyn with William, a lad her own age and a brilliant visual artist in his own right. They were a modern couple. Both were art students in an open relationship—so William was apparently unconcerned about an affair starting between Damian and my ward. In the way I've heard my ward comment on an event that sometimes happens, he and William would maintain their close friendship over the next thirty years, long after Damian had faded from the picture in both of their lives.

Soon after he met her in the park, it was clear to me that Mein Host was falling helplessly in love with the girl—and I have chosen the word *helplessly* with some attention. Sure, he'd loved young Sarah in his time—and Agneta, and Victoria, and Penny, and Jennifer, and Jean. He'd loved them all, or at least he felt he had. He had loved them as much as he was capable of loving.

Yet with Damian, it was different.

Mein Host had always been the one in control, the one perhaps, who was loved more than *he* loved. Damian gave him the opportunity to go through the intensely human experience of falling desperately and helplessly in love with someone who was not as helplessly in love with him. Damian took him to the heights of sexual ecstasy as no one had ever done before; and yet he would also say that no woman had ever ripped his heart open like his Dame.

It was no surprise that their relationship was most likely ill-fated from the start.

They both knew the fire was too hot for it to ever last very long. Neither saw the other one as "a keeper," yet over the year that the affair thrived, my ward found it was one of the most creative and productive periods of his life. It was a time when poetry flowed like quicksilver and his artwork—which up to that time was entirely created in graphite—was transformed, on Damian's advice, to a riot of color.

Damian became a superb muse, though sadly my ward never fully realized it in the moment. It was during this time that she must have given him more than fifty poems, but in one six-hour, unbroken stretch of automatic writing, he received *The Helianx Proposition*—a text that would prove of considerable interest to me—and it drew all of his attention.

Having received the Helianx text in such an usually fluid manner—one word following another as though his hand was moving on its own—my ward decided to illustrate the text and then integrate the writing in a calligraphic font of his own design. He knew it was going to be a massive labor of love and, as such, was going to have to take as long as it took. He soon became completely immersed in the task. He would go on to spend every available moment working on a book that would take him the next thirty years to bring to publication.

It was an irony not lost on him that when his affair with Damian was winding down, it was his obsession with the Helianx project that Damian believed responsible for their breakup. They both must have sensed this was a superficial justification for the split;

a cover for the deeper differences in their culture, age, and race.

Mein Host has since said that he doesn't know if it's any different these days, but back in the late 1970s, walking arm-in-arm with a beautiful dark-skinned girl down a busy street in Manhattan would attract mean looks and snarky remarks from both blacks and whites. Neither of them escaped the racist comments. Some were intended in good faith—as in "your children won't thank you"—and others were made obvious by inference.

She once took my ward to a large party in which he turned out to be the only white person present. He said later he'd felt an impostor. He was also sure everyone else there must have felt he was an undercover cop. This appeared to have made the beautiful young Damian fair game. The girl must have been approached by four or five young black studs intent on proving themselves superior by separating the lovers.

Damian—it should come as no surprise—was an advanced starseed; an incarnated rebel angel with many incarnations behind her. She was as much a natural mystic as she was a sexual provocatrice. She was reckless and independent, with the self-confidence to announce to her lovers that she would be disappearing for a few days—"catting around town," as she put it. She would countenance no curiosity, whether driven by jealously or a genuine interest, about what she was up to when she was doing her "catting around."

Mein Host has said that it was his affair with Damian that most clearly demonstrated the dilemma a lot of starseeds experienced in their choices and in the nature of their sexual relationships. His relationship with Damian was probably the most passionately intense of his life. Given this, he claimed that he learned how tempting it was to become overwhelmed with sexual passion with another starseed and to lose track of what was really important to him. I believe I have mentioned previously that although many starseeds are naturally drawn to one another by deep and often unrecognized affinities, their spiritual functions—as well as their seldom acknowledged drive for personal redemption—will frequently take them in different directions in their lives.

Starseeds also often find their intimate relationships taking a psychotherapeutic turn. I've already mentioned that one of the common factors in the background of many starseeds is their troubled childhoods. The emotional and psychic trauma create an internal pressure that demands attention. Additionally, in starting to untangle the web of lies and self-deception that characterized their childhood, a starseed will ultimately discover who he or she truly is, and why they have incarnated at this point in history.

Rather than staying with one person, starseeds will often be drawn to a series of partners—either sexual or platonic—subconsciously using the particular characteristics of each relationship for both their emotional and psychological healing. This is the draw that attracts them to other starseeds. It is the starseeds who will possess the natural sensitivity, the required intelligence, and the sufficient detachment to enable serious healing work to take place on their emotional and spiritual bodies.

Most starseeds, both male and female, will also have relationships with regular mortals. Yet these relationships will tend to be far more challenging and emotionally turbulent than those with other starseeds. These disturbances most frequently originate in the emotional immaturity and deep insecurity of the regular mortal, and in the jealousy and possessiveness that such intimacy with a starseed can provoke in a regular human being.

For starseeds, these kinds of relationships have more to do with developing and testing their patience and forbearance under the most trying of circumstances (that of an intimate human relationship). I've heard my ward joke ruefully that anyone who has read Doris Lessing's book *The Marriages Between Zones Three, Four and Five* will have a good grasp of this dynamic in action.

In stating this as baldly as I have, Mein Host suggests I'm giving the impression that starseeds are in some way superior to regular mortals. Yet he knows very well this is not the case. Yes, starseeds are of a different heritage than normal mortals. Starseeds might have certain gifts and abilities not readily accessible to normal people. However, as I hope I've shown in this narrative of my ward's life, starseeds have as many—or more—issues and weaknesses than your average mortal.

It is one of the more ironic sights to observe when a mortal woman, for example, starts being jealous or envious of her starseed lover. Or perhaps she convinces herself of his innate superiority, as she sees it, and puts him up on a pedestal of her adoration. This is seldom done—as anyone who has been put up on a pedestal knows—from the purest of motives. It is more often, as some wag put it, "So they can get a better shot at you."

When starseeds choose to have intimate relationships with other starseeds, it will most often be because both know on some level that it's about emotional and spiritual healing and not about what the Process used to call "a cozy tuck-up."

Damian was the last person anyone would associate with a cozy tuck-up. Although my ward's relationship with her would last barely a year, it would start a process that—over time—would make it easier for me to approach him and establish the relationship we have today.

However, reaching this point was never going to be easy or straightforward.

*  *  *

I have since had reason to wonder if prolonging my most recent visit to Zandana—to take the time to meet the captain of the Andromedan ship—may have been a way of delaying my return to Earth. Whether this was a deliberate ploy of Prince Janda-chi's for his own devious purposes—was I now beginning to see him as devious?—or whether it was my own timidity reflecting back to me, I wasn't able to tell. A touch of both, I'd imagine.

However, none of this concerned me as Clarisel and I sat together in the comfort of what turned out to be Prince Janda-chi's personal cabin, watching the landscape speed by below us. The rail here was lofted well above the forested hills that were rolling out beneath us, allowing me a clear view of the coastal plain and the city of Zandan stretching out below. The cobweb of silver rails that formed their transport system flashed in the rays of the suns. Tiny cabins inching along them seemed like shadows relentlessly gobbling up the gleaming rail ahead of them then excreting the light out behind.

I could feel Clarisel smiling beside me, amused by an image that had evidently never occurred to her.

"I've never been drawn to Earth," she said. Her tone, I felt, carried a touch of envy. "Nor any other world. I have never wished to so sully myself."

That shut me up. Yet there was still that touch of envy.

The Prince's house, you'll recall, was perched high in the foothills—in a region shared with the residences of other elites of Zandana. Now, in the broad daylight, I could better see the clever arrangement of the various monorails and how they fanned out to serve the individual residences up here in the mountains.

Then I felt the cabin beginning to pick up speed until we were floating steadily faster and faster down the single rail. We undulated gently up and down, the rail echoing the rise and fall of the rounded foothills below us.

Now this was fun! Yes, I'd enjoyed those long slow rides I'd taken previously—they'd given me time to think—but this was fun! It was a new experience for me. It conveyed the sense of being safe and enclosed, as it must feel to be in a womb. And yet I was also able to observe the beauty of a world speeding by through the unbroken strip of windows surrounding the cabin.

"We're on a dedicated rail here," Clarisel was telling me. "That accounts for our speed. You can see better when we reach the plain; we'll be running parallel to the main grid. No stations on this line, nothing to slow us down . . . you'll see the city over to the east of us when we have to skirt the bay . . ."

Her directions were interrupted when the cabin suddenly—and disconcertingly—lurched back and forth. Then, without seeming to lose speed, it started to lean over at an increasingly alarming angle, which made me grip the laughing Watcher's arm in alarm.

When the cabin had straightened up again, I was able to observe that we were riding a rail that was curving around the bay before cutting through a valley in the mountains, beyond which I believed they'd constructed their new spaceport.

We both sat silently for a while. The bay was stretching out to my left, and the water was glassy calm and of a cerulean blue that faded imperceptibly into the sky. In the distance a single flitter-boat was limping slowly back to safe harbor. The expanding ripples of its wake spread across the still surface—as if the ocean itself was retreating from the stricken vessel. I turned to watch the distant craft that seemed to be gathering water, and traveling slower and slower . . .

But by then, the cabin was entering the valley, and the craggy mountainside cut off any view of the bay, thus obscuring the fate of the flitter-boat.

"Have no concern, sister, they will come to no harm."

"But didn't you see, Clarisel, it looks like the boat was sinking?!"

Clarisel laughed out loud at that. "You forget the shift in densities . . . that boat isn't really sinking."

"It looked as if it was getting lower in the water . . ."

"Don't you have a race of intelligent sea creatures on Earth?" she asked unexpectedly. Then I recalled how I'd once watched whales and dolphins collaborating to form a floating platform for an exhausted fandor and rider back in the days of Vanu and Amadon. How curious that I hadn't thought of that incident for so long. But then again, I'd seen very little of either whales or dolphins back on Earth over the past few thousand years.

"Perhaps the cetaceans wanted nothing to do with your Prince Caligastia—if he's as unpleasant as you say," she remarked with a smirk in her tone that irritated me. It surprised me, too.

I thought I had nothing to feel defensive about—yet here I was thinking the Prince really wasn't *that* bad. How dare a Watcher, who had never even been to Earth, say something so unsavory about Caligastia?!

It was something that *I* could think or say, but not a Watcher from another world! That was plain rude. Have I ever spoken or even thought badly of either Prince Zanda or Prince Janda-chi? No, of course not. But then again, however covertly manipulative I believed Prince

Janda-chi might be—and I still wasn't completely certain he wasn't using me as a spy—I could be sure that he and Prince Zanda had never been as consistently malicious as Caligastia.

Yet her comment still left an uneasy feeling between us. I realized I'd probably been too open and frank with her about my feelings and this could serve as a gentle reminder. Luckily I found the good sense not to blurt out that I didn't think the Prince was really that awful. That would merely have added hypocrisy to indiscretion. So I turned the conversation back to the sinking boat.

"What you were watching," she told me, "was most likely just a rescue drill. It could have been a real rescue, but I think not . . . not since the shift."

"I've seen dolphins—the sea mammals on Earth—rescuing sailors from time to time . . . like that, you mean?" I retorted.

"It used to be like that here," she said. "They'd help if they were close by, if they could. After the dimensional shift, the sea mammals were constitutionally recognized by all governing bodies on Zandana as an intelligent species in their own right. Apparently that changed everything. Now, for example, every flitter-boat is always accompanied by at least two of the sea creatures. They help with the fishing . . . I've heard they can increase the yield threefold. And they're always present if the fishermen run into trouble. I have heard they haven't lost a single boat since the new dispensation."

This was entirely new to me. In all my visits to Zandana, I had heard nothing of these intelligent sea mammals, nor have I ever had a chance to observe them.

"It was a surprise for everybody on Zandana," Clarisel stated with a tone that was still amused. "There were legends of a race that lived in the sea, but no one took them seriously. You know how they have always been fearful of the ocean here. No one had ever actually seen one of these sea creatures. They had kept to themselves, that's all. Then the shift happened, and to everybody's amazement . . . up they popped! They'd been there in the oceans of Zandana all along."

"How could that have happened?" I asked. It seemed very strange to me. "How could they have shared the planet for so long without knowing about this other race living in the sea?"

"The Princes knew about them, of course. They called them the 'Sea People.'"

I did witness, though—shortly before the shift—Prince Zanda calling in a group of psychically gifted individuals from all the island continents. He chose twenty-four of the most sensitive to polish up on their visual telepathy. It was only after the shift that they understood the reason they'd been conscripted. Those twenty-four became the interpreters for a while—that is, until others started realizing how simple and natural visual telepathy was. Now even the fisherfolk can do it!"

I asked, "And that's because of the shift? Is that what made it possible?" This was all new to me. I wondered what the parallel would be on Earth.

"The Sea People . . ." Clarisel started—her tone now more patient. "When it all came to light at the time of the shift, it turned out that the Sea People, as a race, had reached their mental and emotional maturity many millions of years earlier. And like many other aquatic species, they'd chosen to follow the path of exploring the inner worlds."

The light in the cabin dimmed as we sped through a narrow gorge. The cliffs on either side of the cabin were now so high I couldn't see the sky.

"In fact," Clarisel was determined to make her point, "it was the familiarity of the Sea People with the fifth dimension—a natural consequence of their life out of the body—that made them such useful intermediaries when Unava was negotiating the cultural exchange with Andromeda.

"If the Sea People can do that, Georgia, there's really no need to have any concern for a single flitter-boat."

After that we subsided into a somewhat awkward silence until we finally arrived at the spaceport.

We saw it first from the cabin window. The glare of the sun off its silver surface was almost too bright for my eyes when the cabin finally carried us from the gloom of the valley.

The Andromedan vessel was big, of course, but not as big as the arks used by the Pleiadeans when they were transporting the Lemurian survivors. Thus I wasn't nearly as overawed by the craft as Clarisel evidently hoped I'd be.

It amused me at first that she might want me to be impressed by the size of the craft—as if it reflected well on her in some way. Yet there was such a sweet provincial innocence in her need to show off the superiority of her world that I felt no need to press the point. Rather shamefully, I can now admit, I actually felt superior to her for my tactful reticence. I also felt some relief at the implication that Watchers weren't expected to be flawless in the event of a planetary ascension to the fourth density.

The cabin was slowing to a halt before I could take this thought any further, with the doors to one side sliding open. Moving out of the cool of the cabin, a blast of heat hit me. It was reflecting down from the vast silver vessel looming over us. It hung over us, this immense cylinder, even larger now that we stood in the shadow beneath it. It was so long I could barely see where it ended. And what seemed most incongruous was that this colossal vessel was simply floating there above our heads, apparently completely unsupported and looking to collapse to the ground at any moment.

I knew rationally that some form of gravity modulators must be quietly humming away in the belly of the ship. But knowing that wasn't quite enough to dispel the nervousness I was feeling. This feeling was new to me, I might add. It didn't quite amount to fear or terror but rather a kind of nervous excitement. It was as if I was daring myself to be placed in danger.

Now it was Clarisel's turn to be surprised. I realized that for all her talk she'd never actually been here, in the presence of this enormous vessel.

I heard a gasp of surprise behind me, and I turned to see what Clarisel was staring at. Out of the blinding glare that was reflecting off the side of the ship, three humanoid figures were floating down. It was a curiously magical sight, not dissimilar—as I might have joked to someone else—to angels descending from a cloud of heavenly glory. They were limned in light, as if they were glowing, and they only gradually assumed solidity when they floated down beneath the shadow of the ship. As I could see them more clearly, they seemed to be talking and excitedly gesturing to one another. At the same time they were controlling their descent by manipulating a mechanism on their belts with their other hand.

The Commodore and her two aides floated gently to the ground a few yards from where Clarisel and I were standing, and we were still chattering to each other when they moved to greet us. As we were all currently sharing the same reality domain in the lower frequencies of the fourth dimension, there was no problem with a lack of substance. Clarisel and I would have been as solid and materially real to the Commodore and the aides—all three mortal beings—as the Commodore appeared to us.

The Andromedan Commodore was an extremely tall woman who appeared young, yet I knew she must be far older to be holding such a responsible position. Her blond hair was clipped short, and I sensed this was more for efficiency than personal vanity, for she wore nothing to adorn her face. With her high cheekbones, her wide—almost lipless—mouth, and long slim nose, her face had a sculpted look.

Clarisel courteously introduced me and began to tell the Commodore the reasons her Prince had given for my presence. Before she'd finished her sentence, however, the Commodore cut her off by saying she'd already heard from Janda-chi. After the normal courtesies, she thanked Clarisel for accompanying me, telling the Watcher that her presence was no longer required. She also requested that Clarisel communicate her gratitude to Unava, Prince Zanda's chief of staff, for making this—the first of the intergalactic exchanges to have been organized from Zandana—possible.

Lowering their heads to one another in respect, Clarisel took a step back and disappeared into the aether to go about her business, leaving me alone with the Andromedans.

I'd better take a brief pause here to explain something that flies in the face of much contemporary scientific speculation about the nature and morphology of intelligent life in the Multiverse. It's an understandable error—and is one of the unfortunate consequences of planetary isolation. Yet you'll find that, once you start encountering extraterrestrials, almost all of them will appear much the same as you. Some will be taller, some shorter. Some may have more toes and fingers than you do, some may have less. And there may be a few races with an additional eye or two. Nevertheless, you'll find them all—all the space-faring races, anyway—essentially humanoid in form.

There are sentient aquatic races—like the Sea People on Zandana—but with few exceptions they don't develop the technology to travel in space unless transported by another species. There are also a very few intelligent species in the Local Universe whose morphology is completely different from the normal humanoid pattern. However, once again, with very few exceptions, they stay on their planets.

Didn't that young extraterrestrial telepathic mouthpiece that Mein Host and his two friends met in Manhattan's Bennett Park speak of the humanoid as the "most popular" form? And wasn't it "feelings" that all sentient species share—and that represents the potential that unites them?

To fully appreciate what may still seem strange to many, it is necessary to upend some basic contemporary scientific formulations about life in the universe. If I've said this before it's worth repeating. This inversion can be characterized in a maxim coined by my ward: "Planets are made for people, not people for planets." It's crude but essentially true.

Of course individual planetary environmental conditions will have some bearing on how the planet's life-forms turn out, but far less than you might imagine. There's a good reason for this. The humanoid form is the basic pattern that the Life Carriers code into the evolutionary process on worlds in this Local Universe.

It's more appropriate to understand that mortal beings on the inhabited worlds in this Local Universe are all part of one Universal Family. Brothers, sisters, and cousins from other worlds will recognize you—as you will recognize them—as kindred spirits.

The differences among mortals from different planets won't be primarily morphological; they will be more subtle than that. The differences will be in intelligence, in emotional maturity, in psychic sensitivity, in spiritual wisdom, in technological advancement, and in the manner that race has collectively resolved the problems that all races have.

A mortal from an advanced world—as was the Commodore of the Andromedan vessel—would most likely have originated on a world already well established in the higher frequencies of the fourth dimension.

I couldn't imagine what she would want with a humble Watcher such as myself.

# 10

# Of Scrims and Where the Action Is

Extraterrestrial Substances, Peeling Away
the Scrim, Solonon, the Andromedan
Starship, the Heart of Creation, and
the Fourth Dimension

The healing process for starseeds will sometimes take a thoroughly unconventional direction. Damian, for example, was in her own way a masterful healer, and yet not in a way that was immediately apparent. Her gift lay in creating thoroughly unusual situations in which Mein Host was able to experience and learn what he otherwise would never have had access to.

On one occasion Damian took my ward to meet a man she'd hinted was an extraterrestrial living as a regular human being. It was all very discreet and nothing was said openly. Yet when they met, the rare affinity my ward felt with him told them all they needed to know.

I'll call their extraterrestrial host "Andrew" and will relate only that he lived on his own in a magnificent house on a large, rambling estate in the countryside somewhere in the region of Washington, D.C. It was tacitly understood that he moved in the corridors of power of the capital.

Andrew was a beautiful-looking man. He was tall and slim, with fine golden-blond hair worn short, disconcertingly light blue eyes, and skin that seemed almost translucent. He looked to be in his late twenties or early thirties, but it was soon obvious from the quality of his intelligence that he was probably much older than he appeared.

After they came to know one another better over lunch, it emerged that Andrew's interest lay mainly in learning of my ward's explorations into phencyclidine—and perhaps in having the experience himself.

I've heard my ward talking fancifully about phencyclidine and ketamine as "the first of the great extraterrestrial drugs." Those who've explored these substances in any depth will likely understand what he means by this. Not, of course, that the substances were devised by ETs and then dropped into a human mind. No, these were substances intended—more perhaps than the plant-based entheogens—to introduce a distinctly extraterrestrial reality.

We've talked earlier about the unconscious state produced by ketamine and how it is very different from the normal state of unconsciousness. Again, this emerged in the medical community as patients were emerging from operations having spoken with God, or with angels, or having spent time with ETs on their craft. Sometimes worse, they would find themselves roasting in hell.

By the late 1970s, other substances were being added to the anesthetic mix to prevent a patient from remembering what had occurred when they were out. Yet somewhere there must have been a doctor who'd taken note of ketamine's entheogenic potential. It was then that a researcher like John C. Lilly—who fine-tuned the dosages, using amounts as little as one-tenth of a normal anesthetic dose—permitted a fully conscious, out-of-body state.

In terms of phencyclidine, it was unfortunate that it was simple to concoct from readily available precursors, because it soon made its appearance on the street named—appropriately enough—angel dust. Few knew how to use the substance correctly, my ward was telling Andrew. That, so it turned out, was exactly what Andrew wanted to know about.

"All I've heard about dust," Andrew said, "makes it like the devil's own juice . . . terrible stuff! Drives people crazy. When a drug gets such a bad reputation . . ."—he allowed for a theatrical pause before announcing with a wide smile—". . . is when I get interested in it."

"Man after my own heart," my ward joked later to Damian.

"People were plain silly," Mein Host replied. "They didn't experiment. If dust came as a powder, people thought it was like coke. They did a full line and then thought they'd died. They hadn't, of course, but it was pretty hellish for them. That turned them against it . . . they weren't ready to face ego death.

"Thing is, all you need is a match head of the powder to get off. Then if it's sprayed on mint leaf—which is how they like to cook it up in Harlem—you can smoke it with herb as a joint. Two or three good hits is quite enough. I recommend you stop when you hear the angels singing!"

"When you hear the angels singing?" Andrew replied, clearly amused.

"When you hear the angels singing! It's a sort of warbly, high-pitched tone," Damian said. "It can sound like singing."

"You'll know it when you hear it," my ward added.

"After they demonized acid in the press," Andrew said after a thoughtful pause, "I wondered what would be next. Then I heard what they were saying about dust; how awful it was."

Mein Host added: "I had the chance to pull all the research papers on phencyclidine, and how it was being blamed for violence . . ."

"Like those stories about how the cops shoot at 'em, but they just keep on coming?" Andrew interrupted.

"Yeah! And how they gouge their own eyes out . . . I read all the papers, and there were almost always other factors. The guy was known to be violent, or he was already a gun freak, or he was mentally unbalanced—that kind of thing. They were all people who shouldn't have ever taken the stuff."

"It's madness, this drug war," Andrew nodded. "It just makes whatever drug they prohibit that much more attractive to kids. One day they're going to have to wake up—and find that encouraging people to take responsibility for themselves works better."

They agreed the drug situation in America had become absurd. It was just a stick to wave around when a politician wanted to appear tough on crime. Not only was the drug war ineffective, it might well have been devised to make the situation worse. Why the lessons of alcohol prohibition in the 1920s weren't learned, as Andrew suggested, had to be symbolic of America's chronic inability to look honestly at its past.

"Will they never learn?!" Andrew stated as he got up and moved over to the table. "So let's do the dust."

Mein Host prepared a joint, mixing the dust-impregnated mint leaf with the grass in generous proportions. He and Andrew then smoked it, passing the joint back and forth until they were both giggling at the sound of the angels singing. Damian responsibly volunteered to stay straight as ground control. Yet as it would turn out, it didn't seem to make much difference, because Andrew insisted on taking them out for a ride around his estate in his open jeep.

It was an utterly crazy idea, of course. Most people on dust are more than happy to stay very still with their eyes closed. And yet here was this extraterrestrial urging them to join him in his jeep. Damian said afterward she had only gone along with the idea because of who Andrew was, and because she trusted him.

The three of them were soon zipping down the narrow country lanes at absurd speeds. Damian was sitting in the back gripping the roll bars, while my ward was in the front seat riding shotgun. Andrew, of course, was driving, one hand resting lazily on the wheel as he pushed the jeep faster and faster. The sun beat down on them through the jeep's open top. The wind rushed by, searing their faces. The branches of the bushes beside the road were whipping and snapping at them as they teetered around corners, sometimes on two wheels, with Damian standing in the back squealing with delight.

How what happened next my ward still doesn't really fully understand—or have a convenient explanation for. It just was what it was: an unforgettable metaphor. It was a situation, he said later, that could only be appreciated for the value of the experience itself.

When this situation started, I have to admit I was fearful of what I was watching. Andrew and my ward—side by side in the front seat of the speeding jeep, having just spoken to one another—were now no longer looking at the road ahead. They had locked eyes and were looking deeply into one another as the car sped on. It was swerving around corners without dropping speed, on and on, with tens of seconds passing. But my ward and Andrew were still staring—long after others would have broken their gaze—the rolling countryside speeding by them.

My ward told Damian afterward that he realized it must have been a test of trust and faith, which is why he held Andrew's eyes for so long. But he said that wasn't the most extraordinary aspect of it. It was what was occurring while they were looking at each other so intently that had so astonished him. One part of him, he told her, was holding Andrew's eyes for as long as the ET was looking at him, but another part of him was watching something entirely different going on.

He said they were no longer speeding through an actual landscape— that it was more like a film set. There were little men running around with props and scenery. Flats that had the trees and the road painted on them were being shuffled around in a panic, as though they were going too fast for the scenery to be put in place before they got there. He said it was like peeling away the scrim of reality—a favorite phrase of my ward—to catch a glimpse, even for a moment, of how flimsy and inauthentic reality really is.

In fact, it was one of those rare moments when an abstract philosophical concept suddenly becomes experientially real.

The sympathetic reader is doubtless wondering why my ward seems willing to throw himself headlong into situations so ridiculously risky as the one I've just described. There have been other such situations that I've included in this narrative, and some I haven't (as they don't further an understanding of the pattern). I'll add one more example here only because it tells another story as well. This one in many ways is more important than the pattern that enabled it. But first the pattern itself.

If I view my ward's life as a continuum stretching from his birth in

1940 until the present day, it's clearer to see how his near-death experience in 1973 became the turning point around which his life has pivoted. Being told by the Being of Light that he'd done what he came to do—and being given the choice to return—encouraged him to pursue his own interests. And yet it didn't give him an entirely clean slate. What the aftereffects of the NDE appeared to do in this case was to capitalize on a pattern formed in the trauma of childhood.

I've written about the complex of emotions my ward experienced as a child, which is now better known as survivor's guilt. Survivors experience this in different ways. Some feel special, as though saved for some important task ahead. Others might feel they didn't deserve to live. And yet others feel that they'd cheated death. Each of these reactions—or some combination of them, if experienced in early childhood—is likely to shape the future life of the survivor in a particular direction.

In Mein Host's case, one of his reactions—which became hardened with time and repetition—was a deeply buried unconscious drive to place himself in dangerous situations. There was no nobility in this. It wasn't heroism or bravery that drove him. He wasn't daring death to take him. It seemed to me to be more a combination of a feeling of worthlessness, swept away like dirt in someone else's war, and a sense of being special, which needed the occasional reinforcement in the face of life's efforts to show otherwise. He also attributed it to the careless impulse to place no value on his own life and a desire to test himself by going to the edge.

Prior to his NDE, these were the primary compulsions that drove him to be so careless. After 1973—and with the knowledge he'd already accomplished his life's task—his capacity to throw himself wholeheartedly and without care for self into unlikely situations became a valuable asset, both to him and the angels who worked with him.

This wasn't an immediate transformation, but it followed the same essential course during the seven or eight years it took for him to assimilate the profound truths revealed during his NDE.

There were nerve-wracking moments for me: when he sat with his legs dangling out a twenty-fifth floor window in the midst of a minor hurricane in Manhattan, asking the winds to take him if he'd finished his service; the multiple times he confronted muggers by pushing aside their guns; or by swimming into the teeth of a storm in Clearwater Bay, Florida, hoping to be saved by dolphins.

However, by 1980 he reached the turning point—of the turning point—without being aware of it. The pattern that led to the experiment was the same, but the results carried so much meaning they seemed to dissolve the negative aspects of the pattern. After the experiment I'm about to describe, I've heard him say he feels he has a choice whether to throw himself into some outrageous challenge—whether to risk his life for no good reason merely because he placed so little value on it.

I found the concept behind the experiment interesting because it demonstrates my point about this pattern that has reverberated in my ward since his childhood. It was based on some recent encounters he'd had with Walk-Ins. My ward called it an "intelligence accelerator."

The idea was to give over his body and his intelligence to any entity who would make better use of it than he could. Damian agreed to hold the ground while my ward took a substantial dose of ketamine and surrendered himself to the experiment.

Damian sat cross-legged on the floor of his West 85th Street apartment—her sketchbook on her lap—while my ward assumed a half-lotus position on the futon. Here he offered up a prayer for a productive experience aligned with his highest intentions. He added to the prayer that whatever might happen, he be allowed to remain fully conscious and present. If another entity wished to occupy his vehicle then they were welcome to do so, providing he was permitted to stay and share the experience, that is. Then, injecting himself in the muscle of his upper left arm with 1 cc of ketamine hydrochloride, he straightened his back and settled in with his eyes closed for the next four minutes it took the substance to take effect.

Take a moment while the K is coming on to examine his intentions here. How self-aware was he when taking these steps? What was the impulse, or the impulses, fueling this prospective abdication of selfhood?

There was the perfectly genuinely felt altruism in the impulse to hand over his vehicle to any Being who could make more effective use of it. There was also the faith that whatever might happen would be for the best. As well, there was the courage of the counterphobic determined to prove he was capable of facing his fears should the worst happen. And then of course there was the desire of a magician to impress his sincerity on those he knew to be in the higher spiritual dimensions. Oh, and there was also the hope to apply the lens of K to amplify whatever experience would follow and to break new ground. Finally there was the conscious intention of an experimenter to observe what would happen . . . would an entity, in fact, arrive and take over?

Yet beneath these reasonable, even noble, intentions lurked two interconnected and murkier currents. First there was the unconscious conviction resulting from his survivor's guilt feeding into his deep lack of any personal worth. This lay in the shadow of a more conscious belief I'd heard him express. Second, he felt he'd come to the end of a cycle, and he held no fear of death. This was a consequence of the NDE and made him more than happy to step aside.

There are three viewpoints to what followed. Mein Host reported later that as he was sitting there meditating—his hands open and relaxed and laying on his knees, his breathing deep and regular—this effect started. An entity slipped down and overlit him. It filled him up yet left him present. Then another entity slipped down to replace the first, then another, and another, and another . . . on and on. He said he felt he was at the bottom of a transparent tube from which entities slid down into him, only to surrender to another one. He said the sound was like a great flapping of wings and a rushing of wind. As the entities poured down into him, filling him up and then leaving—becoming more and more powerful—he told Damian that he simply couldn't hold onto his conscious awareness and must have blacked out. For when he finally opened his eyes, there she was—still sitting before him—having completed a detailed portrait in pencil on her sketchpad.

My viewpoint affirmed my ward's sensation of these entities descending a transparent tube, although the "tube" is somewhat fanciful—as this is what I witnessed. Entities indeed poured down through him. They were Watchers and rebel angels, beings much as myself—who both fear mortal incarnation and yet accept it as our road to experiential redemption.

My ward, in those short twenty minutes, became the receptacle. He was the material vehicle through which many hundreds of immature rebel angels could have a taste of the emotional density of life in the third dimension. He has never known the identities of those beings who flapped through him until this moment. Thus it might amuse him further to realize that a large number of those rebel angels back in 1980 are firmly embedded in their mortal incarnations in 2012.

As to when my ward blacked out, that's when Damian started drawing and talking to the entity who had finally made his appearance after the flow of angels. The angels stayed for a while to announce his presence and allow his portrait to be drawn.

Solonon was the name he gave, telling Damian that he was a scientist/poet from the forty-first century who had taken advantage of my ward's offer of an open vehicle. His energy, apparently, was too much for my ward to consciously sustain. Thus he had no awareness of Solonon's presence when he emerged from his altered state. And yet when he was able to look at Damian's sketch of Solonon, he said he had the oddest sense of recognition.

Damian was an excellent portrait artist—more than capable of producing a perfect likeness of her subject. So when he first looked at the portrait he said he had a complex of reactions. Somewhere deep beneath the surface he could see his own features, but overlaying them was quite a different creature. His ears were longer, their points rising on either side of his head. His eyes were piercing and full of intelligence, but it was his nose and mouth that caught the attention. There appeared to be a corrugated tube stretching from his brow—between his eyes where a human's nose would be—down to his small, tight mouth.

How he was managing this transformation he didn't say, and, sadly, Damian was drawing and not taking notes. There didn't appear to be any pressure. There was no mention of the science-fiction trope of returning to the past to save the future, none of that.

Was it perhaps more like a brief—or perhaps unusual—unintended vacation for the scientist? Maybe it was trip to the past that would form the basis of one of his poems? Might he have been surprised to have found himself drawn into the spiritual vortex of the descending angels?

This encounter occurred in 1980, at a time when the world was being most threatened by imminent extinction. My ward had been assured once by another extraterrestrial that they "could pick the rockets out of the sky," which had set his mind to rest. However, that was almost twenty years earlier, and the world situation hadn't got any better, even if humanity hadn't destroyed itself yet.

On a deeper emotional level, it was the appearance of Solonon from the distant future that in its own curious way affirmed for him that a distant future did indeed exist. The human race hadn't wiped itself out. Yes, the race had changed and mutated in appearance, but the same sharp, inquisitive, and very human intelligence beamed out of Solonon's eyes in Damian's sketch. And I use the word *curious* here because it seemed to me—even to me—a most unusual way of gaining such emotional reassurance as regards the future of humanity.

\* \* \*

I thought that the Commodore's voice would be harder than it was when she finally turned to me and invited me to join her and her two aides on the bridge. After adjusting the device in their antigravity belts I accompanied them as we floated together up and into the ship.

"You must find yourself surprised to be here," the Commodore was saying as she shepherded me into a shaft. Once we were safely inside, it floated us smoothly up to the bridge located at the top of the ship. As we exited the shaft—and at a wordless command from the Commodore—the two aides returned to their posts. At this she gestured me toward a large and comfortably furnished lounge located behind the bridge.

We settled into chairs opposite one another, and at another sign from her, one of her crew appeared with two glasses and a bottle of what turned out to be one of the finest of Zandana's wines.

The Commodore was smiling while she was pouring the wine. "I see you tasted only the Prince's favorite fruit juice," she said, which made me wonder if I'd been too greedily eyeing the delicious-looking violet liquid filling my glass. "Prince Janda-chi likes to set a good example . . . unfermented, of course!"

I admit it amused me to think the Prince would have felt the need to impress me with his good example.

"He prides himself on the quality of his fruit," the Commodore said quickly. "You know he planted the trees himself. He believes his fruit makes the finest juice on Zandana . . . but this is my preference," she said as she winked and nodded at the wine. "It's this that makes the journey to this world so worthwhile."

And it was good. Very good. I couldn't recall when I'd last had a glass of wine. Since the revolution I've not spent enough time in a material reality to have had the opportunity to enjoy a glass of excellent wine.

"I'm sure you're curious as to why I invited you here . . . Ah, yes! Of course, you believed it was the Prince who sent you."

Now I *was* curious! Whyever would the commanding officer of an intergalactic vessel want to meet with a Watcher, let alone a Watcher from another world—and a third-density world at that? My face must have betrayed me, so I took another sip of the wine and smiled my approval.

"No, indeed," she continued, tipping her glass to me. "I placed my request with Prince Janda-chi to meet you once information reached me that a Watcher from Prince Caligastia's world was currently at my old friend Prince Janda-chi's residence. Well, I thought I'd take my chances . . ."

So it was wasn't me, Georgia, in whom she was interested—any Watcher from Earth would have done just fine. Was that it? For some reason this irritated me more than I thought it would. Hadn't I just come from the residence of one of Zandana's Planetary Princes? I wasn't just any old Watcher, was I? I was a trusted confidante of Prince Janda-chi. Wasn't it my suggestion that had once saved the city of Zandan from the barbarian invasion? Didn't this give me at least *some* importance? Perhaps the Commodore hadn't been informed of my contribution!

I didn't want to betray my annoyance, yet my face must have been tensing up, so I was grateful when she refilled my glass. It *was* an extremely good wine.

"I wish to be perfectly direct with you," she told me while replacing the bottle on the table, relaxing back into her seat, crossing her long legs, joining me in sipping the wine, and smiling most agreeably. Before she spoke again, one of the aides I'd seen accompanying her earlier slipped into the lounge and briefly whispered in her ear before retiring back to the bridge and leaving us alone again.

This gave me a chance to look around the lounge. To my surprise, what I had first taken to be richly luxurious was worn with age and wear upon closer inspection. The chairs were comfortable enough, I suppose, but they didn't adjust to the form in the way Janda-chi's chairs had. And now I could see that the fabric on the armrests was slightly worn and frayed.

"As I was saying . . ." she started, as she waited for the aide to leave the lounge, "and I know this is an unusual request . . . I want to be as open with you as I expect you to be with me."

I nodded my agreement. I saw no reason to hold back. But first I had a question that had been bothering me. "We were taught in our Jerusem seminars," I said, "that the Andromeda Galaxy was not yet giving birth to stars and would therefore possess no inhabited planets. The planets themselves, we were told, were barely yet aggregated. And yet this is said to be an Andromedan vessel and you . . . do you not claim to hail from a world in the Andromeda Galaxy?"

The Commodore was laughing before I finished my question. "What you have been taught in your seminars was clearly an oversimplification. You evidently had no need to know, and this isn't the time to elaborate on the mechanics of planetary engineering. But I said I'd be direct with you, so I'll tell what you wish to know."

I settled back in my chair while the Commodore refilled our glasses.

"I believe I'm correct in assuming that your Jerusem seminars focused almost entirely on the dynamics of third-density life—that is what you would have needed to know."

I nodded. That's the way it was.

"And of course, you're familiar with the many aspects of the fifth dimension," she said—I thought unnecessarily—but I smiled and nodded.

"But what they tell you very little about is the true spectrum of frequency domains in the fourth density. This is correct, yes?" She continued without needing my agreement. "And, no doubt, you will have also observed there is a basic similarity between all the third-density worlds you have visited . . ."

"I only know, what . . . seven 3-D worlds," I said, "and only two of them well, but, yes, from the small sample, it's true there is a certain sameness—rocks, vegetation, animals, and mortals—if that's what you mean."

She responded, "There may be different vegetation and different animals—and the mortals might appear slightly different—but all those 3-D worlds have a similar density . . . the same level of solidity. You have observed that, too, I'm sure."

Again, that wasn't really a question, so I kept quiet. I had the sense I was going to learn something I didn't know, which might even have been held back from us in the seminars.

"They might have been cautious to teach you the full extent of the spectrum of fourth-density worlds," she said, answering my unasked question in a manner suggesting she might be, at least, semi-telepathic. I hadn't been hearing her in my mind, so I'd assumed she wasn't listening—and besides, we'd been speaking together perfectly normally within the domain we were both sharing.

"Here on Zandana," she continued, "we are in one of the lowest of the multiple frequency domains within the fourth dimension. It may astonish you to know there are more than 590 distinct frequency domains within the dimension of the heart, so you can appreciate why they might not have wanted to open that book; not if it wasn't relevant to your tasks ahead."

I was immediately confused. However could that be? Five hundred ninety distinct domains! If that was really true, I had been told nothing of it. I had always assumed the fourth dimension would be more complex, perhaps with eight or ten distinct frequency domains . . . but almost six hundred of them?!

The Commodore came to my rescue. "The simplest way to think about the fourth dimension is to visualize the two essential elements at play in the Local Universe . . ."

"Spirit and matter," I said. I didn't want her to think just because I was a Watcher I was a simpleton.

"Spirit and matter. Quite correct. Now, if the lower three dimensions are those of material manifestation—the third-density planets, if you like—then the fifth, sixth, and seventh dimensions, as you know, are the dimensions of spirit."

Much of this I already knew, but this fourth-dimension material . . . *this* was new to me. I felt for a moment that I was standing atop a high mountain surrounded by an endless panorama of clouds that covered a landscape I knew must be there, stretching away as endlessly as the clouds above. Yet since the rebellion—to continue the metaphor—the landscape below had become forbidden territory.

It suddenly came to me—with the Commodore quiet now and smiling gently across the table—that I'd heard absolutely nothing of the fourth density from Caligastia or anyone in the rebel faction. It seemed to have been taboo. It struck me that I would have known almost nothing of the fourth density if I hadn't been a regular visitor over the millennia to Zandana.

"Are you implying," I asked her, "that Prince Caligastia has no intention of allowing Earth to ascend to the fourth? That he's trapping the world in the third? Can that be it?"

I told her I knew the Prince had modified the grid to trap mortal souls in an endless cycle of lifetimes on his world, so as to become his unwitting slaves. And before I could stop myself I heard my own voice telling the Commodore how I believed that the MA had outwitted Prince Caligastia by substituting and returning rebel angels for mortal incarnation.

"Really? Caligastia truly believed he could control the grid?" she asked. The Commodore certainly sounded aghast, but I couldn't tell from her tone whether she was simply pretending a horrified reaction. As the Commodore was a mortal I was unable read her mind, and she—as the ranking officer of an intergalactic vessel—was obviously well practiced in the arts of social duplicity.

I was self-aware enough to realize that with these thoughts I was starting to become unreasonably suspicious. Yet in my defense, I still didn't know exactly why she wanted to see me, so perhaps there was some reason for the caution that I felt in the moment, but that may seem foolish in retrospect.

"So little information ever leaks out from Earth," she was saying, "this alone has aroused the interest of the Federation; and the quarantine makes it impossible to verify the rumors we hear. The MA has remained silent, so we are left guessing."

"But surely you must know about the presence of Sirian envoys on Earth," I blurted out.

"Yes, yes, the Sirians," she said somewhat impatiently. "We know about them, but they're revealing nothing—even if they did know what was happening, which I doubt!"

We were interrupted again by the same aide as before; the one who'd slipped in and was whispering in the Commodore's ear. I sipped my wine, keeping a thoughtful, abstract look on my face, and appearing as though I wasn't really trying to listen to their hushed conversation—which, anyway, I wasn't able to make out. I was left wondering what was behind her obviously dismissive attitude toward the Sirian envoys.

The aide slipped away as silently as he'd entered.

"Where were we?" she asked as she smiled apologetically at me . . . the responsibilities of a ship's captain. "Yes, of course, the fourth-density worlds. Spirit and matter . . . matter rising from the ground of being, the spirit descending from the highest heaven, and both meeting in the Heart of Creation. Do you understand now?"

I began to feel that she was hurrying me along, or perhaps she was sensing she was saying too much. I needed to step in quickly. "What I still don't understand is why there are so many frequency domains in the fourth density and so few in the third. Didn't you say 590?"

"The fourth-density worlds are the Heart of Creation," she told me. "That's how I think of it. It's where you'll find the great interstellar and galactic civilizations. Every single one of those hundreds of frequency domains will be populated by ascending mortals from the third-density worlds in the Local Universe."

"And the inhabited worlds of the Andromeda Galaxy?" I asked. "Where you come from . . ."

"Were you ever to visit our galaxy, Georgia, I'm sure you would be surprised to find we have some of the most ancient civilizations as well as some of the youngest. My own home world, for example, is relatively new to the fourth density . . ."

"But this ship . . ." I gestured around at what was obviously an extremely sophisticated piece of technology.

"We didn't build it, if that's what you mean. We inherited it from our mentors. I believe that's how it functions on other worlds, too. We were never a space-faring race when we ascended to the fourth density. But after that we were adopted and mentored by an older and technically more advanced civilization from a nearby star system . . . but I'd better stop there. I'm sure there was a good reason why your seminars didn't include information on the fourth density."

"It's good of you to have addressed my question," I said. "Let me make sure I understand you. So it's in the fourth dimension, in all those hundreds of frequency domains, where the real action is?"

Her thin mouth curled into a smile at my choice of words.

"You could say that," she said, laughing. "Just as you could call the third-density worlds the nurseries for mortal souls. So perhaps now you will understand the interest that your home world is generating. And yes, I have heard it rumored that Earth is unlikely to make it to the fourth."

That took me aback. I'd never heard that said before in such uncompromising terms. My first reaction was defensive. I didn't want to hear that such an ugly rumor was being bruited around about my home planet. Yet I still knew so little about the shift from third to fourth densities. All I knew was based on what I'd observed on Zandana and what Clarisel had told me earlier—that I obviously didn't really know the implications of not ascending to the fourth density.

Was that really what Prince Caligastia had planned?

The horrifying thing was that from Caligastia's point of view this would make perfect sense. It would represent the apogee of everything he'd been working toward. If he could delay, ad infinitum, the planet's ascension to the fourth density, then perhaps he was thinking that the MA would cut free the planet—his planet—and finally allow him get on with it.

"I don't believe that is really Prince Caligastia's true intention," I said with as much conviction as I could summon without fully believing it. I don't think I fooled her. As I've said before, we Watchers don't make good liars—and a part of me hoped she would see through my protest.

"I believe you have told me all that I need to know," the Commodore said courteously, "and I thank you for taking your time to meet with me." She got to her feet, signaling the interview was over. She called in an aide, who must have been hovering just outside the lounge, and instructed him to return me to the planet's surface. This left me wondering what it was I'd said that answered her question.

Returning down the shaft together, the aide bid me well and left me to descend to the planet on my own. The second of the Wise Twins had set, and the light had taken on a golden glow, softening and muting the vessel's silvered reflection in the cooling air beneath the craft.

It must have been the Commodore's interest in Prince Caligastia's intentions that made me realize I'd better be making my way back to Earth. After all, wasn't the emotional subtext of the Commodore's curiosity colored by the envy of one who knew where the real action was unfolding, and yet was unable to participate? Well, I could, of course.

It was that thought that spurred me to use the fifth dimension to transfer, without delay, to the Seraphic Transport Center. I'd suddenly felt an unexpected urge to get back to Earth as quickly as possible.

My sister Watcher Clarisel was nowhere to be seen when I left the Andromedan ship. With nothing to keep me on Zandana, I set my intention for the Seraphic Transport Center. An instant later I was in the travel center's lounge facing Eleena's welcoming arms.

"I was expecting you," my special Transport Seraph said in a kindly tone in my mind as we embraced. I believe it was for the first time in friendship, which is curious—now that I think about it—considering how intimate the embrace of a Transport Seraph's heat shield is.

"As mysterious as ever, Eleena! How happy I am to see you!" I thought while she was gesturing me ahead of her to one of the chambers that appeared to be already prepared for her.

Eleena bade me stand closer, unfurling her great wings and wrapping them around me in an embrace that would protect me from being fried by the furious friction of subspace aether. She let me know there was no time to waste as the slight vibrations of her initial acceleration told me we were on our way back to my home planet.

Something was pulling on me to return to Earth. And yet as happy as I felt, I found myself deeply uneasy at what I would find when I got there.

# 11

# Hidden Intentions

Serpents, Nagas and Dragons, the Deta
Factor, Aerial Battles, Akhenaten's Rule, and
the Wounded Mother

In the spring of 1980, three events occurred in Mein Host's life—all within a few weeks of one another—that taken together appeared to drive him into an emotional tailspin. It was the closest to a so-called nervous breakdown that he has needed to experience in his life.

Marion had finally moved out of his apartment, much to his apparent relief—except that now he was running the entire business on his own. Damian had had enough of his obsession with the Helianx and had walked out of his life. And he was being threatened legally by a competitor—the producer of an inferior product for storing color slides.

He was alone for the first time in nearly twenty years. There were no live-in girlfriends, no community, no members of The Unit, no flatmates. He was working harder and harder to keep the business flourishing, and now he was free to write and draw long into the night. It all seemed great . . . until there came a day when he was sitting opposite the head of the audiovisual department of the Metropolitan Museum of Art, selling his Viewpack system for the museum's slide collection—with tears pouring down his face.

My ward was having what others might have called a nervous

breakdown, but it was, in fact, a brutal shattering of any remaining rigidity in his emotional body. I believe he was able to appreciate that this emotional and psychic breakdown represented the ending of a phase during which he reentered the modern world. He'd lived all that the fast life that Manhattan had to offer. He'd gotten high and danced the night away at Studio 54. He'd had numerous lovers. He'd run a successful business in one of the hardest cities in the world, marketing a system of his own invention. And he had made new friends and sampled many of the recently developed "designer drugs," substances like MDMA, which were beginning to prove so effective in psychotherapy. He'd done all those things human beings tend to do after they'd lived the life of a monk, and when they finally had a little money of their own, in a city as fast and wicked as New York.

Yet something vitally important was missing.

His awareness of the Great Spirit, which was so present during much of his time in the community, appeared to have moved into the background. He was now able to set his own agenda and read and study what he chose and what most interested him most deeply. *The Helianx Proposition,* for example. Its story line encompassed three-quarters of a billion years. That and the ancient entities traveling from the second to seventh Superuniverse had radically deepened his sense of the distant past, as well as expanding his understanding of intelligent life in the Multiverse.

I don't think his interest in *The Helianx Proposition* lay so much in his conviction that the story was necessarily true in any objective sense. This was due to the fact that it had a narrative power and an intuitive insight that wove together the myths and legends with the stories of wise serpents, nagas, and dragons. He had been receptive to *The Helianx Proposition* and the way it came through and then found it intriguing enough to study its implications. This had in many ways prepared him for the depth and complexity of *The Urantia Book,* its 2,097 pages still unread and gathering dust on his bookshelf.

In fact, it was shortly after receiving *The Helianx Proposition* that he first turned to *The Urantia Book* with every intention of reading it seriously. Starting at the beginning—which would have seemed logical—he quickly discovered just what a task he'd set for himself. My collaborator suggests we give an example from page 5 of *The Urantia Book*'s foreword, in which the celestial author (more on the UB's authorship later) writes the following paragraph in addressing reality.

> REALITY, as comprehended by finite beings, is partial, relative, and shadowy. The maximum Deity reality fully comprehensible by evolutionary finite creatures is embraced within the Supreme Being. Nevertheless there are antecedent and eternal realities, superfinite realities, which are ancestral to this Supreme Deity of evolutionary time-space creatures. In attempting to portray the origin and nature of universal reality, we are forced to employ the technique of time-space reasoning in order to reach the level of the finite mind. Therefore must many of the simultaneous events of eternity be presented as sequential transactions.

I've not chosen this passage because it's particularly dense or complex but because it demonstrates what the reader will be dealing with for the next 2,092 pages.

The first impression striking the reader—and I'm deriving this from my ward's reactions; different people may well find it otherwise—is that the paragraph seems to make coherent sense. There's clearly a logic to the writing, even if terms like *Maximum Deity* and *Supreme Being* and *Superfinite Realities* have yet to be explained. The basic concepts presented appear sensible enough, as my ward remarked. There clearly have to be realities beyond the merely human. And if this information purports to be relayed from the celestials, then it makes sense that celestials have to downstep and finesse it for human understanding.

Yes, it certainly made general sense as far as he could understand it, but it must have seemed too daunting a read to take on right then when there was so much more to read and learn.

Even two years after leaving the community, Mein Host was still living on the high energy and the twenty-hour workdays to which he had become accustomed during his thirteen years in the Process. Now that he was on his own again, he was able to indulge in his capacity to get carried away in his long hours of focused work. And as the Process had its high-flown ideas, so also did he take this bold and expansive approach into the long analytical essays he was starting to write.

As regards an article written in June 1980, the title is enough to suggest where his thinking was taking him. It was titled "Some Speculative Scenarios on the Future of the Human Race" (reprinted on pages 402–13 of *The Return of the Rebel Angels*). It was an intriguing and well-reasoned analysis—if a little dry—but I was encouraged to see that my ward was able to think outside the box. A second essay, titled "Sidestepping: F-Delta Superimpositions and the Hologrammic Reality," went even further to propose that—under certain extreme and life-threatening conditions—it is possible to sidestep to a parallel reality in which the immediate threat no longer exists. He included three examples of true events in which Occam would have ruled sidestepping legitimate.

Other essays and articles followed: on Benjamin Creme's Maitraya, another on dolphins and underwater birthing, and another probing review of contemporary channeling. All these were written when he was taken up—and was actually paid three cents a word—by the good and kind Tam Mossman.

Once editor of *The Seth Material,* Tam had broken off on his own to launch and edit the elegant but sadly short-lived magazine *Metapsychology: The Journal of Discarnate Intelligence.* My ward also served the journal briefly as book reviewer. Other essays were published in the magazine *Connecting Link,* as well as one for the English publication *Kindred Spirit.* For this he wrote an essay titled "The Angelic Dimension," which turned out to be his first serious examination of angels since his near-death experience seven years earlier.

In retrospect, writing on a wide variety of subjects that interested him—and that were being accepted for publication—gave him the confidence to feel he might have something of value to say that could be of interest to others; even if the interest was measured at a modest three cents a word. Diana, his mother back in England, who was concerned naturally for her son's welfare, was generally encouraging of his writing, always trying to impress on him the importance of getting paid for his labors.

My ward, in his turn, found that writing for money was an unnecessary distraction. Besides, what mainly intrigued him was not the stuff of bestsellers. He'd made it clear he didn't think of himself as a professional author, nor did he particularly wish to be one. He believed he was a capable writer simply because he'd been well educated in the English tradition and—perhaps more importantly—because he'd always loved reading and was therefore extremely widely read.

Since leaving the community at the end of 1977, he'd been keeping a detailed journal—his Black Books, of which there were a total of seventy-five. So in 1981—when he considered putting the strange experiences he'd been having into a book—he discovered he had the first four chapters already sketched out in his journal.

This first book he completed within a couple of years, writing in longhand and then laboriously pecking out the second draft on a portable typewriter. He was living in the coastal town of Netanya in Israel with Melinda when he'd completed that draft. It was a substantial book of more than four hundred pages. Upon closer reading of it, he and Melinda had decided that it would work better if it focused on the experiences they'd been having with angels, dolphins, and extraterrestrials. In addition, they felt it should also contain an original and provocative analysis of the Lucifer Rebellion as it appears in *The Urantia Book*.

The book was consequently cut in half when it was published in 1984 as *The Deta Factor: Dolphins ETs & Angels*. With it my ward made the resolution to write a trilogy of books under the general title *Adventures among Spiritual Intelligences*. His expressed intention was to publish a volume every ten years, charting from personal experience the help that Earth was receiving from nonhuman intelligences.

He succeeded in completing this assignment, publishing *Dolphins, Telepathy & Underwater Birthing: Further Adventures Among Spiritual Intelligences* in 1992 (and republished in 2002 as *Adventures Among*

*Spiritual Intelligences*) and completing the trilogy in 2011 with *The Return of the Rebel Angels.*

I have heard him say he thinks of those three books as his service to his fellows, as his giving back something of what he'd received. It was only after he'd completed his trilogy and was accustomed to writing with angels—he credits Zadkiel and Zophiel for their encouragement during the writing of the second two books—that he was free to be open to work with me. But a great deal more needed to occur over the next thirty years to make our collaboration possible.

Returning to America from Israel in the spring of 1982, the couple stopped off for a visit to my ward's mother in London.

Diana was now living in a ground-floor apartment on Warwick Avenue, close to the canal that gives Little Venice the name awarded it by ambitious realtors. Although a single canal does not a Venice make, the area did have a certain tired elegance. It contained large houses that were all painted cream, some with columns on their faux-Georgian facades, and most now subdivided into apartments. Other houses—mansions, they might have been called by your ambitious realtor—with a single monied owner could be spotted by the high walls surrounding them.

Warwick Avenue—a street of some three hundred yards in length— is relatively unusual in London because it is a true, if inadvertent, avenue. Mature trees line either side of it, the sidewalks are uneven—riven by tree roots—and there is a central median that had long been a taxi stand. Trains could be felt rumbling underground and stopping at Warwick Avenue station at the one end of the street.

Two particular features, a garden and a garage—both of which were much envied by Londoners—allowed an apartment that Diana bought in the mid-1970s for thirty-seven thousand pounds to be sold upon her death in 2001 for more than thirteen times as much. Although it had only two rooms—as well as a large and comfortable bathroom, a tiny kitchen, and a breakfast nook—the two rooms were large and spacious.

The French doors in the living room at the back of the house opened onto a shaded patio with clusters of lavender and purple wisteria flowers, together with bunches of grapes hanging from a trellis. Sunlight filtering through the greenery overhead and falling on the grapes lit them up as if from within. This gave them a bioluminosity more normally seen on an underwater reef. A small lawn stretched beyond to a wall at the end of the garden that was always draped with a variety of climbing, flowering plants.

A miniature apple tree, onto which Diana had grafted three different types of apple—and that miraculously was producing the three different apples when in season—was a pride of Diana's garden. She was always sure to point out how well the violets and primroses had taken and spread—plants that she and my ward had dug up wild on one of their trips into the country some years earlier. All this, together with Diana's natural skill and love of gardening, conspired to give the apartment a restful Mediterranean feeling.

When Diana came to look over my ward's manuscript, it was loaded with awkward corrections, and many partially enclosed characters were now blobs of typewriter ink. Unfamiliar with typing, my ward had done his best, but even he had to admit it was an uneven mess. Diana kindly offered to retype the manuscript using her new electric typewriter to clean up its appearance. Although she never stated it out loud, I could tell her real interest was to read the book and find out what her son had been up to.

If my ward pecks out ten or fifteen words a minute with his two fingers (*Note: and a thumb! —TW*) on a good day, Diana's typing sounded from the next room like a machine gun. Words spat from her typewriter at what seemed like two hundred a minute. Within a couple of afternoons she'd completely retyped the book's now 220 pages, returning the new, sparkling fresh manuscript to her son with a phrase that remains—as my ward likes to say—burned into his cerebellum.

"It's nicely enough written," Diana told her son, "but it's pretty thin stuff to build a career on!" These were her precise words!

As with my ward's housemaster Jock Reith and his dismissive comment when my ward was leaving Charterhouse, he took his mother's remark as a challenge to prove her wrong. When the housemaster had told Diana in his presence that all her son was good for was a job in a bank, she, too—whether or not she was aware of it—must have believed on some level that to get the best out of a rebellious personality, it is advisable to taunt and belittle them.

That, anyway, is the most charitable explanation for her dismissive attitude to what was most close to his heart, for it made him determined to get the book published and make a success of it.

What he couldn't have understood at the time is that Diana's traumatic childhood and the disappointments and fears of her adult life—all firmly repressed under the veneer of a proper English lady—were starting to edge their way to the surface.

Diana's repressed trauma—when it finally showed itself—would manifest in an explosion of violence during which her most shocking and most deeply repressed impulse would burst forth, ultimately permitting a catharsis that would greatly improve the relationship between mother and son.

Diana—in a blind fury and witnessed by at least twenty people—would try, with her own two hands, to strangle her son to death.

\* \* \*

Eleena the Transport Seraph and I didn't communicate much on my return trip to Earth. I sensed she might have been tired. Regardless, I could hear her trying out her new melodies. However, she failed to bring any of them to the level of sonic brilliance for which she was now becoming recognized—or so she'd told me—by her seraphic sisters.

That was fine by me. I had a lot whirling around in my mind after this particular visit to Zandana. I welcomed the time in peace to attempt to assimilate all that I'd just learned from both the Commodore of the Andromedan vessel and from the time I'd spent with Prince Janda-chi.

I was all but certain that the Prince had been scanning me telepathically during our discussion, but that concerned me less than the meeting with the Commodore. Why had she appeared to be so keen to see me and had then spent almost the whole time we were together answering my questions? Had I underestimated her? What might I have missed? Had she accepted my ridiculous claim about Prince Caligastia's intentions? Or was she perhaps probing me to see where I stood? What if I had told her the truth; that I thought Prince Caligastia's plan might well include a complete secession from the MA's theocratic grip? Would I have learned more from her if I'd said what I truly believed?

These were the span of thoughts and questions that pressed on my mind when Eleena left me off at the Seraphic Transport Center in the Middle East. The fact that she brought me here and not to the North American Seraphic Transport Center was not lost on me. I didn't think she did this maliciously, or necessarily even on purpose. She was simply following the natural flow of events. I doubt if she had even given it any thought.

Regardless, here I was, deep in Caligastia's territory.

I knew I wasn't ready to see him just yet—I had too much to resolve in my own mind. I needed to go somewhere to clear my head, a place where Prince Caligastia or one of his minions wouldn't stumble across me. My peaceful times in Crete—in the Gorge of Samaria—came back to me. Within moments I was there again, carried almost instantaneously through the aether on the wings of my intention. I knew I would be safe there—in the fifth dimension—in a location I was familiar with and loved. This was the dimension in which I would only find other celestials, or Watchers like myself. All of us were sensitive enough to know better than to disturb me in my meditation.

So settling back against a rock—with the sun setting behind me and Venus shining as large as a dinner plate in the rarified atmosphere of the fifth dimension—I attempted to make sense of all my competing thoughts and feelings.

Caligastia was aware of my trips to Zandana, of course, and had expressed some interest early on, but that seemed to have come to a halt—he hadn't quizzed me about my last two times there. That's why I could have been sure I had never heard him speak of the fourth density. Was he even back then plotting his secession from the MA?

And if that was the Prince's basic intention—to make the world such a hellhole that the MA's official stance would be to throw up its arms in despair and leave him and the Earth alone—then, in the Prince's mind, wouldn't this justify any action concocted to appall the MA's bureaucrats?

This was heavy stuff. These were questions I'd never contemplated before—I'd never dared to think before—and the questions just kept rolling in, one leading to another. Might this have better explained the Prince's divulging the secrets of the atom and fomenting the terrible war that followed, for example, than the motive given that the whole ugly episode had been fueled simply by his intended vengeance against Vanu?

And was it the Prince's dream of secession that lay beneath his outwitting and humiliation of the Material Son and Daughter, who, as you might recall, were the pair of intraterrestrial biologists whose mission on Earth Caligastia had so effectively sabotaged within a few centuries of the pair's arrival? And what about the Prince's relentless self-promotion as God of the World? He must have known how that would have angered the MA, yet it never stopped him; it never even slowed him down. It just made him more uncompromising and remorseless in his demands for total supremacy.

Before I left for Zandana this last time, I was aware the Prince was already having some success with imposing his version of monotheism by working through his favored rebel midwayers on an increasing number of the nomadic clans in southern Palestine. I knew he'd been having considerably less success in other parts of the world with his proclamations of divinity, due mainly to the embedded interests of the local rebel midwayers. They had been playing their faux-divine roles for such a long time that even though Prince Caligastia was their superior, many of them turned against him at that point.

Astar had told me of some of the conflicts that raged between the midwayers who succumbed to Caligastia's pressure to fight for his cause and the midwayer pantheons who'd rejected the Prince's demand for absolute dominion. By all accounts, there'd been some terrible aerial battles with both sides reactivating the flying machines that were moth-balled soon after the rebellion. Astar told me one of her sisters reported that some of the most vicious and destructive of these battles occurred over the northern regions of the Indian subcontinent.

In the face of an open midwayer rebellion, the Prince had retreated back to the Middle East and redoubled his efforts to spread his doctrine of a single, angry, punitive, and jealous god. This god would be an issuer of terrifying threats who would punish the slightest deviation from his word. A god, in short, to be feared.

I think the Prince must have believed that it was only by contrasting the strict austerity of his desert monotheism with the profligate indulgence of the midwayer pantheons that he could stir up the people's self-righteous anger toward their midwayer overlords. It appeared that Caligastia was correct in this assumption, because the Semitic clans falling under his spell found themselves in almost constant conflict with their polytheistic neighbors.

If I was to survey the spiritual state of this world at the turn of the third millennium, I would have to say that—from what I have observed—it was probably in the worst condition I'd seen in the almost two hundred thousand years since the rebellion. The hostilities breaking out between different factions of rebel midwayers had forced them to reveal themselves, further terrifying populations with their destructive power.

This was an era when those rebel midwayers capable of remaining visible to human perceptions relentlessly wielded their power and influence among the rapidly expanding mortal population. It was a time in India when Krishna could tell the confused Ajuna, concerned about the massive prospective death toll in yet another battle: "Who lives? Who dies?"

It was when the conflict among the rebel midwayer factions in the Mediterranean region would become recorded by the ancient Greeks as the Battle of the Titans. The Nommo were appearing and spreading their belief system in North Africa, and the five Oannes were busy teaching the arts of civilization in Mesopotamia. Both the Sumerian and Egyptian pantheons were at their most vital in this period, imposing themselves in the lives of their people through their priest-kings.

These pantheons would maintain their hold over their populations until the droughts of the second millennium. The radically changing climatic conditions during this millennium could cause a drought that continued for as long as seventy-five years and completely dislocate a budding civilization. The most devastating drought lasted all of two hundred years. It occurred approximately 2,800 BCE and stretched across North Africa to devastate the Egyptian culture and disperse the survivors back to scratching out their living from dry desert dirt.

The terrible drought conditions stretched across the already desertified Arabian Peninsula. It affected the land all the way east to bring down the Sumerian civilization in the Land of the Two Rivers, and then even farther east to affect much of Persia and Afghanistan.

As crop fertility and the general tribal well-being was believed to be so fully in the hands of the gods, a destructive drought or a massive flood had the tendency to chip away at the credibility of their gods and goddesses. The stories that can be found on Sumerian clay tablets telling of their gods' anger and frustration at human behavior suggests the profound unease that had grown between humans and their gods. Enlil, the god of weather, simply got tired of human complaints and called down a flood, for example.

Although midwayers may have had sufficient knowledge to be able to predict when a devastating flood was imminent, they were certainly not capable of calling down—or creating—a flood to destroy people. As the clay tablets had been inscribed by the priests of the Sumerian deities, the priest-scribes would have found themselves in a theologically ambivalent position. The droughts and the floods were utterly traumatic for the people affected. They decimated the population and pushed progress back for hundreds of years. And yet it was their gods who had to be held responsible, just as it had to be human misbehavior that must have triggered their gods' disfavor. Thus the tablets had to relate the discussions held by the gods arguing for and against the destruction of humanity—as if for one moment it was actually within the midwayers' power to carry out such an atrocity, which of course, it wasn't.

The Sumerian priests' resolution to the ambiguity they faced was not original. Priests of every cult and religion have every reason to promote natural catastrophes as a punishment from the gods for human misbehavior. However, in the case of the droughts and floods, it was harder to make it stick.

If, for example, an earthquake reduced a town to rubble, the priests of the local divinities would have been better able to make a plausible case for the anger of the gods being the cause of the disaster. But a catastrophe as overwhelming and all-encompassing as a flood of such biblical proportions so as to leave only one family and their animals alive . . . evidently this needed a more thoughtful explanation. The flood story, as recorded on the Sumerian tablets, suggests that the priestly scribes were hedging their bets by introducing a conflict among the gods as to whether to destroy humanity.

Of course, this was all pure priestcraft, a way of trying to turn a natural disaster to their cult's advantage. Yet one of the possibly unintended consequences of this was to reinforce the polarization between the "good god" who argued to save the human race and the "evil god" who couldn't wait to destroy it.

I realize I'm becoming somewhat didactic here, but as my collaborator—having himself emerged from a contemporary polytheistic cult—has expressed his interest in hearing my views in this area, I've decided to continue.

Although most polytheistic cults have chosen to include a destructive deity in their pantheons, different cults handled this inclusion in different ways. Some have treated this entity as a test or a challenge to be met and overcome. Some cast the entity or entities as seducers or temptresses. Other cults have framed them in adversarial terms. In others still, they became the devil or the demons who then, not surprisingly, proceeded to bedevil the minds of their faithful followers.

As time passed I observed the more mature polytheistic

cultures—such as the Greeks some fifteen hundred years later—assigning to their deities both positive and negative aspects to their personalities. This may have more accurately reflected the conflicted human condition—itself a sign the deities were becoming progressively more humanized. And yet these same sublime divinities frequently dished out their rewards and punishments with such cavalier whimsy as to betray the total lack of concern the rebel midwayers really felt for the well-being of humanity.

There was another, perhaps more serious, dynamic at work here. The humans may have been projecting their own more complex emotions on their gods and goddesses. At the same time, the midwayer deities were, in their turn, becoming progressively more exposed to the denser and darker human emotions—emotions that midwayers were not built to handle.

Some pantheistic belief systems, on the other hand, have portrayed the negative entity as a trickster; not inherently evil, but prone to stir up trouble wherever trouble was needed. It was this archetype—more than the others—that carried with it the promise of a human to use his or her wits to challenge and outwit the trickster.

Over the millennia, the characteristics—both positive and negative—of these midwayer faux divinities could radically change. They could be worshipped in one era and reviled in the next. Set, for example, in the Egyptian pantheon, was originally the god of the desert, of storms, and of foreigners. Later he became the evil usurper when he killed and mutilated his brother Osiris. This led to the conflict that followed between Set and Horus (the son of Osiris) becoming symbolic to the Egyptians of the competing cosmic principles. The pharaohs' function was then to balance and harmonize these principles so the land might remain fertile and blessed by the gods.

However, the process of accepting the interdependence of these opposing, or competing, cosmic influences would gradually lead—over the millennia, and through its various iterations and convolutions—to a monotheistic reformation. This blossomed briefly in the fourteenth century before Christ, when the pharaoh Amenhotep IV attempted to promote Aten—a minor solar deity of his own choosing—as the Supreme God. Formerly, individual pharaohs were understood to have had their preferences, but it was always expressed as devotion for one god among many. Before Amenhotep IV never had a god-king not only promoted a single god as supreme over all other gods but also did his best to stamp out the worship of any other deity.

It happened that the pharaoh's attempt to impose Aten as the sole and Supreme Deity also ran in direct opposition to the state religion that had traditionally formed around Amun-Re. It should be no surprise, therefore, that Amenhotep's monotheism had less to do with his religious convictions. Rather it was a purely political move to wrest power away from the entrenched and immensely powerful priesthood of Amun-Re and restore it to the pharaoh, the god-king.

Regardless, the pharaoh certainly wanted to appear sincere. He even changed his name from Amenhotep to Akhenaten—meaning "the living spirit of Aten"—and began a building program at Thebes that included a new city and temples dedicated to Aten. Placing his city and the temples dedicated to Aten to the west of the Nile River also had another purpose. This was to separate his new religion from the age-old tradition of locating temples of the old religion—as were the pyramids on the Giza Plateau—on the east side of the river.

Akhenaten ruled as pharaoh, however, for a relatively short seventeen years. Had he ruled longer he might have been able to make his monotheism take hold. Yet within ten years of his death, traditional Egyptian polytheism had once again reasserted itself. The priesthood of Amun-Re worked tirelessly to try to restore itself to its previously dominant position in Egyptian life. They attempted to deface any image of Aten. Amana—the city Akhenaten built and dedicated to Aten—disappeared beneath the desert sand until rediscovered in the early nineteenth century. The god's temples were torn down and the stones used to build temples to other deities—and Aten was demoted back to being just another solar deity.

It was my observation, however, that cracks were already starting to appear in the traditional Egyptian belief system. The priesthood of

Amun-Re, for example, was never able to fully recover its previously dominating influence over the lives of the people of the Nile. Yet much to the frustration and anger of the priesthood, the spirit of Akhenaten obstinately lived on. More and more of their priestly power devolved to the god-kings, forcing an uneasy tension between future priests and the god-kings.

There are generally two signs, in my opinion, of the decline in the spiritual vigor of a belief system. Egyptian religious life after Akhenaten demonstrated both of them.

As the god-kings increasingly asserted their political power—making magnificent monuments to their grandiose self-importance—worship of the gods to the average Egyptian was becoming increasingly subordinate to the worship of the god-kings. This is the first sign, and pharaohs then used the devotion of their people to build yet more lavishly constructed temples and tombs for their own glorification, exacerbating the belief shift of the followers.

The second sign that a religion is losing its hold on the spiritual needs of its people—and that runs concurrently with the religion's progressively materialistic manifestation—is the divide that opens up between those who remain faithful to the authentic spirit (however inauthentic it actually is) of the original religion and the belief system of those in power. In the latter case, the people's religious instinct would be sure to be manipulated to serve the interests of the powerful.

Over time these two threads start to define themselves as either the exoteric, those aspects of the religion designed to manipulate the multitudes, or the esoteric, the sacred truths of the religion preserved in secrecy by a dedicated few.

There seems to be an overwhelming impulse in what I might call "human religions" for their originators to place their stamp on material reality in the form of some sort of splendid structure designed to be that much more impressive than a competing religion's building.

It has been this process of the institutionalization of religion, regardless of which religion—and its use by those in power for their own ends—that has been among those factors leading over the centuries to the cynicism and skepticism so common today.

When any relatively large group of human beings gathers together to live in a town or a city, there will invariably emerge any number of subgroups. Some of these—for a variety of different reasons—will build walls of secrecy around them.

Yet it is a curious fact to see how many secret societies that have flourished over the past two thousand years have sought to find their roots in the secrets of the Egyptian priesthood.

There are those who believe Akhenaten's monotheism represented an authentic attempt to reintroduce the religion of the One God as taught by Vanu and Amadon, but from what I observed this was not so. Some believe they can see the basis of Judaism in Akhenaten's monotheism and claim that Moses was a priest of Aten who escaped from Egypt after the death of Akhenaten. Others have painted the pharaoh Akhenaten more sentimentally as a precursor of the Christ—as a Christ who came too soon—because he liked to call himself the "Eternal Son of the Heavenly Father."

While I've no wish to be a party pooper (*Note: I couldn't stop her using this one! —TW*), there is more romanticism than truth to all these assertions. A more accurate understanding of Akhenaten can be formed from the manner in which he tricked Tushratta, a local king, out of the bride price promised by his father Amenhotep III, when his father married one of the king's daughters. The pharaoh's father had promised the king immense riches and a statue of himself and his daughter made out of solid gold. Akhenaten withheld all the riches and sent Tushratta the two statues. However, they were made of wood and merely plated in gold.

Akhenaten was not only an ambitious and competent politician, but he also understood better than most the psychological power of the religious impulse. Whether the pharaoh himself was genuinely in touch with the God of his Heart, only he would know—and I've no desire to call him in to find out. Frankly, I think—from what I observed of him, his spiritual authenticity was most unlikely—although I've no doubt he was filled with his own sense of divine privilege. He was the only one, along with his wife, Nefertiti, who was permitted to actually worship the Heavenly Father—everyone else in Egypt was expected to worship him, their god-king, the pharaoh Akhenaten.

Akhenaten was also unconventional in that he ruled with his wife, Nefertiti, beside him. There were a small number of female pharaohs in Egypt's history, but Akhenaton and Nefertiti's coregency was an unusual arrangement. It has also been pointed out—accurately I believe—that the various artistic representations of Akhenaten and his family are remarkably relaxed. As such, they avoid much of the formal stylization typical of the wall paintings and sculpture of the other pharaohs.

What I can say to clarify the nature of this enigmatic man—and you may not be altogether surprised to hear it, having read this far—is that the pharaoh Akhenaten was, of course, an incarnate rebel angel. And this "Heavenly Father" of his was none other than Prince Caligastia in yet another of his guises.

Prince Caligastia, as we're coming to learn, was not only obsessed with asserting his sole sovereignty as God of this World, but he was also more than willing to hedge his bets in his bid for total dominion. The fact that any hint of Akhenaten's monotheism had disappeared so soon after his death would have been an irritating blow for Caligastia. Yet by that time I've no doubt the Prince already had his eye on Moses.

* * *

It would be unfair of me, dear reader, if I was to leave you with the cliffhanger of Diana's astonishing attempt to throttle her son—at least without soon addressing the event in question. Of course, any event that culminates in such an intriguing and unexpected drama will be sure to have its own tangle of precedents . . . some of which will have already become obvious over the course of this narrative.

I have touched briefly on Diana's difficult childhood and something of her background: her work at MI6 for British Intelligence, her brief marriage, her business acumen, and her complex relationship with her only son, my ward.

In the summer of 1980—when Mein Host was still with Damian—Diana traveled to New York City on one of her rare trips to visit my ward. By saying the trip was rare is not meant to imply any lack of caring between mother and son. It was only that both lived busy lives on different continents, and transatlantic flights were much too costly to overindulge in. If anything, their arrangement appeared to be colored as much by their mutually thrifty nature as by any unexpressed disinclination to see one another.

The event that climaxed in the throttling occurred in two stages, the first of which young Damian was instrumental in bringing to a head. I suspect Diana and her son might have been content to let sleeping dogs lie, but Damian, with her acute sensitivity, must have picked up on the density of the suppression that underlay Diana's relationship with my ward. She therefore created a situation in which the truth could be told.

The backstory seems to be a simple one.

Ever since early childhood, Mein Host has had an irrational horror of eating raw bananas. It's irrational because he can eat dried banana chips and baked bananas with no problem, and yet never once in his life had he eaten a raw banana. It was all very curious, as Diana loved bananas! It was one of her favorite foods!

Given that a bunch of bananas sat on the table of Diana's hotel room, Damian must have felt this strange anomaly was a good place to start working out this difference. She knew of my ward's phobic reaction to raw bananas and was as baffled as he was by its irrationality.

There's little point in trying to reconstruct all of their dialogue. It's probably best to say their discussion was extremely awkward. It was heated and explosive, and yet what emerged was a key that unlocked the first of Diana's many guilty secrets. It also stripped away the primary layer of her suppressed shame. As such, it would lead directly to the event that would finally expose the truth.

On Damian's prompting, Mein Host addressed for the first time his odd and unaccountable distaste for raw bananas. He said he knew he was being silly and unreasonable, but he just couldn't do it.

"But you've always hated bananas!" Diana said. "Even when you were a baby you wouldn't eat them. I'd try to make you but you just wouldn't open your mouth."

"So even back then I didn't want to eat the things? What happened to the bananas?" Mein Host asked innocently.

"*I* ate them, of course. You didn't like them, and I didn't want to see them going to waste. It was in the middle of the war, for heaven's sake! What else could I do?"

"During the war?" Damian asked, genuinely surprised—and too young to have thought World War II would have figured into the banana issue. Then she asked, as much as anything, to diffuse the situation: "What was it like during the war? The food?"

Diana answered, "We were a little luckier than most, I suppose. I moved out of London and down to Kent after the divorce, which was . . . when? Early summer of 1941 . . . around then. Being in a country village helped a bit with the food. My sister and her family lived nearby, and Norman had an allotment down near where he worked on the coast . . ."

"Whatever's an allotment?" Damian asked.

"It's a kind of tiny veggie garden," my ward chimed in, "divided off from other allotments, all in the same place. Like one big garden but divided into separate people's sections. I don't know if people still do it in England, but certainly during the war and after it, families in small towns had these little allotments . . . you'd see 'em out of the train window. Maybe ten or twelve in a couple of rows, each neatly partitioned off with a trellis or whatever. Uncle Norman had his in Folkestone . . . it's where all those disgusting beans came from!"

"You see!" Diana pounced. "You hated beans just as much!"

Mein Host calmly replied, "That was different, Diana. I was older, four or five . . . and Norman made me eat them—or else. I had to taste those dreadful broad beans, for instance. I knew I didn't like them. I'd retch the damn things out at the table! Lotta good that did me with Uncle Norman! But bananas were something else . . ."

"But I did try to get you to eat them! I did!" Diana responded, her protest suggesting she hadn't tried very hard.

"But I was just a baby," my ward said. "Why wouldn't I have liked bananas? I like them dried, and I love those Jamaican fried bananas. Why not raw ones? Isn't that a bit weird?"

"I don't know what you're getting at . . . some babies simply don't like some things!" Diana snapped, but with a tone that wasn't as firm as she probably hoped.

"But, Diana, how did I know I didn't like them? I never tasted one! Beans I knew I loathed!" he retorted.

"Why don't you eat one then, right now, in front of your mother," Damian dared him. "If you don't know what they taste like, then go on! Try it!"

Tearing a single banana off the bunch, my ward squatted in front of where Diana sat. He cut off the top and with studied deliberation pulled down the skin in segments. He held his mother's eyes while he slowly ate the first banana of his forty-one years without showing any obvious distaste. It was this action that caused the first crack in the dam. Amid Diana's tears the guilty truth slowly emerged: she had liked bananas far too much to share them with her son.

It wasn't difficult for her to persuade herself that the baby's slight hesitance—let's give her the benefit of the doubt—permitted her to eat his bananas. And if that wasn't bad enough, the bananas were only intended for the children. They were never meant for the adults. Bananas didn't grow in England; they had to be shipped into the country at a time when U-boats were blowing the transport ships out of the water. It was because the fruit was thought to be so nutritious that bananas were reserved only for the children.

And yet there was Diana. She'd convinced herself that her baby son had some sort of instinctual dislike of bananas, and she was scarfing down his weekly quota whenever ships managed to squeeze through without being sunk. Men were dying by the thousands to deliver the food that, they might have hoped, would keep the children alive and strong enough to fight in the next war.

Whatever would impel a loving mother—and Diana was as loving a mother as she was capable of being—to do this? What could have been behind such an action?

When the high emotions had cooled off somewhat and they were able to discuss the banana issue more sensibly, it was quickly obvious that—despite her tearful confession—Diana hadn't yet fully taken in the implication of what she'd done. For that she would evidently need the actual experience of acting out the most shameful of her repressed desires.

# 12

# What Lies Beneath Our Fears

Nonviolent Resistance, Catharsis, the Basis
of Religion, the Left-Hand Path,
Yazidi Cosmology, the Peacock Angel,
and Brutal Thoughtforms

It was a couple of days after the banana business and Mein Host and Damian were taking Diana to a party given by Armand in her honor.

I've written of my ward's friend Armand before, because he was so helpful with providing the information that allowed my ward to disentangle—and finally to integrate—his multiple personalities.

As a psychotherapist, Armand had recently been treating a handful of patients suffering from serious cases of multiple personality disorder (MPD). So although my ward never went to him for treatment, he was able to pick up enough from his friend to work on the issue for himself. Besides, his case was mild compared with a full-blown case of the disorder. He'd long been aware of when he would switch personalities, and during his time in the community he had actually used it—when donating, for example—to his advantage. However, it was Armand's experience treating MPD patients that led him to understand there was always one personality—Armand called it "the angel"—who was aware of all the other personalities. He said it was in conscripting this angel's help that the integration could finally take place.

It was this advice that had taken Mein Host out onto the great rock in Bennett Park—where he'd seen the UFO—this time well after midnight for a meditation. During this meditation he was able to call forth his seven subpersonalities and ask them to tell their stories; who they were and how they came to be there.

However, on the night of Armand's party, Mein Host's integrative meditation was still a year in the future and—although my ward probably wasn't aware of it—he was still manifesting the hard, glittery surfaces of his Jesse personality.

The party for Diana wasn't a large party, composed of perhaps sixteen or eighteen people, most of whom Mein Host knew and liked. Almost all were psychotherapists—or in some way connected to the mental health profession—and Armand's gatherings were known for their unpredictable surprises.

The party was held at Armand's penthouse apartment on Lexington Avenue. When the three of them arrived, the guests were already spread out on chairs and sofas, overflowing in small groups onto the richly carpeted floor. Making sure his mother was comfortably seated with a drink—close to Damian and chatting with friends—he found himself a space on the floor next to his friend Bobby Faust. Faust, as my ward likes to call him, ended up being one of my ward's closest friends for more than thirty years, but on the night of the party they'd only known each other for less than a year.

It is important for this event to know that Robert Faust is a dwarf who'd made a name for himself in films, as well as being featured on one of the most controversial album covers of the time. He was highly intelligent, extremely widely read, had a delightful sense of humor, and had a side business that required courage, daring, and considerable ingenuity.

It was soon after my ward first met Faust that they found they both shared a lifelong interest in exploring altered states of consciousness. Both of them had separately discovered the profound value of phencyclidine at a time when the substance—quite unreasonably they agreed—was being so maligned in the press. Even confirmed psychonauts had been put off by the stories being spread about the substance, so he and Faust regarded themselves as fortunate to have found one another. There was another person in their entheogenic triumvirate who will feature in other anecdotes, but he wasn't present at the party.

It was a gathering of close friends who all knew each other and had similar interests. Because of this, Faust and my ward rolled up a couple of joints of mint leaf with phencyclidine. Making sure everyone knew to take at the most three hits and to stop when they heard the angels singing, they passed the joints around and continued chatting. It was all quite casual, with most people taking their tokes and a few simply passing the joint along without smoking it. Diana, who was never a tobacco smoker, took a couple of cautious tokes when the joint came around to her, which turned out to be all she needed.

One of the effects of phencyclidine I have observed—that can be so valuable if it's not overdone—is that it can give a person a deep sense of confidence in themselves. However, it will also bring out what has been repressed in the personality. While this is obviously of enormous value to anyone authentically seeking to know themselves, it's equally obvious why it would not be a good idea to have people totally unaware of this effect running around with an ax in hand, releasing their repressed violence.

At some point in their conversation Faust announced—and not for the first time—that he was a reincarnation of Mahatma Gandhi. This was familiar territory for my ward—as they'd frequently discussed reincarnation together—but this evening he clearly wanted to push Faust to the limit. He said afterward that although he'd heard his friend's claim before, for some reason he felt like testing it this time.

He knew Faust had been a student at the University of Buffalo during the student unrest of the late sixties. Being a small person, his courage in facing the police batons had been an inspiration to other students. He was well-known for his bravery—there was never any question about that.

Faust was talking about nonviolent resistance, how effective it was, and how he'd never respond to violence with violence.

"Let me get this straight," said my ward. "You don't believe in any violence, even defending yourself, right?"

"Perhaps if someone tried to hurt Boogie (Faust's pure white German shepherd), and if nothing else worked . . . then, perhaps I would . . . only if Boogie couldn't defend himself."

"But if somebody hit you, Faust. What you're saying is that you'd never respond with violence, even if you felt like it?" my ward asked.

"No!" Faust responded with supreme confidence. "Never!"

He was standing now and drawing himself up to his full height. This put him on eye level with Mein Host, who was sitting on the floor, his back straight, in a semi-lotus position.

"Easy to say, Faust. Who's going to hit a dwarf?!" my ward retorted. It was a cruel thing to say and was clearly a deliberate provocation to get his friend angry.

Faust's reply: "Fuck you, man! 'Course I've been smacked around. You try growing up a dwarf! And to answer your question: No, I wouldn't. I was Gandhi. I totally believe in passive resistance."

What occurred next happened very quickly, and yet Mein Host said afterward that the dust seemed to slow down the whole action in the strangest way.

Mein Host, completely unexpectedly, uncoiled his right arm and hand like a snake and slapped his friend Faust hard on the left side of his face. The smack reverberated like a gunshot in the immediate silence, and every head turned toward them.

Yet it was only an instant later that they were watching Diana, who'd been sitting about eight or ten feet away from my ward, launch herself into the air in a long, curving dive over an intervening coffee table and straight for her son. Mein Host said afterward that he could see his mother coming at him mid-dive out of the corner of his eye and that she seemed to him to be horizontal, as though hanging in the air.

It would have been an extraordinary feat of gymnastic power and grace for an Olympian athlete. Yet to observe this seventy-year-old English lady hurling herself through the air and then landing so elegantly on top of her son with her hands so cleverly grasped around his throat—this could only have been in the realm of Hollywood special effects.

Mein Host allowed himself to fall backward from his sitting position so as to effectively cushion the impact of his mother's momentum. He then spread both his arms out to the side on the floor in a position of complete submission as his mother's fingers were tightening their pressure on his throat.

"Go on and do it!" he said quietly, looking deep into his mother's furious dark eyes. "Go on, Mother! It's what you've always wanted to do. Go on, do it! Do it!"

The pressure increased, and for one moment it appeared that she *was* going to do it. But then, he later said, his mother's fingers started to relax when she must have realized what she was doing. By that time a couple of the men were peeling her off her son and helping her up and back to her chair.

My ward straightened back up and he and Faust shook hands and hugged, laughing together as all the conversations in the room started up again and everything returned to normal—as if a little old lady had never thrown herself across half a room in an attempt to strangle her son.

It was just another party at Armand's.

Let me say in advance that as unconventional as this piece of psychodrama was, it turned out to be most effective in transforming the relationship between mother and son. There would be other family secrets to be spilled as time went along, yet nothing would be as shameful as Diana's repressed desire to kill her son. The catharsis they experienced in those moments of intense eye contact—when Diana's hands were tightening on his throat—allowed each to see the other clearly and with compassion.

Diana, as I've previously noted, shared a number of the qualities attributed to the Greek goddess Diana. She was certainly a fierce huntress, a trait that served her well in her business life. She was also emotionally damaged in a way like so many people affected, directly or indirectly, by war. The suicide of her beloved father—a World War I victim of shell shock (PTSD these days)—when she was just thirteen years old was her first betrayal by a man. Her husband's infidelity at the most sensitive of times, when she had a small baby and a war raged all around them, was her second confirmation of the worthless unreliability of men. There were, I'm sure, more stabs in the back. No doubt there were also small personal betrayals over the course of her everyday life that were less significant—accumulatively damaging all the same.

Diana would find it hard to accept that depriving her baby son of bananas was tantamount to starving the child. But of course it was. It was a manifestation of her unconscious desire to rid herself of the image of the male betrayer. She subsequently had a number of lovers over the course of her long life, and—despite considerable pressure from the men in question—she never remarried, always preferring her own independence.

In light of this it wasn't surprising to hear her say that what made her leap was seeing her son hit a small person. In her mind she was protecting Bobby Faust from him—and bless her for that, the protectress of small things.

Yet when I consider this situation in retrospect, I can only once more give credit to the elegant coordination on the part of the companion angels of all those present. Can you think of a safer environment for such a violent catharsis than a room full of savvy psychotherapists? Or the elegance with which Damian was able to help strip away that first layer of Diana's repressed shame?

The incident at Armand's party was one of the single most significant events in Diana's and my ward's life as mother and son. There was more to go, of course, but now there was no way back.

And Mein Host? What of him?

He has said that even while he was striking his friend he was aware it was really about something far deeper. He didn't understand what it was, only that the dust had allowed both men to know it was nothing personal. Faust hadn't made any move to respond with violence in those moments immediately after the slap—and before Diana cast herself into the air—thus proving his point about his nonviolent response.

Now that Mein Host was free from the constraints of the community, we will meet Diana more frequently as she plays a more active part in his life. Her business would continue to prosper and expand, allowing her the financial freedom to travel more widely.

Mother and son would continue to live on different continents, but there would be more transatlantic visits—as well as an intriguing arrangement they made between them to meet for a week every few years for an adventure in different and interesting parts of the world.

* * *

Some readers might question whether my inclination to focus on religion as much as I do in this narrative is simply a consequence of my angelic nature. I am sure there is some truth in this but it's only a lesser aspect of a far deeper issue that gets overlooked in the modern age. When the power of the religious impulse in humans is ignored, or denigrated, religion will tend to rear its head in its most extreme form. Thus a situation emerges in which the actions of an Islamic suicide bomber, or a Buddhist self-immolator, or a Christian fundamentalist who shoots up an abortion clinic become difficult to comprehend rationally, and the people can be dismissed as manipulated dupes or sociopaths.

The view of many contemporary atheists that religion is the cause of most of the violence throughout human history may well be true, but it totally misses the point if their only solution is to rid the world of religion. I know I'm not the first to make this observation, but the problem isn't religion itself—it's the manner in which it is promoted and practiced. The more modern atheist nations of Soviet Russia and Communist China are perfect examples of countries that tried to get rid of religion as a solution to curbing violence among humans that simply didn't work.

Like it or not, religion is here to stay, and I don't say this with any moralistic attitude. Religion is here to stay because human beings are spiritually endowed with worship circuits. These spiritual circuits—of which the worship circuit is but one—are embedded in a mortal's subtle energy body. They are as real in their own realm as the sympathetic nervous system is in the physical body.

However, worship can take many different forms. It's the worship circuit that can become activated, for example, when a human being gazes up at the stars at the magnificence of the universe—just as much as the miser counting his coins is also worshipping in his own way. The gods and goddesses of ancient Greece were openly worshipped in temples dedicated to them, and yet the celebrity culture that dominates the modern popular mind will be feeding off the same worship circuits. The difference between these two civilizations also demonstrates a profoundly changed psychological view of the object of worship. The Greeks, for better or worse, accepted the fact that their divinities had their faults and were worshipped as much to avoid their anger as to obtain their favor. However, the contemporary worshipper of a celebrity will generally reject the celebrity when he or she is exposed as having feet of clay.

When human beings die to the flesh, it becomes self-evidently obvious to them that they are spiritual beings who merely don physical vehicles for their lifetime as mortals. It is at this point that all arguments that promote human supremacy in a godless universe have to dissolve in the face of the unimaginable grandeur of the inner worlds.

The religion that was originally brought by the Prince's staff placed its emphasis on two main spiritual insights. The first was that they counseled mortals to worship the invisible Father Creator in a temple dedicated to him. The second was that they taught that all human beings of sound mind were indwelt by a fragment of this same Creator God. This second "admonition" was rendered more complex, for no member of the Prince's staff—as is also true for us angels—possessed this Indwelling Creator fragment. It is this that makes mortals so particularly special to those who serve the mortal ascension program.

Most human religions accept that mortals possess an eternal soul, even if there's little agreement on what the eternal soul actually is. A great deal rarer are those religions that teach that humans are indwelt by a Divine Spark, because it's evidently far easier for priests to locate what is to be worshipped outside the self.

In general, this pre-personal fragment of the Creator—the Atman in Hinduism comes closest to describing the Divine Spark—plays a backseat role in the choices and decisions a human being makes over the course of this lifetime. Yet it will be this Atman who will be accompanying him or her throughout their many lives. It will come to play a progressively more vital role in one's life as the soul ascends up through the levels to don the appropriate vehicle that will allow the soul to fully interact with that reality—the frequency domain—in which that soul finds itself.

It was this ascension of the soul that Prince Caligastia was trying—without great success—to short-circuit with his Reincarnation Express. One of the consequences of the Prince's meddling with the ascension program was a gradual increase in the number of rebel angels the MA's authorities in Jerusem were substituting for the ascending mortals.

While this may sound as if the MA was playing straight into Prince Caligastia's hands, it seldom turned out that way. As these were the angels who had once rebelled against the MA's rigid theocracy, they didn't take easily to the Prince's bullying ways. Granted some were swept up into one of Caligastia's cults. Yet for others—driven by a desire to know themselves—it became a consuming desire to explore what was forbidden by the strictures of theocratic monotheism. In this you can see one of the origins of what has come to be known as the "Left-Hand Path."

Throughout history there have always been a few freethinkers—even if many of them came to sticky ends. However, with the arrival of progressively more rebel angel incarnates during those three thousand years before the birth of Christ, a number of other alternative spiritual paths opened up. Over time these would manifest as religions and cults as diverse as Zoroastrianism, Mithraism, and, more interestingly from my point of view, Yazidism.

The Yazidi are known now as a Kurdish ethnoreligious group with Indo-Iranian roots, but their actual roots go deep into the past with the arrival of those early rebel angel incarnates. Perhaps the Yazidi are best known—to the extent this highly secretive group is known—as being most misunderstood as "devil worshippers." This was due largely to later Islamic propaganda over key differences in their belief systems. And it's just these differences that reflect the influence of those early rebel angel incarnates.

My collaborator's research finds the following reason given for this misunderstanding in the *Encyclopedia of the Orient:* "The reason for the Yazidis' reputation for being devil worshippers is connected to the other name of Melek Taus—Shaytan—the name the Koran has for Satan."

The Yazidis have always been confirmed monotheists. They were able to sustain this belief in the One Creator God at a time when the rebel midwayers were proclaiming their own divinity throughout the Middle East. The Yazidi say that the Creator entrusted the care of this world to seven Holy Angels, of whom Melek Taus—the "Peacock Angel"—is the most important. While this belief is not entirely accurate, their reference to the Seven Master Spirits—that we were taught in our seminars on Jerusem were assigned to care for this world—was a profound cosmological insight.

Yazidism is so ancient—with its origins long preceding Zoroastriansim—that later emergent religions both absorbed and assimilated some key Yazidi beliefs, while also defining themselves by opposing other beliefs. It was Melek Taus, for example, much revered by Yazidis, who became the Satan of Islam and Christianity.

Why should this be so?

Islamic belief claims Shaytan refused God's command to bow down before Adam, and by his prideful failure to do so he was condemned to hell. The Yazidi believe that Melek Taus, as a direct emanation of God's illumination, was originally ordered by God not to bow down before any other beings. Thus the command to bow before Adam was in actuality a test, which Melek Taus passed with flying colors.

Yazidi give no credence to any transcendent "evil being" and wisely attribute the origin of "evil" to the thoughts and acts of human beings. They reject any idea that Melek Taus was actually a fallen angel and revere him as the leader of the seven archangels.

Angels in Yazidi cosmology are regarded as existentially real, and, most tellingly, their seven Holy Angels are believed to reincarnate periodically as human beings. Their emphasis on spiritual purity; their rejection of hell as a reality; their belief in reincarnation for mortals; and their knowledge of the soul's journey after death—all these are clues that the Yazidi belief system finds its origins in the influx of rebel angel incarnates in that area of the world during the three millennia before Christ.

I was intrigued to see that Prince Caligastia tended to leave the Yazidi to themselves when he could have so easily assumed the identity of Melek Taus—chief of the archangels—and manipulate the Yazidis in the same manner by which he was impressing his own monotheism on the Semitic tribes in Palestine. I attributed this at the time to the firmness of the Yazidi faith in the One God—formed from direct personal experience of the god who indwelt them.

Mein Host informs me that—in his opinion—it is only through the direct personal experience of the Indwelling God that a mortal can know the deep truth of monotheism. He says this is one of the most astonishing revelations to emerge from a direct experience of God—that the Creator of the Multiverse is a single being. Regardless of whether different monotheistic religions may believe the Creator is composed of a Trinity, the essential revelation is the absolute singularity of the Creator.

My ward says this is such a mind-blowing revelation—that the entire Multiverse is the creation of a single being—that after having a personal experience of God it is utterly inconceivable to think otherwise. The Muslims, he tells me, have it right when they claim: "There is no God but God."

Yazidism put down its roots in the mountains of Iran about a thousand years before the Vedas appeared in North India in the mid-second millennium. This makes Yazidism the most ancient religion still to be actively practiced. However, being as old as that has seen a number of Yazidi religious beliefs appearing in later religions. In this way, some modern scholars claim erroneously it is Yazidism that is syncretic in blending elements of Mithraism, Zoroastrianism, and pre-Islamic religious traditions from the Land of the Two Rivers—and even some elements found in Christianity and Islam. Yet this is a modern conceit as it is clearly the other way around. The later religions were obviously the ones that borrowed from the Yazidi original. By adapting or reacting against some of the Yazidi key concepts, the later religions defined the limits of their beliefs. Much later we'll find a number of Yazidi beliefs appearing among the Gnostics of the second and third centuries after Christ. Later still—in the twelfth century—the Adawiyya Sufi Order living in the Kurdish mountains were so profoundly influenced by the Yazidi belief system that the order could no longer be considered to be following the norms and traditions of Islam.

I've had to greatly simplify the Yazidi cosmology here, but it was the central elements to their cosmology that I found to be of most relevance to the point I'm making.

There are other telling elements, too, in the Yazidi belief system that ring true to my Watcher ears. The knowledge that good and evil exist solely in the mind—and represent a constant decision to choose good over evil—is a profound psychological and spiritual insight. This can be seen as the root of self-responsibility because there's no transcendent evil entity to conveniently blame for the sins of the world.

Then there is the Yazidi belief in their direct descent from Adam, which suggests that they have a genetic relationship with the infusion of violet blood. Their strict religious laws regarding endogamy would have ensured that whatever violet blood resulted from their Adamic infusion would stay within the limits of the Yazidi community. All this makes the Yazidi the keepers of the first revelation on this world to be brought forth by rebel angel incarnates.

I should add for the record that the Yazidi community has had an appalling time over the previous century. Many of the Kurdish villages destroyed by Saddam Hussein, for example—their inhabitants gassed and their houses reduced to rubble—were people of the Yazidi faith.

The Syrian conflict, shown nightly on the news, has so badly affected the Yazidi living in the country that it has forced thousands of survivors to flee to Turkey. All the while, Turkey itself is currently carrying out a military campaign against the Kurds—many of whom are Yazidi—who are demanding their own autonomy.

At this point there are probably far more Yazidi living in Europe and other countries than there are still living in their traditional mountainous locale.

It is my fondest hope that the senior Yazidi Sheikhs and Pirs will decide—at some point before too long—to share more broadly the valuable insights of their religion, knowing that such a decision would be a choice for the good of all and not merely what is good for the Yazidi.

I imagine the window of opportunity for this decision—if it ever were made—is unlikely to remain open for long, as progressively more Yazidi become assimilated into contemporary Western secular life. If the Yazidi elders realized—and I can only hope they do—that one of the deepest currents running through Western society in the twenty-first century is the drive for transparency and openness, they might possibly become more yielding with their secrets.

It is a time in which the sacred secrets of the religions and mystery schools—as well as the corruption baked into so many aspects of human activity—are rising to the surface for expression and inspection.

Yet when a religion has survived intact in the face of almost constant hostility for more than five thousand years—mostly by keeping its own counsel—I am not, as my ward might say, exactly holding my breath for this to occur.

\* \* \*

The four years that my ward lived with Melinda would turn out to be seminal for much that lay ahead of him. They were years of experimentation and exploration of both the inner and outer worlds. Having learned how to make close and reliable contact with his companion angels, he filled Black Book after Black Book—his 11 × 14-inch hard-back journals with black covers—with the communications he was having with his angels. My collaborator tells me he was rather amused to discover in his research that one of the Yazidi holy books, the Mishefa Res, translates as "the Black Book."

Naturally I observed his progress with a growing sense of excitement and the feeling that my time of working with my ward was drawing ever closer. However, he still had much to learn and experience before he could become clear enough to devote himself to this work.

When a mortal starts working consciously with her or his companion angels, perhaps the most important and necessary elements required are reliability, personal honesty, humility, the courage to face the worst in one's self, trustworthiness, patience, and an intense desire to know the truth. In fact, they are many of the same qualities you would hope for in a spouse, a close friend, or a lover.

However, these qualities remain unknown until they are tested. Then, as my ward says, "You know who your friends are." It is the same with angels. We have no more desire to waste our time with an unreliable mortal than you would wish to continue a friendship with someone who is boastful, cynical, and untrustworthy.

This is one of the reasons that so much inner work is required to clear out all the psychic and emotional debris that a human being accumulates over the course of a lifetime. This takes some explaining for those not yet aware of thoughtforms and how they differ from spiritual entities.

Human beings, like all mortals, are by nature creative beings. They can't help it. They create all the time—whether or not they know it. Simply thinking a thought is in itself an act of creation.

Beneath their level of conscious awareness, humans—like all animate creatures—are co-creating the world they perceive around them. In a modest way, the physiology of sight will illustrate this. The photons bouncing off objects in the environment are converted into electro-chemical impulses that the brain then reinterprets as a coherent external reality. Setting aside any problem with the eye itself, it is in the brain's reinterpretation of the impulses that this deeper level of creativity can be observed.

My ward's art partner, June Atkin, tells a story that illustrates this well. Her husband had an accident some years ago in their apartment in which one of his arterial veins was pierced. This resulted in a stream of blood arcing out across the room. June, who says she was right there with a sheet and trying to help, turned out to have been unable to see this stream of blood pumping across the room. In her intense focus on helping, her brain had simply edited out the jet of blood and all that was irrelevant to the immediate task. Psychologists have called this "inattentional blindness." Yet by focusing on the blindness, the brain's creativity can tend to be devalued.

This innate creativity becomes clearer still in dreams when the brain changes its electrochemical state, directing its focus inward, to manufacture autonomously entire landscapes and coherent narratives.

Because human beings are inherently creative it's in the kingdom of thought that the forms are first initiated. When a thought is given utterance, it can truly be said that "the word builds"—as the word has no choice but to create its impact on the environment in which it was spoken. It might be a word of wisdom imparted at exactly the right time, a word that precipitates a war, or it could be the word that "breaks the camel's back"—or it could be a word of love.

If I'm stating the obvious, it's because the concept of thoughts taking form within the astral occurs in much the same way. What makes the difference between a thought that merely comes and goes and an intensely emotional thought—or an obsessionally driven thought pattern—is that the latter can assume a form in the planet's astral plane. These are thoughtforms, and they are generated and sustained by the projected energy of mortals. It might be someone's silent fury with their boss that is feeding the anger thoughtform, just as it will be the loving thoughts of a mother that fortifies the maternal thoughtform.

Powerfully emotional thoughts of love, hatred, envy, jealousy, compassion, or anger, for example, will create—or contribute to— preexisting thoughtforms already in the astral plane. It will be these negative thoughtforms that can appear as the demons bedeviling the inner worlds of the guilty or the mentally unbalanced. This has been the case with the appearance of Mother Mary over recent years, which has been an astral thoughtform of the Holy Mother Spirit materialized by the people and the intensity of the love directed at her.

I wrote earlier—quoting one of the angels in Gitta Mallasz's book—that the word builds. If an angry thought is then expressed in angry words, it compounds and solidifies the thought. As an architect might design a house in his mind and then externalize his design into material reality, so also can focused thought affect another person's mental state. This occurs on an ongoing basis. Most human beings learn automatically over the course of their childhood and adolescence to tune out the mental cacophony. It is fortunate that so few people are capable of concentrating and focusing mental energy in the manner, for example, of some Australian Aboriginal shamans who have been known to kill at a distance by "pointing the bone."

It's been shown that a sensitive clairvoyant witnessing a violent verbal row between two people is often able to perceive clairvoyantly that sharp objects—knives and daggers—are flying back and forth, embedding themselves in the subtle energy bodies of the antagonists. These astral daggers are examples of fear-impacted thoughtforms. And unless these thoughtforms are released they will lodge, generally in the emotional body. Then, over the years, they can develop into a physical disease or mental imbalance.

And herein, of course, lies the rub.

The simple process of growing from a child to an adult means that every human being is carrying around with them an entire host of these fear-impacted thoughtforms. It might have been a teacher who hurled a hurtful insult across a classroom, the vicious remark of a belittling uncle, or perhaps the envy of a peer or the spiteful fury of a rival. But they are all there, stuck in the subtle energy bodies, creating a psychic and emotional armor around the personality. This armoring can be thought of as an unconscious attempt by the individual to protect the tender inner self from any similar abuse.

It is generally this psychic armoring that produces a distancing effect—keeping people at arm's length. Unless this is tended to—and the thoughtforms released—it will sooner or later appear in one of the largely unacknowledged serious personality disorders of the modern age, what the eminent Scottish psychiatrist R. D. Laing named the "divided self."

This is a condition in which what a person manifests on the outside—in their dealings with other people—is at odds with what they are really feeling on the inside. What starts as hypocrisy can easily become internalized as the dissembler seeks to convince herself or himself of their own lies. It is this that can feel as though a permanent battle is being fought in the psyche of the individual. Again, if this condition isn't recognized and dealt with, it is more than likely to develop into some form of cancer or mental breakdown.

Cancer, viewed in this light, can be thought of as the body at war with itself—aggressively consuming itself. This is true whether cancer develops environmentally or in some other manner. Either way, it will be the body attempting to take itself out of circulation.

The mental breakdown that often dwells at the end of the divided self can manifest as a complaint as common as a midlife crisis, all the way through to an imbalance as serious as a full-blown schizophrenic episode.

Needless to say, the implications and the effects of the divided self as a destructive social phenomenon is unlikely to generate much intellectual currency among social scientists. This is because the consumer milieu continues to benefit from the hard currency lifted from the pockets of an impressionable, insecure, and compliant public. If that selfsame public goes on buying the lies of merchandizing wizards, hypnotized into believing they'll feel fundamentally better with a bigger car or smarter clothes, there's unlikely to be an end to this sadly corrupt and corrupting practice.

Thoughtforms can be both personal or impersonal, though the line between the two states is easily blurred.

Ultimately all thoughtforms are manufactured in the human creative imagination. A thoughtform like anger will have existed in the astral regions as a quasi-life-form being fed energy for as long as humans have been angry. These meta-thoughtforms possess a primitive urge attracting them to their own kin—and this is where things can become confusing.

It's worth reiterating that thoughtforms are not spiritual entities. They are not angels or guiding spirits. They are not neuroses (though they may appear in that form). They are not hallucinations, nor are they tricks of light—though they may frequently be dismissed as such.

Thoughtforms under normal circumstances are generally experienced rather than perceived. My ward once had a direct experience of this with the thoughtform of jealousy in which this became all too clear.

I have observed over the course of his current life that Mein Host is not normally subject to jealousy. He has shared girlfriends—as he had with Damian and William—more than once, with no sense of possessiveness clouding his emotional body. Rather the opposite.

Yet there was one particular girlfriend who set out to deliberately make him jealous in a manipulative attempt to revive a relationship with him. By seductively flaunting herself—and then outrageously flirting with one of his friends in front of him—she did manage to stir up some jealousy in him. He said afterward that because he'd never really felt jealous before it was an unpleasant surprise, but by no means was it overwhelming. He said he could see what she was up to and was determined to not be affected by it.

However, about a day later—and with the situation still unresolved—he said he suddenly felt his jealously unaccountably increasing until it almost overpowered him. This continued for three days of emotional torture. It was only by finally consulting Joy—one of his companion angels—that he learned he'd been joined by the meta-thoughtform of jealousy. The knowledge that it was merely a mental phenomenon encouraged him to use his spiritual intelligence to project love into the situation. When he did so, to his relief, the thoughtform evaporated. It was from this painful situation that he learned he could dissolve any demonic manifestation with a beam of love from his heart chakra.

There are certain metaphysicians who have made a study of thoughtforms. Carl Jung's writing on archetypes can also be understood as referring to archetypes as creations of human mentation. According to my ward, the metaphysician and occultist C. W. Leadbeater's 1901 book *Thought Forms*—written together with Annie Besant—is one of the best primers on the nature of these thoughtforms.

Most indigenous shamans are aware of thoughtforms, generally naming them demons. In fact, much of a shaman's healing work is concerned with the removal of these demonic thoughtforms. As fear-impacted thoughtforms are given no credence in modern psychiatry, they become suppressed in patients beneath the soul-deadening weight of medications like antidepressants and antipsychotics. There won't be any significant changes while such medications offer what appear to be effective short-term solutions to a seriously overwhelmed health care profession.

Mein Host, as should be clear by now, had an extremely challenging childhood and adolescence. He had accumulated a number of these fear-impacted thoughtforms, each of which needed to be located and identified. These are what consumed him for the two years it took to make reliable contact with Joy. And of course, the contact didn't stop then. Their discussions became a constant process, developing over the next decade.

Joy shared with him a series of simple meditations that turned out to be so effective that my ward later codified them. With the help of his two other authors, they included it in their 1992 book, *Ask Your Angels,* under the working title of the G.R.A.C.E. Process.

Joy emphasized that the process needed to start off with a Grounding meditation. She advised visualizing roots sent down from the base chakra deep into Mother Earth to stabilize the psyche. Having completed that, one should use the inner eye to survey the subtle energy bodies for the troubling thoughtform. Once located, she recommended examining it for color and form. The more clearly the thoughtform is visualized, the more effective the process when it comes to moving it into the heart chakra. There it can be dialogued within the security of a loving heart. What most often emerges is the thoughtform itself believed it was serving the person.

The most virulent thoughtforms frequently attach themselves during childhood, a time when someone is the most vulnerable to the heavy-handed influence of others. By adulthood many of these thoughtforms have outlived their usefulness. Joy counseled treating these fear-impacted thoughtforms with kindness and respect and to express appreciation for their devoted service.

Thoughtforms are not complex entities. They are usually capable of being only what they were created for. And yet in lodging in the auric body, they can either become protective of the individual they've chosen to attach themselves to or they can become further exacerbated by a similar situation later. Those unfortunate warriors who have suffered from post-traumatic stress disorder will be familiar with the automobile's backfire that instantaneously invokes the crack of rifle fire and broken, bloodied bodies. This projects the warrior right back into the action. That reaction is the fear-impacted thoughtform jolting awake.

Thoughtforms—however horrifying and overwhelming as they might seem while being experienced in the moment—are simple entities. They are not hard to persuade to leave when the hosts realize their original functions, whatever they were, have long since been fulfilled.

We have seen that the first element of the G.R.A.C.E Process is Grounding. The next element is Releasing, followed by Aligning, Conversing, and Enjoying the connection.

The Release element is what concerns us here. At this stage, the thoughtform, with its agreement, could be directed by intention and—with the cooperation of the companion angels—could be released. She recommended using the breath while toning the thoughtform, down through the roots, to be returned again to Mother Earth.

Joy liked to say that Mother Earth enjoyed reprocessing the thoughtforms, joking that the fragile things were completely biodegradable!

Let me relate an incident from my ward's life that illustrates this particular psychic dynamic at work. And for this I've needed to ask John C. Lilly for his blessing to recount what I observed of this situation. His reply was much the same as when my ward asked his permission—while the good doctor was still in the flesh—to include in a book one of the ketamine sessions they had shared together.

Dr. Lilly replied to me as brusquely as when he was alive: "Write whatever you want."

The event in question occurred at a small seminar held in Key West in the late 1980s in which John C. Lilly, Michael Hyson, and a couple of other notables addressed the issue of dolphin intelligence.

My ward had come to know Dr. Lilly fairly well by now, as they shared an interest in both cetaceans and ketamine. They'd also met a number of times when both were speaking at dolphin and whale conferences.

Dr. Lilly had already read my ward's first book, *Dolphins ET's & Angels*—twice he said—before they ever met one another in 1985. He expressed his appreciation of the book in the following sparkling endorsement: "It's a great book," he had written, "a marvelous book, very creative. It's fun to read. If a bigot reads it, he'll get more bigoted. If a free man reads it, he'll get freer. I recommend this book highly."

My ward was a first-time writer, and I'm sure you can imagine how thrilled he was to have received that accolade from a man he so respected for the pioneering work he had done in his lifetime, and the courageous positions he'd taken. This was serious scientist at the top of his field who, like my ward, had a direct personal encounter with the angels. He had camouflaged his encounters—not naming his communicants "angels"—when writing about the interchanges in his 1978 book *The Scientist: A Novel Autobiography*. In person, however, he was more open to admitting they were angels.

As mentioned, both he and Dr. Lilly shared an interest in ketamine. Yet at some point earlier Lilly had become involved in serious research of cocaine. He had become entranced by her, and then finally became addicted and ravaged by the tentacular charms of the White Lady. At the time of the seminar, Lilly's macabre dance with cocaine had clearly become self-destructive. People close to him were beginning to become concerned about his increasingly erratic behavior.

However, there was another element that worried Mein Host as much as Lilly's deteriorating health. People were aware of the doctor's ketamine use, given that he'd written about it, but almost no one knew of his addiction to cocaine. The word going around was that his decline was due to the excessive use of ketamine. Although that substance may have played a small part, it was in fact his freebasing and his use of cocaine by injection that was really at fault.

I heard Mein Host saying to his friend Carolina that he thought it was giving ketamine an undeserved reputation.

"K may have its issues," he was saying, "but it's not physically destructive like coke. Also, it's not addictive like coke is. Even after a binge I've never had a problem with stopping. I'm sure it's the coke that's fucking him up . . . not the K."

Carolina had known John Lilly since the 1960s and had been an occasional companion of his. Thus she was one of the few people who was aware of and desperately concerned about John's deteriorating condition.

"Something has to be done," she said, "or we'll lose him."

"Maybe he has an entity attachment that's causing the problem. I don't know if it'll work, but we could try to release it . . . like the angels showed us. You think he'll go for it?" Mein Host asked.

"Let me talk to him first," Carolina said after a pause. "I don't see why he wouldn't give it a chance. I know he really wants to get rid of it."

So it was that in one of the breaks in the seminar, John Lilly—accompanied by Carolina, my ward, and a couple of others who were closest to him—found a quiet room in the rear of the house. My ward made sure John was lying comfortably on the couch, and they all prepared themselves for what was to come.

After holding a brief meditation they passed the pipe around, and my ward explained the basis of the releasing process. He said afterward that John must have been so easy to work with because of his familiarity with shamanism and altered states of consciousness.

The process quickly revealed that John had been joined sometime back by a discarnate entity, a dead cocaine addict who called himself "Cokey Joe." Cokey Joe had been lodged in John's emotional body and had been moving steadily down into the denser vibration of his physical body. This is what had been causing John's physical decline.

The problem soon became obvious. Cokey Joe refused to leave. He was quite happy with John soaking up all that coke. There was no cocaine where Joe was, and he was getting high vicariously by embedding himself in John's subtle energy system.

Cokey Joe was adamant. Speaking through John, he said he was onto a good thing and wasn't about to leave. No, sir! Not when John was hosing it up by the ounce.

It was then, as my ward said later, that he remembered an account he'd heard from a friend who'd been part of a circle in Australia that made it their job to release those souls trapped in the astral and help them move along after their death. She'd said she had particular difficulties with a man so bowed down with grief, terror, and self-loathing that he resolutely refused to move toward the light. He'd been frightened and mistrustful of every suggestion until it emerged that his only friend had been a white horse he'd known and had felt loved by when he was a child.

My ward's friend said she'd then manifested a beautiful white astral horse (a thoughtform, of course) who'd then led the poor man into the light.

"Cokey Joe," Mein Host said, addressing John's reclining form. "I sure know what you mean about coke. Ain't it the greatest thing?! Never get enough myself . . . I just wish I could get high all the time. I tell you, Cokey, I'd never stop doin' it."

This evoked some grunts of surprised appreciation from old Cokey Joe, who was not the smartest guy in the world.

My ward continued, "It must be a real drag when the doc can't get any dope!"

"Fuckin' right it is!" Cokey Joe responded, his tone turning quickly resentful. "Fuckin' hell it is! Horrible, whatever I fuckin' do to kick his ass, nothing . . . like he doesn't care for me anymore . . ."

At that my ward pounced. "So, Cokey Joe! Sounds like you ain't never heard 'bout the beach."

"Heard 'bout the beach?" queried Joe.

"Yeah, 'bout the beach. They call it the Beach of the White Lady . . . surprised you never come across it. 'Stead of sand, it's all cocaine, far as the eye can see, deep as far as you can dig. You really never heard of it?"

That, of course, grabbed Cokey Joe's greedy attention. From then on it wasn't a case of persuading Joe to leave John—he couldn't wait to get out and dive into all that delicious cocaine. And that is precisely what old Cokey Joe did. He went off to find the beach, which was conjured up by my ward's vivid and tempting visualized description—most of which I've left out here for brevity's sake. By all accounts, Cokey Joe never jumped back into John again.

John C. Lilly, one of the most brilliant minds of the twentieth century, lived another fourteen years and died in 2001 at the venerable age of eighty-seven, surrounded by his friends.

As my ward said after hearing of John's death, and knowing of his long use—some would say misuse—of ketamine, it gave them all a whole lot of leeway.

"No one," he said, "was ever likely to do as much K as old Doctor John, and it didn't harm him in the end! The guy was lucid and brilliant until the day he died."

Mein Host went on to explore for himself the alternate states that were accessible by ketamine. He was grateful for—and guided by—John's pioneering and meticulous research into the effects of the substance and was therefore able to use it wisely enough to avoid the most serious of its pitfalls.

Ketamine, he would agree—of all the entheogens he'd experienced—had proved the most valuable at allowing him to probe beneath consensus human reality to gain some experiential knowledge of the workings of the Multiverse. In addition to this, I believe there are two resolutions he made when he began working with ketamine that have allowed him to navigate the shoals without endangering himself.

The first decision he made was to avoid chasing after the substance and instead to allow it to come to him. That way, he liked to say, he would always know when to do it. The second was to cross-check—as much as possible—what was revealed to him in an altered state of consciousness with what was already known in consensus reality.

When he felt the dolphins in Clearwater Bay indicated they'd performed a small surgical procedure on him using focused sound, he'd talked to both an acoustic engineer and a surgeon as to how this might have worked. Both experts agreed in principle that it should be within the dolphins' potential to focus intense beams of ultrasound.

The surgeon in particular became excited at the possibility of *zapping* (his word) tumors by crossing different beams of ultrasound. He explained that each beam would not be harmful. But if the beams were carefully tuned so as to increase the frequency at the designated spot when they crossed—then, yes, they might be able to burn out the tumor.

Both the engineer and the surgeon agreed that to be a successful sonic operation, the ultrasound beams would have to be extremely precise and finely modulated.

In 1981, modern technology, they said, simply hadn't advanced that far.

# 13

# The Related Spirit
# of Events

## Midwayer Conflicts, Threatened with Extinction, Machiventa Melchizedek, the Conference-in-Spirit, a Rebellion Reconciled, and Hypnotic Locks

I have written earlier that the power of the religious drive is mainly based in the worship circuits embedded within the subtle energy bodies of all mortals. However, there is another element to religion's influence that will inevitably play its part.

It seems not to matter who or what is worshipped but rather a shared belief system—for better or worse—will always unify its followers. This is hardly an original observation in the twenty-first century. It's been so clearly demonstrated by the unified Islamic antipathy for the Jewish people, or the devoted followers of David Koresh. The latter were unified in staying to die with him in the conflagration that destroyed their Mount Carmel temple, killing seventy-six Branch Davidians. There are also the examples of Jonestown, or Heaven's Gate, or North Korea for that matter. However, it seems to remain a mystery to those not involved as to what could have created and sustained these violent extremes of religious fervor.

In the three millennia before Christ, this element was made far worse by the fragmented nature of the population into numerous tribes. Many of these tribes defined themselves in opposition to other tribes in their neighborhood. Some tribes—like those of the Yazidi people and the Semitic clans who were now worshipping Jehovah—solidified their tribal and religious unity by sanctioning that marriage and childbearing could only take place within the tribe.

By this time the rebel midwayers had spread across all the inhabited regions of the planet and much of their time and energy was being expended in forming and reforming alliances with others of their kind. Frequently this would produce conflict, some of which erupted as battles in the air as recorded in Hinduism's sacred literature. In other situations, opposing rebel midwayers would urge their followers into unnecessary tribal wars for their pride and vanity's sake.

The constant tension, hostility, competitive ambition, and all the shifting affiliations among the rebel midwayers further coarsened their emotional responses. The glorious promise of greater independence— that originally convinced the midwayers to follow Prince Caligastia into Lucifer's rebellion—had by now completely faded from their collective memory. In its place was selfishness and cynicism.

This period saw a deepening in the corruption among the rebel midwayers as they battled each other for primacy. Not only that, but it also imprinted a standard of acceptable belligerent aggression—and greed—among those human beings who rose to power within the tribes. While I can hold the rebel midwayers responsible for this steady decline in human values, I can scarcely blame them for it. When they had only their superior, Prince Caligastia, to set an example, what hope, really, did they have! The loyalist midwayers might well have a more sardonic view about that, however!

These different rebel midwayer groupings each had its own belief system centered on their gods and goddesses. And each tribal pantheon was intent on convincing its followers in the absolute rightness of its own cause, while demonizing all those they opposed. The appalling efficacy of appealing to the lowest and densest human emotions—and then to stir up fear and hatred of the "other"—appears to work as well today when applied by cynical politicians and priests as it did in the past at the hands of the priests and rulers subject to the rebel midwayers.

Some might attribute this aggressor/victim polarity to a flaw in human nature. Although there is some truth to this inheritance from a more tooth and claw era, most humans left to themselves desire only to live in peace. This is true, unless, of course, they are faced with aggression or injustice, or if they are cynically manipulated by those in power over them.

The flow of rebel angels into mortal incarnation had accelerated to match and cancel out the impact of Prince Caligastia's meddling. Yet it also had a less obvious but equally profound impact on the spiritual well-being of life on the planet.

I believe it was Astar who commented that she thought the rebel angel incarnates of that era were like weights that dragged down any chance of general spiritual well-being. She had pointed out how frequently it was the incarnates' need to strengthen their emotional bodies by testing themselves against the most extreme conditions that set in motion much of the intertribal hostility.

So ugly had the general situation become that one of the other Melchizedek Brothers was known to express his horror. I quote him here, when he was heard to complain that "revealed truth was threatened with extinction during the millennia that followed the miscarriage of the Adamic mission . . ."

Truth threatened with extinction! That serious!

However, much was about to change and the Middle East would once again be in the forefront of this new development.

I was there in the Palestinian desert 1,973 years before the birth of Christ to observe the arrival of Machiventa Melchizedek. It was a remarkably quiet and modest affair for the arrival of such a high celestial being.

So who is this Machiventa Melchizedek?

He is known in the Bible from a couple of brief references to him as the King of Salem and from the blessings he bestowed on Abraham. Considering what an important figure he actually was, this is really somewhat sparse.

Mein Host reminds me that one of the rare representations of Melchizedek is in the form of a finely wrought statue—one of a number of sculptures of church fathers and other dignitaries—in the portal of Chartres Cathedral.

Machiventa Melchizedek was, in reality, an angel of a high order of celestials known by the MA as "Emergency Sons." As such—and as their title suggests—they stepped into difficult or failing planetary situations to restore equilibrium on the inner planes. Machiventa was one of twelve Melchizedek Sons who arrived here soon after the rebellion. Yet because they were affiliated with the planetary Seraphic Overgovernment, I observed very little of their activities. Watchers have never been made welcome among the loyalist seraphs functioning in the overgovernment. My only contact with them after the rebellion was when I needed to acquire permission for my interplanetary jaunts.

I had heard from Astar some time ago that the twelve Melchizedek had then left the planet, only to have to return when Prince Caligastia sabotaged the second intervention thirty thousand years ago. After that, the twelve receivers remained here, working with the Seraphic Overgovernment.

There appears to be a curious paradox here: An overgovernment of loyalist seraphs appear to have permitted a steady deterioration in the spiritual state of the world in their care. However, the Seraphic Overgovernment is more of a coordinating agency for all the angels functioning in the fifth dimension on the planet. It seldom, if ever, involves itself with life in the third dimension.

Subsequent to the rebellion, both Planetary Princes—Caligastia and Daligastia—were shunned by the Seraphic Overgovernment. To my knowledge the seraphs in the administration never intervened in the decisions and actions of the Princes, however outrageous they became.

Now I have to rely on another Melchizedek for his report on what occurred next. I'm paraphrasing his comments when I say he tells of two crucial issues that had drawn the twelve receivers into earnest conference.

The first I've already mentioned. "The light of revealed truth"—how the worthy scribe expressed it—was rapidly being extinguished. This situation was becoming progressively more serious after the collapse of the second mission.

The second reason, and the one that both astonished and concerned the twelve Melchizedek receivers, was the news that Michael—the Creator Son of this Local Universe—had just chosen Earth as the site for his seventh and final incarnation . . . this one as a mortal of the realm.

As I've previously mentioned, we were taught on Jerusem that a Michaelson and a Mother Spirit oversee the creation of their Local Universe—one of the one hundred thousand Local Universes in each of the seven Superuniverses. They create the different orders of life-forms within their domain. These life-forms are both celestial and material. They follow the patterns descending from the Central Universe—the hole in the middle of the torus—by modulating the energies pouring into their Local Universe on an ultimatonic level.

Whereas the Mother Spirit is not required to incarnate in person, the Michaelson incarnates once on each of the seven primary levels of sentience in his domain. Even back in the Jerusem seminars we were told that our Michaelson had already completed six of his seven incarnations.

To give some sense of temporal scale let me pass along what we were taught about the first of Michael's incarnations. The Jerusem tutor first put this in the context of Michael and the Mother Spirit originally organizing this Local Universe around four hundred billion years ago. The tutor went on to say that his first bestowal (incarnation) as a Melchizedek occurred about a billion years ago. One hundred fifty million years later, Michael appeared as a Lanonandek Son, serving as a replacement System Sovereign following a rebellion in another constellation within the Local Universe.

His next four bestowals followed, so we were told, at approximately

150-million-year intervals, including one as a Material Son and another as a seraphic teaching counselor. But one, the fifth, seemed to particularly intrigue the lecturer. This was a bestowal as an ascending mortal who had already reached Uversa, the headquarters world of this Superuniverse. We never did discover at the time why this so interested our lecturer. It was only when we heard Michael was planning to incarnate as a mortal on this very world that I realized what the tutor was trying to figure out.

You see, no one knows when a Michaelson is going to incarnate—or where he'll choose to do it. And those who function alongside him are also unaware of his true identity. This occurs apparently to allow the Michaelson to fully experience that particular incarnation without being treated any differently from any other Seraphim or Material Son.

The only incarnation that remained was his seventh—as a mortal on one of the ten million inhabited planets in his Creation. Again, what was never taught was when or where Michael would decide to make his play. And it was precisely this that so discombobulated the twelve Melchizedek when they were informed it was going to be on this planet that Michael had chosen to live out his final lifetime as a human being.

I'm sure you can imagine the confusion and excitement among the Melchizedek when they heard the news while surveying the appalling spiritual state of the world. It was an immense privilege that Michael had chosen Earth, of course. Yet it remained a complete conundrum as to why he'd decided on a planet as troubled as this one. And although they were now aware of his choice, they were not told *when* to expect him.

Apparently, after a long discussion, they'd petitioned the Most Highs of Edentia as well as their own superior, Father Melchizedek. Yet the reply they got was that they should continue as usual; they wouldn't be receiving any outside assistance. Left to themselves, the twelve resident receivers decided it was within their brief for one of them to directly intervene in an attempt to return some of the light of truth to a planet almost completely locked in darkness. They were finally given permission to move ahead with this, and it was Machiventa who volunteered for the mission.

Individuals within the Melchizedek Order of Sonship are unusual in that they're one of the few orders able to manifest and personalize in the form of a mortal. I think it was Astar who told me that what Machiventa was doing in personalizing as a mortal had only been needed on six previous occasions in this Local Universe.

Neither Astar nor I were privy at the time to what the Melchizedek receivers knew about the possibly imminent incarnation of the Creator Son. Thus the arrival of Machiventa on that warm spring day in the hills of southern Palestine seemed like merely another exceptional event in what felt like a long history of exceptional events.

Yet for all the unusual events that had happened in the past, I still didn't know—and I don't believe Astar knew either, for all her access to inside information—just why this planet was receiving such special attention. It would never have occurred to either of us that this chaotic and tormented world would ever conceivably host the mortal incarnation of the Creator Son of an entire Local Universe.

Yet had we known it, it was precisely this condition of turbulence and torment that made this planet such a likely proposition for a Michaelson wishing to demonstrate to the rest of his universe the true value of love, mercy, and forgiveness in the face of the most unjust and brutally cruel opposition.

All I really knew at the time as I relaxed on that scented Palestinian hillside was Astar's promise that if I waited with patience I would witness the rarest of events. Yet I still had no idea who or what I was waiting for so patiently.

* * *

My ward would always claim that the concept of the Conference-in-Spirit dropped into his meditating mind as a complete gestalt—as though cut from whole cloth. Holding a conference in which all participants were requested to meet in an out-of-body state in the Queens Chamber of the Great Pyramid of Cheops on a particular date was always intended as an experiment. This is due to the fact that it was also sure to raise some controversy in some more straight-laced quarters. The concept particularly appealed to Mein Host. He'd said more than once how he felt burned out by putting conferences together in the 3-D world—when so much depended on whether there was an audience paying their way and filling the seats.

My collaborator has written more extensively about the Conference-in-Spirit in his 2011 book *The Return of the Rebel Angels.* My point is merely to provide a graceful segue to the late summer of 1981 in which we found Melinda and my ward making their way from Israel to Egypt.

They'd never intended to actually travel to Egypt for the conference, but—as they would discover later—their angels had different plans for them. It was this that resulted in their last-minute decision to attend the Conference-in-Spirit on the full moon of October 11, in the close vicinity of the Great Pyramid. And because Melinda's parents were living in Israel, the trip would also give Mein Host a chance to spend some time getting the feel of the Holy Land before the pair crossed into Egypt for the conference.

However, there was a deeper purpose to this trip that Mein Host was less aware of, so focused was he on the event going smoothly. This deeper purpose to the trip was that it was to be one of the first occasions in which Mein Host was actively used by the angels to spread the news of the reconciliation of the Lucifer Rebellion. He hadn't yet written of this revelation in his first book, *The Deta Factor: Dolphins ETs & Angels,* which was published three years later in 1984. Thus this proposed journey to the Middle East would act as a test of Mein Host's commitment. It was one of the reasons the angels supported and smoothed the way for the conference to take place. They had also been responsible for the inner promptings the pair had received to travel to Egypt and Israel. The angels' intention—as far as I was able to make out—was to set a challenge by which they would be able to assess the integrity and reliability of their two messengers.

And quite a challenge it turned out to be.

The conference was due to be held on October 11. However, five days before, on October 6, the president of Egypt, Anwar Sadat, was gunned down by Islamic fundamentalist army officers, and all access to the country was closed down. It was due only to Melinda and Mein Host's patience and persistence that after four days of frustration waiting for the ports to open, they were finally able to enter the country accompanied by Palestinian daily workers on a ferry across the Suez Canal.

Whenever a head of state is assassinated—no matter in which nation the murder happens, and regardless of how the person assassinated is popularly regarded—a black cloud of depression will invariably hang over the populace. Anwar Sadat's eleven years as the president of Egypt had made him a particularly controversial figure internationally, but even more so within his country. He was revered by some, but as my ward discovered in speaking to people in the street—to shopkeepers, men in buses, and taxi drivers—he was heartily loathed by many others for all the changes he'd wrought. Finally, that President Sadat should have received the Nobel Prize for negotiating the peace treaty between Egypt and Israel had effectively sealed his fate in the hearts of many native Egyptians.

Mein Host was not in America in November 1963 when President John F. Kennedy was assassinated in Dallas. Yet for those who can remember it and the days immediately following the killing, they will be able to recall the deep sense of psychic disorientation that resulted from the intense emotions brought to the surface and stirring around in the country's collective psyche. Those behind the killing of JFK were a small cadre of powerful people. The shooting of President Sadat by Islamic fundamentalists reflected the wishes of a much larger proportion of the population. This created, if anything, an even greater sense of dislocation in Cairo—where the people were still wandering around a week after the event as if in a hypnotic trance.

I should add, though, that this curious state of mind also produced some surprising and amusing results. A touching example of this occurred on the night of the conference. I can't do any better than have my ward repeat what happened as he described it in *The Return of the Rebel Angels* (pages 45–46). He wrote:

The walk from the Mena House Hotel to the base of the Great Pyramid was farther than it appears, the vast size of the pyramid deceiving the eye. It was also a long hill, this evening lined with heavily armed troops. The moon was so large every detail of the landscape stood out, and we could see the soldiers' eyes following us as we plodded up the deserted road.

Around a bend we came to a barrier across the road and a gaggle of soldiers with machine guns, smoking and talking between themselves. As we came to the barrier a young officer detached himself from the group, walked toward us gesturing, and said in cultured English: "Reasonable people would not walk near the Great Pyramid at this time of night."

I replied that we were *not* reasonable people. There was a surprised pause before he roared with laughter, and ordering his troops to lift the barrier he ushered us through, saying, "In that case it's fine for you to proceed."

So proceed they did as the friendly laughter of the troops, on hearing their interchange translated, pursued them up the hill and toward the Great Pyramid.

It was under the title the Future Studies Research Group (FSRG) that Mein Host and Melinda had gathered a small group of friends to select two hundred people in various fields who would be likely to respond positively to the experiment. I heard them talking about their choices as bringing together "two hundred of the coolest people on the planet." Naturally, they all included themselves among the two hundred invitees! Very cool indeed.

They'd then sent out the two hundred well-designed invitations anonymously in the hope that at least some of the invitees would get the point and try to attend in spirit. The feedback they received afterward—when the FSRG finally released their address—indicated that a surprising number of people had indeed participated.

Whether the Conference-in-Spirit could ever be considered a success was entirely dependent on the level of participation of those involved.

The late Elisabeth Kübler-Ross, for example, was such an enthusiastic participant that she'd asked a number of her friends to join her in the group meditation. A notable and now deceased scientist, however, responded with irrational fury at even being asked to attend a conference in an out-of-body state—a state of consciousness, of course, that his scientific community had scornfully refuted.

However, what the 1981 Conference-in-Spirit achieved was more hidden by nature. It introduced the novel concept into the World Mind—as well as into the minds of many hundreds of influential people—that such out-of-body gatherings were not only possible and plausible but also would most likely be a fixture of the future.

Mein Host and Melinda had only scheduled a short trip to the Middle East this time, as they'd made the travel arrangements so close to the event and needed to return to New York to fulfill other obligations. Yet what Melinda was introducing into my ward's life was, for him, almost like a new way of being.

My ward would likely claim he had been following his heart and inner guidance before he'd joined the Process community in the early 1960s. While this was perfectly true, what he hadn't been so aware of was that his years in the community were more about learning first to follow, and then to lead. Another key lesson that he was to learn was that by exchanging the many small decisions constantly needed over the course of everyday life for one large overarching decision to join the community—however heartfelt and guided that may have been—was not quite the same as having to deal with the deluge of choices faced in everyday life.

Taking vows of obedience, poverty, and chastity had clearly made life simpler for a while. Yet by focusing so consistently on renunciating material values, my ward had unwittingly deprived himself—as much as did the others in the community—of the maturing process that can result from having to handle the endless challenges of daily life. Then, by surrendering his individual autonomy to Mary Ann, he had never felt the sense of personal freedom to which Melinda was now introducing him.

Melinda had long lived the life of an artist; a woman who had always been completely devoted to her art and her spiritual studies. Being intensely curious by nature—and having lived in many countries during her life—she loved traveling and thought nothing of suggesting they take a cross-country trip that very next week. Now that my ward had sold his business and had a small stipend to last him for a few years, he was entirely free to follow his heart and make those hundreds of decisions, large and small, by which mortals can grow in spirit.

This impulse felt by both of them to take to the road in America was inspired by their mutual desire to spread the word of the reconciliation of the Lucifer Rebellion—as told them by the angels in Toronto. This they intended to do to some of the individuals and groups of people who had studied *The Urantia Book*. These were, after all, the people most likely to understand some of the implications of this startling revelation.

This was the early 1980s, and many of those in the loose-knit Urantia community greeted the news with some caution, having been previously burned by poseurs with their own agendas. Most of the individuals with whom they talked weren't ready to accept that there could ever have been a true reconciliation of the rebellion and simply parroted the unforgiving attitudes toward Lucifer held by certain of the celestial communicants in *The Urantia Book*. Yet there were a small number of bold individuals in the various Urantia study groups who were prepared to break with the rigidity of the Urantia belief system and give serious thought to what this reconciliation might mean.

Now, roughly forty years later, there are many more people who are living the truth of this reconciliation in the course of their everyday lives.

As Mein Host has stated, the Supernaphim Shandron's reference to the final reconciliation of the rebellion actually made a great deal of rational sense. This was despite the fact that it was as astonishing to those present at the time as it was to those subsequently contemplating what Mein Host and Melinda had to say. Shandron had reported that forgiveness for Lucifer had been found in the hearts of mortals. This carried the stamp of divine revelation and resonated with the tone of mercy and forgiveness characterizing this Local Universe.

It was, in fact, the most elegant of resolutions to an apparently intractable problem that had lingered for millennia.

I was glad to observe that neither Melinda nor Mein Host made the error of falling into the trap of becoming fanatic true believers in this revelation—obsessed with convincing others of their truth. Rather, they were doing it more to prop up their own conviction.

When Mein Host was speaking to others about the reconciliation, he used all he'd learned when he was conducting the First Progress. (The First Progress was the introductory course he'd led for those interested in the Process Church.) He never insisted on the absolute truth of the reconciliation, for example. Instead he only said that it was something both he and the others experienced under unusual circumstances in Toronto and he thought others should know about it. His approach was all very laid-back.

I watched him as he drew out readers of *The Urantia Book* on what they made of some of the curious contradictions in the book's account of the Lucifer Rebellion. And what did they think about the oddly vindictive attitude expressed by the Melchizedek Brother writing about Lucifer and the rebel angels? And didn't it seem a little simplistic to dismiss Lucifer—a high angel—as insane?

Rather than imposing the concept purely by force of his personality, he clearly preferred presenting what he knew as a proposition, as a matter to be seriously mulled over. Because if the reconciliation was true and real, it was probably one of the most significant events of the past two hundred thousand years.

As my ward explained to Melinda after she'd completed her weeks of work transcribing the tapes of the Toronto angel sessions, in an ultimate sense, how could he or anybody know for certain that what the Supernaphim had told them was true? Or whether Edward—like any channel—could be trusted to be entirely accurate? Or indeed, whether they had perhaps misunderstood Shandron's admittedly enigmatic message?

Taking all this into account and weighing up both sides of the discussion, he said he'd decided to proceed on an "as-if basis"—as if it was an accurate transmission.

"If it's really true," he reasoned, "we'll be able to see signs of the changes in the world . . . the angels gave us a whole heap of predictions to check out. On the other hand, if the whole thing is bollocks then we'll probably get our asses kicked by the angels soon enough!"

They were laughing at the image of a celestial ass-kicking when Melinda added that she couldn't see it would do any real harm if it was wrong. "It might even get more people to think about such matters . . . besides, the angels bid us be bold, didn't they? What's the worst that could happen?"

"And if it is true," my ward added, "and I'm choosing to hold faith that it is unless the angels tell me differently, then it's going to be something really important. It'd change everything, wouldn't it?!"

Melinda was nodding thoughtfully. "Then why don't we just see what goes down? Let's see what happens if we live our lives holding this vision."

My ward must have been amused—so many years later—to read with what an innocence he plunged into a spiritual journey that, after so many adventures, would bring us together, ready to accomplish this work.

I don't believe he had any reason to dismiss the message from the Supernaphim Shandron, nor to doubt the integrity of information they received from the other angels over those ten days of inspired contact in Toronto.

The angels had told them that with the reconciliation they should expect the exposure of the deep corruption baked into so many human institutions and organizations. They added that it would be a rough ride for everyone over the next score of years and that it was going to be dark as pitch before the dawn.

They predicted there was going to be widespread fear and confusion as the old, corrupt structures crumbled. They said some would fight to maintain their status quo while others would fight to establish their new freedoms. They also spoke about the coming new global communication system and the rapid and unpredictable changes to society that would bring.

There was much else spoken about that the interested reader will find transcribed in more detail in chapters 8 and 10 of my ward's first book, *The Deta Factor: Dolphins, ETs & Angels*.

I should add merely that I, Georgia, had nothing to do behind the scenes with making this encounter occur—that would have been the function of their companion angels—but I was extremely encouraged to observe that it was happening.

It was the first time in the seven years following Mein Host's near-death experience—in which he'd witnessed angels as real beings—that he was ready for the full effect of angelic contact. His subsequent decision to take the angel's counsel for each of them to develop their own line of communication with their companion angels, and then for him to spend the next two years working to accomplish this, only further encouraged me.

However, by this time I wasn't quite as trusting as I once was that what I'd hoped would transpire would really happen. I became concerned whether, in fact, my ward and I were going to have the chance to work together. I'd already observed that he preferred to live much of his life on the edge. Would he fall off his perch before we'd ever have the opportunity for me to tackle this work?

As I wrote that paragraph I realized—with a shock—that I was beginning to frame my ward's life and development in terms of our eventual collaboration. That's not fair. I will try to avoid doing that in future, but you can probably deduce from my words that I faced what was to come with some degree of anxiety.

What I wasn't to understand at the time was that this feeling of constant nervous agitation and worry for the future—my future—was the same state of mind that held so many human beings in its thrall of fear.

The game was far from over.

* * *

Astar must have had some high-level contacts, because it was she who suggested that I would see something interesting if I was to spend some time in the Palestinian desert. I've never understood quite how she managed it, but it wasn't the first time she'd pointed me in the right direction.

It was one of those brilliantly clear spring days in the rolling hills of Canaan in southern Palestine. I could smell the salty breath of the Mediterranean blowing in from the sea in the far distance. I was as surprised as ever at how the scents of the world penetrated up into the astral. By midday the sun was high in the sky, sending the few shepherds I could see in the distance scuttling for the untidy shade of a grove of tamarix trees (*Note:* Tamarix aphylia. —*TW*), to be followed by their sheep ambling after them.

I moved down to a wide flat valley stretching below me, with a fine mirage flickering liquidly over the barren dusty sandscape. Rocks and shrubs appeared to disappear only to reappear a moment later as though washed clean by their moment of invisibility.

I seldom allowed myself any restful pleasure, so I found myself a large flat rock already warmed by the sun. As I was contemplating this sibylline landscape—already so deeply impregnated by history and the shadow of what lay ahead—I felt not the relaxed pleasure I'd lazily anticipated but instead a sudden and unexpected frisson of excitement that was a little too close for comfort.

What a fearful creature I was—perhaps I still am—if with any hope, now somewhat less so. I knew I needed to have the courage to move toward the fear, to know what lay beneath it, and to understand what lurked in the minds of men. These were the thoughts troubling me while I was staring idly into the fluidly rippling mirage stretching out before me.

Yet in those brief moments of understanding there was a purpose to my being brave, and I found my fears dissipating. They were replaced by an excited curiosity as to why Astar might have given me this odd tip to be in the desert—and why she wasn't here with me. I was starting to become concerned that Astar might be setting me up—although I couldn't think why she would do it—when something caught my eye. A dark pole, I thought it was; a momentary vertical interruption in the rippling horizontality of the mirage. It was there one moment and gone the next. Was it a tree I hadn't previously noticed? A stand of rocks? Some large, unrecognizable animal?

But no. The form was moving toward me as if wading out of a deep surf. The mirage first obscured the figure's torso, midsection, legs, and long robe, leaving only a majestic head and broad shoulders to float for a few moments—magically legless—above the flowing mirage. Then the image appeared only as a pair of sandaled feet and the flapping of the bottom of a dark blue robe, which suddenly seemed comically disembodied as the sandals padded toward me. I really shouldn't have laughed at the sight, but fortunately the figure was still too far away to have sensed my presence.

I could now see it was a tall, remarkably well-built man of indeterminate age, with a full dark beard and a firm stride. His robe was somewhat the same as those worn by the local tribesmen. Later, however, when I came to look at his clothing more closely, the lightness of the material and the superb regularity of the stitching were of a far finer quality than the robes of the other shepherds. I was also surprised at the man's choice of a robe. He wore such a dark color in the desert heat. And yet in the many times I observed him over the years I never saw even the smallest bead of sweat gathered on his face or hands.

Drawing closer I could see from the way the man carried himself that he exuded self-confidence. I thought he must be one of the local sheiks, yet he traveled alone without a camel or retinue, and I could see no caravan in the distance from which he might have strayed.

I remember now it was when the sun glinted off a metallic shield worn on his breast and I saw embossed on it three concentric circles—familiar to me from symbols I'd seen back on Jerusem—that I realized who this commanding presence had to be. It could only be a Melchizedek, right here, on this world, in the flesh.

I believe it was then that it struck me this world must be in even more desperate straits than I had previously imagined. And yet with this renewed sense of dread came another feeling that, by now, was so foreign to me I almost didn't recognize it. I am embarrassed to admit it, but I felt hope.

After all, posting a Melchizedek to this ramshackle planet had to be a sign the MA hadn't entirely forsaken this world. And along with this arrival also came a hint that the MA might even be preparing the way for some important future event.

Here it's hard not to be wise after the event, because by now I doubt if it will be much of a mystery for whom this Melchizedek was preparing the way.

* * *

Mein Host was unable to account for the immediate and fierce affinity he felt for the land of Israel—a feeling that only grew stronger the longer he was there. The country was relatively peaceful—as least on the surface—in the early 1980s, during the time of his two visits there. I placed the emphasis here on the *land* of Israel, because it was my ward's sensitivity to the spirit of the land itself that appeared to awaken a dormant aspect of his inner life.

He had a number of profound insights on his first trip, when he and Melinda had the chance to travel around the country while waiting for the borders to open after President Sadat's death. The death had shaken both of them, because Anwar Sadat was one of the only two politicians on the list—Jerry Brown, the governor of California being the second—of the two hundred invitees to the Conference-in-Spirit. The two hundred "coolest people on the planet!"

Preoccupied as they were with getting into Egypt, I heard them questioning whether Sadat's unfortunate death—and now the country's closed borders—were signs that boded ill for the conference. Perhaps they wouldn't be able to get to the pyramids in time. I was amused to hear them express concern about this. One of the reasons my ward had stipulated that the conference be held in an out-of-body state was to stay clear of the stress of actually producing it in 3-D reality. It was the stress he was feeling while waiting for the border to open as he and Melinda were being driven around all the archaeological sites by her proud parents.

My ward has missed the irony of this—and the fact that they could just as well have attended the conference from Melinda's parents' apartment in Israel—until this very moment. And as he says, he had thought and written a great deal about the conference. It was complicated trying to make it into Egypt. And yet so focused was he on getting into the country that it never once occurred to him he was simply repeating the stress that he'd created the conference to avoid.

I don't want to make too much of this as there were days when my ward was able to get away on his own—walking and meditating on those Canaanite hills and clambering down the sandy cliffs to the shore of the Mediterranean.

Melinda's parents, both of whom had retired, lived in a recently built, high-rise apartment in the small coastal town of Netanya. They had moved from France to Israel in the late 1960s as a token of support for the troubled fledgling nation. Melinda's stepfather in particular had been growing increasingly disgusted with the deteriorating state of affairs in the country and seemed quite unable to stop complaining about it—in voluble French. Yet her mother was kind and caring, and—having been a war correspondent—she was also intelligent and worldly. She was obviously overjoyed at the rare opportunity to see her daughter, even if neither parent knew quite what to make of Melinda's boyfriend.

I could see that my ward was genuinely interested and trying his best in his schoolboy French to keep up with the stepfather's constant caviling. The man's anger and impatience and his scorn—common to many French people of his time for someone who didn't speak fluent French—made their halting discussions minefields of misunderstanding. Although it was clear from the start the stepfather didn't like my ward one little bit, Mein Host's attempts to comprehend what the stepfather was saying only seemed to make the man angrier and more frustrated. However, as the days passed, it turned out that Melinda's stepfather didn't like anybody.

It was the language issue that gave my ward a good excuse to slip away on his own, allowing the three of them to rattle away in French together. It was on one of those occasions he was able to get away for a whole afternoon and evening that he had an experience that profoundly opened up his life in the most unexpected way.

You will have noticed I've written almost nothing about Mein Host's father in this narrative, and there's been good reason for this. After the age of two—when Diana divorced her husband—my ward had never seen his father again. There'd been a chance when he was about eleven years old and away at boarding school when George had turned up at Diana's London apartment hoping to meet his son. This hadn't been possible. When Diana finally confessed to this visit to my ward when he was in his forties, she justified it by saying she didn't want to dislocate his life. But she clearly felt troubled about her decision because it took her so long to own up to it.

When Mein Host was in his late teens, Diana heard that George had remarried, had another family, and had recently died in Australia. Yet it must have seemed so inconsequential to my ward that he recalls nothing of being told about it—only that a fifty-pound note had been left to him in his father's will.

Diana was not the sort of woman who spoke poorly to her son about his father's failings, but she did this by not talking about George at all. I've heard my ward say he can barely remember ever thinking about his father when he was growing up. He has claimed it was only an acid trip in his late thirties that woke him up. Up to then, he says, he felt he was in some sort of hypnotic lock created by his mother's rigid denial of George's place in his life. The acid trip that broke open the lock was a profound emotional upheaval that left him weeping for hours.

Now he was in Israel facing off against Melinda's stepfather's irrational dislike of him and no doubt reasoning—and not for the first time—that he was fortunate not to have a father if that's what fathers were like. It was not a particularly mature thought given that all fathers are obviously not like that angry French curmudgeon. The sad truth was that my ward's deepest feelings about his father had been frozen at the stage of a two-year-old.

Yet all that was about to change.

# 14

# Dissembling the Lies and Rebuilding from the Ashes

## An Astral Encounter, Self-Healing, Amdon the Shepherd, Machiventa Melchizedek's Mission, the Dome of the Rock, the Healing Grotto, and Small Miracles

It had been a pleasantly warm day for October, and the light in Israel in fall—cleaned by the previous day's rainfall—was clear and golden. I could see how happy my ward was to be out on his own and away from what seemed to be a constant family drama.

The south side of the town of Netanya ended abruptly. It was almost as though there were a wall around it. And it looked like that, too. It featured featureless apartment blocks, all of the same height and shape, their white paint peeling and stepped back in a soldierly line perpendicular from the block closest to the water. The apartment blocks overlooked the rolling sandy brush—an undeveloped wilderness stretching down to Tel Aviv in the far distance. The lights of the city were just visible when they sparkled over the horizon at night.

Mein Host has said he had no thoughts of his father when he set off down the beach that late afternoon. He was quite alone as he walked steadily south; the few remaining Israeli tourists preferred to stay back on the town's beaches a couple of miles behind him. He'd commented to Melinda earlier that day how Israelis invariably seemed to cluster together. He'd rarely ever seen any of them on their own and they were always chattering away together like birds in a tree.

The slope of the cliffside to his left rose about a hundred feet at an eighty-degree angle and was pocked with rocks. These rocks were both large and small, exposed by erosion, and threatening to fall to join their fellows in the jumbled heap at the cliff's base. It was a narrow beach and Mein Host had to clamber over slippery water-washed rocks while keeping his eyes open for the falling debris loosened up by the previous day's rain.

After walking for a couple of miles he came to what he'd called the sacred circle. It was eight or ten feet larger than man-size rocks that had fallen off the cliff to embed themselves in the sand in an almost perfect circle. He had meditated there before, sensing in the regularity of the positioning of the rocks something of the artistic hand of the midwayers.

This particular afternoon it wasn't the sacred circle that drew him. Thus he continued walking farther and farther until he found a large flat stone at the edge of the water and settled down on it for an evening meditation. The sun was low in the sky and dropping fast. The water was flat, smoothed, and silvered in the evening glow, her waves barely a ripple in this tideless sea.

What occurred next was as surprising to me as it was to my ward.

I should say in advance it's extremely challenging to get across in words just how malleable reality can become in the fourth-dimensional frequency domains. These realities are far more evidently created and shaped by the needs and desires of those who inhabit those realms than your third-dimensional domains in which your reality appears consistent and stable. My ward subsequently likened the experience to a lucid dream. However, it was far more solid and real than any lucid dream he'd ever had. It occurred, he said, almost immediately after he'd closed his eyes to meditate.

There was no sense of movement, no dislocation of senses, no ringing in the ears that he'd noted happening when detaching from his body on ketamine. There was no singing of angels . . . no warning at all. And yet there he was, sitting in a beautiful walled garden, with the reddest of roses climbing a trellis against a wall to his left. The sun seemed unaccustomedly bright, yet it was a friendly light—soft, he said, to the inner eye. The garden furniture—the small round table and the two upright chairs—was of cast iron and painted white. That—my ward said afterward—seemed somehow familiar. In fact, he speculated, the whole mise en scène appeared to have been created so as to ensure his maximum psychic ease and comfort.

A man sat in the chair opposite him.

His face was tanned, his hair and short beard both gray, and his eyes a soft cerulean blue. He was slimly built, and from his upright sitting posture he was clearly tall. He wore a white tropical suit, impeccably tailored, and my ward recalls he had his left arm resting on the table, with his tanned hand and ringless fingers relaxed and easy.

It was one of the most intimate of encounters of my ward's life—as profound and lucid as his NDE—and as he has never written publicly about it. This is how he recalls it:

> The transition happened so quickly, it was like closing my eyes on one reality and then opening them to find I was in another reality entirely. It seemed to be that fast. But for some reason I wasn't bewildered. It wasn't weird or unsettling, which was also strange when I think about it now. Something like this had never happened to me before for all my explorations of entheogens, and—similarly to my NDE—this was happening when I was straight.
>
> At first I didn't know who the man was, except I remember thinking how he looked oddly like me—or perhaps more how I'd like to look. He was a beautiful man, and he had this smile of such sweet poignancy—such a mixture of regret and sadness, joy and pride. Yet it was as if I was feeling all this mix of emotions along with him.
>
> It was then I must have realized it was my father—the father I'd never met or even thought about very much. And then we spoke

together. I don't know for how long, but I do know all that needed to be said was said. Everything was resolved between us in the most tender way. My father's regrets at not being around during my childhood; his sadness at being prevented from seeing me (yet there was no hint of blame of my mother); his sorrow at dying without resolving his differences with my mother; his happiness at being able to finally meet me; and his pride at how I was turning out.

And then there was my joy at finally seeing him; my utter astonishment at being known and loved in a way I'd never felt in my life; and the profound sense of basking in his love—a love that would never be withdrawn. Any feelings of abandonment I might have been harboring completely dissolved in his love. There was no talk of forgiveness—there was nothing to forgive. We both knew I had chosen this incarnation, as he had chosen his. We both knew my mother would never have flourished in the way she had if she'd remained in the marriage. She'd chosen her path every bit as much as we'd chosen ours.

I don't recall how our meeting ended but when I found myself back on the rock, I felt like an entirely renewed person. It was as though a missing part of myself—a part I didn't even know was missing—had suddenly filled out.

It's been said that a man doesn't become a man until he's a father. As someone who's declined fatherhood, I became that man when I met my father. It changed my life, giving me the security and courage to dig deeper into the adventures I was beginning to have with spiritual intelligences, then to write about them with all the honesty and grace of which I'm capable.

In fact, it was soon after meeting my father that the notes I was keeping in my journal started evolving into the early chapters my first book.

Mein Host's mention here of the added sense of security and courage he was feeling was the direct result of the healing of his base chakra. This was the hole he never knew he had. Up to this time he'd always had to use his will to overcome his timidity—to engage his counter-phobia, if you will—to override his fear. As a consequence, he has had a way of driving himself to take on impossible (and foolish) challenges simply to prove to himself that he was courageous. In this same way his public performances—whether speaking or leading a band—could also appear somewhat forced.

This lack of the security that is normally transmitted by the consistent presence of a loving father had—unfortunately in Mein Host's case—played into the mild personality fracturing he'd experienced as a child during the war. It contributed to his sense, as he'd say, of being a lightweight, of never being quite sure of who he was. He'd occasionally remark how fortunate he felt at being able to wheel out the appropriate subpersonality to fit the task. But it was a hollow claim.

What he'd never understood until this meeting with his father was his own mercurial personality—his ability "to wheel out the appropriate subpersonality"—was in reality a coping mechanism. It was a way of compensating for his lack of a stable sense of self. Even his almost masochistic tolerance for pain and suffering—his public school beatings, his diving into self-flagellation at Xtul as well as Mary Ann's many humiliations—all these were accepted unconsciously by my ward as a way of proving to himself that he *had* a self.

He has said he sometimes used to be a bit like Kurt Vonnegut's innocent antihero, Billy Pilgrim, who felt he was lost in time. My ward's concepts and designs at architectural college were so advanced the technology has yet to catch up today. And I heard him joke on a radio interview that he writes for people a couple of hundred years in the future. He claimed this conceit was said and hopefully understood as a joke. Yet there was a time while he was writing his first book over thirty years ago that this wasn't such a joke. Back then it was a way of threading a path through the tangle of scornful literary brambles and the thoughtless dismissal of people contemptuous of other realms of existence.

This sense of floating in time for a reincarnate is largely due to this deep sense of insecurity in the base chakra. One of the reasons I've focused here on this aspect of my ward's life is that he has shared this base chakra insecurity with many other rebel angel incarnates. Choosing a difficult childhood will most often result in a wounded base chakra. Yet it will also permit a starseed the opportunity to discover for herself or himself the profound self-confidence allowed by a stable and healthy base chakra.

This seems to echo a dynamic common to many mortals and reincarnates on rebel-held worlds. Spiritual healers, for example, will frequently choose to incarnate into a damaged physical body so as to know and thoroughly understand the healing process from the inside.

Learning to heal the self is deeply embedded in the psyche of all starseeds and can be thought of as the first step on the path of their personal redemption as a mortal Being.

Self-healing for an angelic incarnate involves far more than merely correcting complaints in their physical bodies. The healing needs to reach deep into the individual's subtle energy bodies as well as the work of identifying and clearing out any residual psychic debris from previous incarnations. As my ward has been pointing out in his books—along with other contemporary spiritual writers—as each individual heals himself or herself, so will the world restore a more equably balanced dynamic tension.

There's an issue here that requires clarifying, and it is of particular relevance to starseeds. The desire to "change the world"—or "save the world"—is a common identifying feature of starseed consciousness, and it's a noble enough ambition for a young person. With maturity, starseeds will hopefully discover that this impulse is a projection of their own subconscious distress and pain and will choose to work first on themselves.

This can be a harsh realization for those already on the way to achieving their change-the-world ambition when—for some completely unexpected reason—they fall flat on their faces or disgrace themselves in some appalling way. Preachers, politicians, athletes—often people proud of being role models—are particularly prone to a sudden downfall as their iniquities are revealed. Even as I write, the disgraced bicyclist Lance Armstrong—who's unlikely to be soon forgotten for trying to change the world of cycling in his own chemical way—is having to grovel to those he lied to for so many years.

The necessary corrective for this dynamic for a starseed to avoid falling into the trap is simple: authentic self-knowledge. Much of what needs to be known and accepted to achieve a real clarity of consciousness, as my ward says, can be extremely painful to confront. And yet the only way of truly moving along is by accepting full responsibility for all past transgressions.

It is in this way that rebel angel reincarnates can affect the world authentically for the better—and without drawing unnecessarily attention to themselves. There will always be those with vested interests who are opposed to change. As such, it's best that they maintain their ignorance to the extent they have already been infiltrated by starseeds.

Mein Host was told by his angels back in the early 1990s that there were about 90 million rebel angels who had adopted a mortal incarnation and that there were "more coming in every day." As I write these words, more than twenty years later, I'm happy to say the figure has reached around 120 million—and they are embedded at all levels in every culture on the planet.

It's not a large number of people in a world of more than 7 billion souls. However, as each individual starseed awakens and attends to her or his own self-healing, so also will the world become incrementally realigned with its glorious destiny.

*  *  *

The figure was still some distance away when he turned away from where I stood, clearly unaware of me, and made his way to the tamarix grove where one of the shepherds had pitched his tent.

I couldn't resist looking in on this encounter, and I slipped into the tent a moment before the Melchizedek. I was just in time to watch the shepherd's face as he looked up to see what must have seemed to be a giant filling the open flap of the tent. The giant stood silently—almost entirely blotting out the blistering sunlight—before introducing himself in the native tongue of the Chaldean herder.

The shepherd, his mouth still agape, finally managed to struggle upright. He'd fallen when one of his sandals caught in the hem of his robe, sending him sprawling to his knees in front of Melchizedek. He quickly bowed his head in astonished respect. Had he known he was the first human being to greet a personified high angel in this world for more than thirty-five thousand years he might well have not made it upright!

I only realized afterward how Melchizedek's greeting neatly encapsulated both his identity and the promise of his mission. "I am Melchizedek," he'd announced in a deep and resonant voice. "I am Priest of El Elyon, the Most High, the One and Only God."

These were superstitious times, and Amdon the Chaldean would have had every reason to believe he was facing a demon. And yet there was evidently something in the dignity and bearing of the stranger that was all too real. After the shepherd covered his nervousness by ordering one of his wives to bring out sheep's milk and sweetmeats for their guest, the poor flustered man was able to settle down. It was at this point that he started showering Melchizedek with questions.

He was still asking his questions when dusk fell. Thus he implored his eminent guest to stay for dinner, ordering a sheep slaughtered for the occasion. Word had passed rapidly around the half dozen other shepherds camped nearby Amdon's tent. By the time the food was prepared, the smell of cooking meat had drawn all of them to join Melchizedek and Amdon around the steaming cauldron in the center of a rug set out in front of Amdon's tent.

Melchizedek offered a blessing over the cauldron of mutton. It was to El Elyon, the Supreme God in heaven. Then each of the shepherds reached in with their left hand to pick out a piece of meat. I noticed how each of them avoided the choicest morsels. They were leaving them for Melchizedek and Amdon, who were the last to feed themselves as they ate in silence. Flat rounds of unleavened bread were passed around. At the same time, Amdon's finest silver bowls were constantly being refilled with either fresh well water or warm sheeps' milk by two of the proud host's younger sons.

Amdon was an unusual man. Although he now herded his sheep in the rolling hills of southern Palestine, he was originally from the Land of the Two Rivers and had grown up there in the family of a once-successful trader. The widespread and long-lasting drought that struck Sumeria had ruined the business, leaving the family to eke out their living while the region was slowly recovering. So it was before Amdon had reached the age of twenty that he had set out—as so many had before him—on the long journey across the desert to the still-fertile hills and valleys at the eastern end of the Mediterranean.

His once-prosperous family had sold many of their saved valuables to finance their eldest son Amdon's caravan, placing all their hopes on his starting a new life in Palestine. As the shepherd explained nervously to Melchizedek, his family was once an important and influential force in Sumerian life. Given this, it was as he was leaving his homeland that his father had presented him with these fine silver bowls from which they were now drinking. They were the last of the family's valuables, he said. I appreciated then why Amdon would be nervous at how his guest might react to such an ostentatious display for a humble sheepherder. Talk of the bowls had the other shepherds—who had clearly never seen such elegant silverware before—lifting them carefully up for a closer and more covetous examination.

The bowls were indeed beautifully crafted. The curved silver body of each bowl was sensuously smooth, prompting the shepherds to caress them and stroke them against their bearded cheeks amid their giggles of delight. I wondered if they would be quite so gauche if they understood who their unusual guest really was. Yet Machiventa seemed to take it all in his stride, laughing and joking along with them. I liked him for that. I thought he would do well here if he could adapt to the local silliness that quickly.

Looking more closely at a silver bowl, not only were there no signs of the metal being hammered into shape but the regularity of the bowl's form proved the impressive strides in metalwork that had been made before the drought and the collapse of the culture. Half an inch below the lip of the bowl were two embossed horizontal ridges. Between them small polished carnelians were set in a row half an inch apart and positioned to prevent the bowl from slipping through the fingers.

As the meal was ending, the shepherds agreed, with much nodding and mumbled compliments, on the beauty of the bowls, which were once again refilled by the boys.

I think it was then that it hit me I was watching a drama I'd never seen before; something extraordinarily rare. Up to this point I'd focused on the rarity of finding a Melchizedek in the flesh. Yet seeing those elderly shepherds giggling like children reminded me it was every bit as extraordinary for them to be in a high angel's presence.

The meal finished, the cauldron was picked up by Amdon's wife, who'd been sitting quietly in the darkness in the depth of the tent with her three daughters. When the women finished picking through the remains, the eldest daughter was sent outside to throw the scraps and bones to the dogs I now noticed must have been slumbering in the shade of the tamarix trees.

It was only when the rug was cleared and all faces were turned expectantly to Melchizedek that the Priest of El Elyon began to talk of his presence here and his plans for the future. He spoke simply and with a natural dignity that gave his words an indisputable authority.

He was here, so he said, to restore the knowledge and worship of the One True God. Gesturing to Amdon, he spoke of the gods and goddesses of Sumeria as being mere demons and interlopers who had drawn a veil over the eyes of their worshippers. He warned them of the many temptations and all the wickedness abroad in the world—tribes fighting tribes, their different gods provoking their followers to further frenzies of violence.

He taught the shepherds of a time long ago—long before the ancestors, before the drought—when all men worshipped the One God. He spoke of this Father God as the Creator of all they could see; as a god of justice and truth, who asked only to be known by his children. Speaking as simply as possible—sometimes switching languages to clarify a point to one of the shepherds—Machiventa Melchizedek talked until dawn. He took great care to frame his answers to their tumult of questions, and yet he always returned to the One God, the Heavenly Father. He had introduced his revelation when he'd turned to Amdon, and—with a great sweeping gesture—told the little group: "El Elyon, the Most High, is the Divine Creator of the firmament and even this very Earth on which we live. He is also the Supreme God of Heaven."

\* \* \*

Mein Host said later that he'd found himself unaccountably emotional in Jerusalem. He was becoming more sensitive to the deeper vibrations of place, and Jerusalem—of all places—had a history stretching far back beyond Melchizedek's time.

In addition to this natural affinity for the city, my ward had discovered in his short time in Israel that he had an equally strong affinity for the Palestinian Arabs. When he was much younger he'd traveled widely in North Africa and the Middle East. Invariably he had found he had a natural rapport with the Arabic people he met. It was this conceit of an empathic fellow-feeling that was sorely challenged one afternoon at the Dome of the Rock.

Melinda and my ward caught the local bus from Netanya to Jerusalem that morning. The sky was overcast, and as they traveled down the coast they could see dark, violet-streaked storm clouds clustered over the horizon, turning the sea as gray as boredom.

The sky was clearing when the road turned inland. The storm had moved off to the east and a weak October sun now peered through the dissolving haze as the bus rumbled over the arid hills. It creaked to a stop at every excuse. A constant stream of people, mostly poor, were getting on and off. The men greeted one another with nods and harsh barks of Arabic, and their women sat like silent ghosts in black burqas. Only their dark eyes communicated with the outside world. Some were glazed, some were all-seeing, and others were covetously comparing themselves with others. All this I could see—and more—in their eyes.

As the bus approached the city of Jerusalem, the sky had finally opened up and a small miracle was taking place that—as they both agreed—seemed singularly appropriate. They happily entertained the notion it was being arranged by the midwayers for their pleasure.

A single ray of sun had broken through the clouds and was falling directly on the golden surface of the Dome of the Rock. The sunlight was reflecting off the dome's gracefully curved surface and diffusing in the air around it, enveloping the whole structure in a golden aura. This luminescent glow extended outward. It lit up the Dome of the Rock's immediate surroundings and gave the center of the city the ethereal quality of a vision.

The Dome of the Rock was completed toward the end of the sixth century CE to honor the great rock—known to the Muslim faith as the Foundation Stone—and over which the structure was built. The shrine was set as the central focus on Temple Mount, and—as Melinda remarked—the dome's golden glow made it quite clear it was the power center of the city.

A little research by my collaborator revealed that the golden finish on the dome was not gold at all but an aluminum bronze alloy made apparently in Italy and put in place in 1964. It was only in 1993 that the dome was refinished in real gold—all eighty kilograms of it. This was made possible by a donation of $8.2 million from King Hussein of Jordan, who sold a house in London to cover his gift.

Mein Host hadn't been back to Jerusalem since the 1980s. He reasoned that if a bronze alloy could create such an ethereal golden glow, he couldn't wait to see what eighty kilos of real gold would do.

The bus edged its way through the crowded, noisy streets, letting off its stream of passengers to join the melee in the narrow alleys and the covered souks of this bustling city. After seeing from afar how the presence of the Dome of the Rock commanded the spirit of the place, there seemed little doubt in the two travelers' minds as to where to go first to pay their respects.

The Dome of the Rock is one of the most significant of the Muslim shrines and is known to them as Haram ash Sharif. It was built, as most know, on top of the site of the Second Temple of the Jews in commemoration of the prophet Muhammad's Night Journey. Yet far more intriguing for Mein Host—who has a lifelong love of rocks—was the great rock standing under the structure. It was the rock after which the shrine was named, the rock that Muslims believe was indented with the mark of the prophet's foot when Gabriel lofted him off to heaven.

It's not in my brief to dispute the authenticity of the prophet Muhammad's Night Journey—nor whether it was Gabriel who accompanied Muhammad. However, it was evident that my ward, having had his NDE and his own visit to heaven, felt a certain natural affinity for the prophet's experience. This is not to say he felt the same draw to the religion that emerged from the prophet's writings in the Holy Koran, but merely that his NDE inclined him to give credence to Muhammad's out-of-body experience.

Yet it wasn't so much the astral flight that intrigued him as the rock itself from which Muhammad was said to have sprung. My ward had already started a series of graphics featuring what he liked to call the Great Rocks of the World. I knew it was his desire to sketch the Foundation Stone that was magnetizing him to the wooden walkway near to the entrance to the Western Wall.

Descending into the grotto, there was the rock on the left-hand side of the cave. Half a dozen Muslims were standing reverentially in the dank half-light of the few yellowed bulbs. Mein Host made straight for the rock, which was roped off, making it impossible to touch. As he said afterward, there was something rather special about it—even if was just from all the attention it had received over the millennia.

Melinda was standing back behind him when my ward sunk down into a semi-lotus sitting position on the stone floor before the rock. He was evidently starting to quietly meditate facing the Foundation Stone and opening himself to the rock's gentle and stabilizing energies. He knew how to do this. I'd watched him do this over the years. Whether it was with one of the standing stones of Avebury, England, or one of the great menhirs of Brittany in northern France, he'd worked with the energy of the rocks while sketching them.

It shouldn't come as a surprise that my ward's attraction to rocks was his intuitive impulse to use the rock energy to compensate for the frailty of his base chakra. It was a tribute to his finely tuned intuition that he would do this long before he discovered, from the angels he worked with, that the base chakra is the portal to the Rock Kingdom.

Now, with the healing he'd just undergone as a result of his meeting with his father, which he hadn't fully understood or appreciated yet, it wasn't really necessary anymore to draw energy from the rock devas. It's just that he wasn't aware of that yet.

My ward said afterward that while he was starting to meditate he was vaguely aware of a disturbance of what sounded like angry whispers behind him that he'd dismissed as noise to be tuned out.

A few minutes passed as my ward sat meditating while the whispers among the faithful grew louder into the furious buzzing of a disturbed nest of wasps. Attracted by the noise, the guard outside came clattering down into the crypt, clearly as furious at the buzzing that, with the guard's arrival, was rising to a new pitch.

"It is forbidden! No pray here!" The guard's voice was harsh. He came in at full blast; there was no room for negotiation. Either my ward didn't hear him—which was unlikely—or he deliberately chose to ignore him. Perhaps he was shouting at someone else.

Mein Host made no movement. The guard was stepping closer, his voice louder and even more grating. I didn't have to be in the man's mind to guess his inner dialogue: *Who was this infidel idiot? Didn't he know this was a sacred place and no infidel was permitted to pray here? Was he mad, perhaps?*

"It is forbidden. You no pray here." He was still angry, but his voice dropped slightly in his concern for the infidel idiot.

Still no response. Now the idiot was really starting to strain the guard's patience.

Suddenly my ward opened his eyes and, still sitting, turned to look up at the guard on his right. The guard stepped back sharply, suddenly aware how close he'd gotten.

"I am not praying," Mein Host said calmly. "I am meditating."

"You praying... It is forbidden." There was a moment of hesitation—the guard evidently didn't understand or know what meditation was—before his anger picked up again.

"But I'm meditating with God . . . we both believe in God . . . in the same God." Mein Host's voice was calm and firm, sounding all the calmer in contrast to the guttural fury of the guard. My ward obviously had no idea how seriously the guard was taking the Islamic prohibition against non-Muslims praying anywhere on the Temple Mount. Not only could they not pray but they couldn't carry any religious artifacts. Worst of all, they weren't even permitted to display anything carrying Hebrew lettering. For long periods of time, non-Muslims were never even permitted on the Temple Mount.

In fact, the area was closed to non-Muslims until 1967. At this point it was opened with many restrictions, which were in effect when Melinda and my ward were there. It then closed again soon after their visit and during the troubles of the 1980s and '90s. It only reopened in 2006, with extremely limited visiting hours.

My ward was completely ignorant of all this as his preference had always been to avoid the guidebooks and absorb the experience for himself—whatever it was going to be—untainted by outside influences. All Mein Host had known about the Foundation Stone and the prophet Muhammad's Night Journey—not a great deal—was derived from his general reading.

My ward was standing up by now, having given up in trying to speak reasonably about everybody worshipping the same God to a man who didn't understand a word he was saying. And if he had, he would likely have objected even more vehemently to such terrible blasphemy.

Mein Host had done his best. He'd stood his ground as long as plausible under the circumstances. Despite being at least six inches taller than the guard—a genetic advantage that generally cooled the opposition down—this only seemed to drive the bearded guard into further paroxysms of fury.

My ward told Melinda later it was about this moment—when the guard was shouting and pushing at him—that he had the sense something larger was being acted out through this drama. He said he didn't know what it was, but something was keeping him there.

The clutch of Muslims in the back of the crypt were now surging forward and joining in the guard's shouted orders. *The natives are getting restless!* What an English thought! But Mein Host still believed that the guard had chosen quite arbitrarily to attack *him.* So when it came time to retreat—when the only move left open to the guard was to use his baton—my ward was still baffled by the strangely unwarranted level of rudeness and aggression that the man displayed.

It was a sad awakening to the nature of Islamic exclusivity, but nothing that my ward shouldn't have expected. He would have more contact with various Sufis later in his life, in which he would experience a very different and welcoming response.

I wish to confirm there was a larger issue that was being expressed and worked through with the guard and Mein Host, but I find that right now I'm not permitted to divulge any further details.

* * *

Melchizedek's august presence, his obvious sincerity, and the immense authority with which he taught had evidently touched the hearts of the shepherds. This was evinced by the fact that, over the next few days—and then months—more and more people gathered to hear him teach.

After two years passed, he'd collected enough pupils and supporters to move farther south to the hill village of Salem and began to set up what was to become his teaching center over the ninety-four years of his life. It will be from Salem that he would send missionaries to all regions of the world teaching of the One True God.

If my patient reader believes I may have focused too much here on Melchizedek's arrival, it is because of the profound—though still largely hidden—influence he had on the history of the Middle East at a key time, and subsequently on both Judaism and Christianity. And thus, of course, his influence has extended right into the very core of Western civilization—although I doubt if he would have appreciated how it has all turned out.

A word about Machiventa Melchizedek himself. As I've previously noted, the appearance of a personified Melchizedek on the surface of a third-dimensional planet was so rare it's only occurred six times in this

Local Universe. To make this possible I have heard a special body needed to be constructed for him in much the same way that the bodies were created for the Prince's staff. Unlike the bodies of the staff that could be maintained endlessly as long as they continued to eat from the Edentian shrub, this time there was no shrub to sustain the Melchizedek.

Yet it was a fine body indeed that the Avalon surgeons constructed for him, created in the mold of a Chaldean priest. It could absorb food and drink, it needed little sleep to refresh itself, and it was entirely impervious to disease. Over time, however, his vehicle was going to finally deteriorate. I've heard that this was the reason Machiventa gave for choosing to curtail his mission after ninety-four years and leave behind his material body before it began to fall to pieces.

Melchizedek's body, unlike those of the Prince's staff, was unable to produce progeny. Thus no children remained after his disappearance to claim or fight over his position. Nor was he ever known to have taken a wife, or wives, as was the way of the times. I have sometimes overheard his contemporaries say that the very idea of their stern teacher ever taking a woman to bed would simply never have occurred to them.

What I admired above all in this formidable figure was that he appeared invulnerable to Prince Caligastia's wiles.

As a Melchizedek, he was far more intelligent than a Planetary Prince—a mere Lanonandek Son. The latter had been created to have a sufficient shared emotional bandwidth with mortals to be able to comprehend them. It was this shared emotional bandwidth with human beings that dampened Prince Caligastia's mental intelligence. Allowing his ambitions to overwhelm his better judgment was a weakness I'd seen acted out all too many times before. Machiventa could always be relied on to outwit the Prince, frequently by completely ignoring him.

Even placing his teaching center among the hills of Salem, so close to where Caligastia had dreamed into being his magnificent palace in the fourth dimension, was interpreted by the Prince as the worst of insults. I heard this was made even more humiliating in the Prince's vainglorious mind by Melchizedek's refusal to meet him, as would have been the convention under normal circumstances.

Over time, Prince Caligastia would have cause to become far more infuriated with his hated King of Salem.

At first, the Prince ignored Melchizedek's influence when people were joining him in small numbers. It was only when entire clans turned away from worshipping Prince Caligastia as the Supreme Deity and toward the teachings of Melchizedek that the Prince finally understood what was really going on. These were the very people who Caligastia's priests of Jehovah had bullied into worshipping him, together with his own brand of narcissistic monotheism.

And now they were turning away from the Prince in droves.

Machiventa Melchizedek was using all those thousands of grim years when Prince Caligastia was held supreme to piggyback his own belief system on top of it. It was during these years that he had impressed his monotheism on the gullible tribes of southern Palestine.

For Caligastia this was the final insult. It was as if he had been unwittingly working on the behalf of the MA all along. It would never have occurred to him that Melchizedek was merely attempting to make the best of a thoroughly difficult situation. Even I could appreciate that Machiventa needed to start his mission somewhere. At least the priests of Jehovah had done something toward paving the way for his teaching of the One True God.

Of course the Prince was infuriated by this, but there was little he could do about it. For the first time in almost two hundred thousand years, Caligastia found he was no longer top dog. The Prince quickly discovered he was essentially powerless against the Melchizedek, and although he tried his utmost to sabotage the mission, he was never able to do any serious damage.

The Prince's loss of personal power was as though his balloon of bloated self-importance had suddenly deflated. I didn't encounter him during this time but Astar told me she'd been quite shocked by his condition. His midwayers had long since dismissed the Prince as a megalomanic and had carved out their own fiefdoms in the landscape of the minds of the people. And yet even their influence had been steadily diminishing over the recent millennia as human beings became progressively more independent minded.

Astar said that the Prince's right-hand aide, Daligastia—who'd always served in Caligastia's shadow and had suffered his many abuses—finally summoned the courage (if that's what you could call it, said Astar) to turn his back on the Prince when he saw his superior's power evaporate in the face of Melchizedek's authentic integrity.

Prince Caligastia was now utterly alone. Satan, the only authority to whom the Prince had ever shown any respect, had failed to visit Earth for a long time. So long, in fact, that Astar reckoned he didn't want to appear connected with Caligastia's betrayal of the rebellion.

As Melchizedek's revelation of El Elyon the Most High God gained progressively more purchase on the religious sensibility of the Semitic tribes who'd previously worshipped him, Caligastia became a shadow of his former strutting self. Deprived now of the psychic energy he'd extracted from being worshipped, and yet still inflamed enough to try to pull down Melchizedek's mission, he was reduced to merely doing his worst to make a nuisance of himself wherever he could.

At this time, Melchizedek simply built on the Prince's monotheism—regarding it as just another adversarial challenge to be met in the journey of life. Caligastia must have realized he'd been out-classed and outwitted and began fading to the periphery of the action.

There would be times over the next few millennia when Prince Caligastia's fortunes would rise and fall as unscrupulous priests and preachers of a variety of religions tried to use transcendent fear to ter-rify their flocks. The Prince would find himself painted as the devil, reigning over an imaginary region called hell—imaginary because it exists only in the imagination of human beings.

The Prince will be confused with Lucifer and Satan by people ignorant of the true situation. He will be painted as the king of lies and the prince of darkness. He will find himself reviled and blamed for all the sins of the world until the time came that the once-glorious Prince Caligastia would no longer be believed to have ever existed—all but erased from the history of this troubled planet.

At this point in history the collective consciousness of human beings would expand sufficiently to see the wisdom of taking responsibility for their own thoughts and actions—without requiring a devil to blame for making them do it. At this same time, humanity will evolve into adulthood.

\* \* \*

When Melinda and Mein Host left the Temple Mount, my ward allowed the anger he'd suppressed in the altercation with the Muslim guard to come out. By expressing it, he'd released much of his frustration by the time they'd walked deep into the Old City and came across an obviously ancient church. Its facade was plain and undecorated, broken only by some Romanesque arches. Like so much else in the city it seemed to be built atop an even earlier structure.

This was the Church of St. Anne. Built and completed in 1138 CE, it was constructed over a grotto. Later research noted that the Crusaders believed this was where Anne, the mother of Mary, was born. Once again, I seem not permitted at this stage to say any more about the authenticity of this. (It isn't my purpose here to burst any legendary balloons when to do so would cause unnecessary pain for no relevant gain.)

What was of interest to my ward when he discovered it far later, was that the Byzantine basilica that had preceded the Roman Catholic St. Anne's Church was itself built over a pagan shrine dedicated to two gods of healing. In an earlier era, the grotto had been a shrine to Serapis, the Egyptian god of healing. Later it was where to find the Greek god of healing, Asclepius. I say this in advance because of what my ward and Melinda experienced when they slipped into the cool air of the church, found the entrance to the grotto, and followed their uneven steps down into the still cooler air of the grotto.

When I followed them I found the cavelike space with its uneven whitewashed walls to be a place of great peace. I could see from my ward's emotional body that he was starting to relax. They'd found a stone bench in the empty grotto and were sitting together, silently contemplating the simple unadorned beauty of the place.

My ward commented afterward on the profound healing vibes he felt coursing through the cave. And yes, it was in his base chakra he said he was feeling it. What he couldn't have known was that two midwayers who have specialized in healing were present. However, in this case, they were not those known as Serapis or Ascelepius, neither of whom were on duty at the time.

Here is Mein Host on what happened next. He writes:

> After the heat and dirt and the noise of those packed alleys of the Old City, the feeling in the grotto was akin to slowly sinking from the tepid surface of the Caribbean into the cooler water beneath. The primitive beauty of the place; the intimacy of the space with its gentle rounded corners; the friendly smell of whitewash paint so reminiscent of other caves and grottoes. We both settled into the atmosphere, feeling it tangibly wash over and through us.
>
> It was a moment of utter perfection, one of those rare perfect moments, per facio, "thoroughly made," in which it's beyond the human imagination to make the moment any more perfect.
>
> And yet . . . and yet . . . the sounds began so quietly I believe I thought the perfection of the place might be inducing a synesthetic trick in my mind, transducing visual beauty into music. Into music? And then into song? Other singers joined the plaintively beautiful chant, layers and layers of them, as though the whole angelic host was filling the space with sound.
>
> "How could this be? How could perfection be rendered even more perfect? Is it turtles all the way up? Can perfection be ever more perfected? Are we looking at the upside of Von Newman's Catastrophe of the Infinite Regress*? Can it be only me and my limitations that prevent my climbing this ladder of perfection?

---

*Robert Anton Wilson's definition follows off Von Newman's Catastrophe of the Infinite Regress as recorded by Paul Hughes in his essay *Super Free Will: Metaprogramming and the Quantum Observer,* included in *Exploring the Edge Realms of Consciousness,* edited by Daniel Pinchbeck and Ken Jordan and published by Evolver Editions, Berkeley, California, in 2012.

Paul Hughes quotes Wilson, writing: "A demonstration by Dr. Von Neumann that quantum mechanics entails an infinite regress of measurements before the quantum uncertainty can be removed. That is, any measuring device is itself a quantum system containing uncertainty; a second measuring device, used to monitor the first, contains its own quantum uncertainty; and so on, to infinity."

Dr. Wilson then adds the central insight of the quantum physicist to this apparently alarming, dice-playing, quantum nature of the Multiverse. He writes: "Wigner (*Note: Eugene Wigner, the Hungarian American theoretical physicist. —TW*) and others have pointed out that this uncertainty is only terminated by the decision of the observer."

I managed to get the questions out of my head as the choir, who must have been singing in the basilica above us, surged in volume into a series of elegant crescendos. It's a cliché to say I was carried away by the chant and washed clean by the beauty of it. And yet the cliché remains the most simple and evocatively familiar metaphor to describe this precise sensation, a feeling everybody is likely to experience at least a few times in their lives. Besides, after Georgia's pleasure at her own cavalier use of clichés, I trust she'll allow me one of my own!

Melinda and I must have sat in bewitched silence for as long as the chanting continued, and then for a time afterward. We were assimilating the modest miracle in which we'd both participated as mute and joy filled participants, unknown to those in the church above us.

It was only afterward, as we climbed back out into the noisy streets, that I wondered, not entirely seriously, whether it was Melinda and I who, by hearing those perfect harmonies drifting down to us from on high, were the ones collapsing the uncertainty wave function and as observers, it was us making all this real.

And, of course, a question always wise to ask in such a magical place as Jerusalem: Was there really an actual choir of people up in the church? And if so, was it the choir that was collapsing the uncertainty wave function by singing? Or was it perhaps us, down in the grotto, who were collapsing it by listening?

Indeed, it was all very fascinating, this application of the position of quantum observer to such a tender situation. I didn't know at the time that my ward was thinking along these lines. Once again I have to credit his intuition for taking him in this direction—and his companion angels for fostering his layman's interest in the physical sciences. Being able to think in quantum terms, and then applying the concepts in real-world settings supports the metaphysical truth that each person is totally responsible for themselves and the reality they co-create.

More important, in Mein Host's case anyway—although he was unaware of it at the time—becoming adept in thinking in quantum terms allows some familiarity as to how fourth-dimensional reality is so immediately responsive to the spiritual and psychic needs of the observer.

The next stage of my ward's journey would take him further still into unknown territory in both the inner and outer worlds. He would travel widely to Switzerland, Australia, Japan, Hawaii, New Zealand, Peru, all over Europe, and back again to the Middle East and Israel, where his first book would be written.

He would find himself progressively more involved with the angels, working with them to accomplish small shifts in people's thinking. He would go on to write more books and he would finally manage to leave New York City for the high desert of New Mexico and a more solitary life.

Diana would finally come clean with secrets she had been holding back for all these years, including handing over a letter from his father—the only letter he would ever receive from his father. For reasons known only to her, Diana didn't give the letter to her son until he was in his forties; it would explain much that my ward needed to know.

In spite of the various clues my ward had been receiving it would still be some time before he could come to terms with being an incarnate rebel angel. It would take him a full twenty years before he would be ready to accept it. And it would ultimately take him working with me to finally confirm it.

As for me, Georgia, I would start making myself more and more known to my ward, which would take us both into some challenging, as well as some thoroughly entertaining, situations. It would take us another twenty years before we could stabilize our working relationship sufficiently to collaborate on this work.

Yet they would be twenty of the most fascinating years for us both.

# An Exciting Future

True Angelic Collaboration, Starting a
Second Life, the Islands and the Ocean, and
the Experiment Continues

I started writing with Georgia having no clue as to what to expect. I certainly didn't know it would continue this long—and she tells me there is more to go. How many volumes she won't say, even if she knows.

I thought to begin with that Georgia might have the narrative already mapped out in her mind, but as we have progressed it is becoming increasingly clear this really is a true collaboration. Neither of us really knows where it's going before the words drop onto the page. And yet the volumes appear to be so well-structured they require only the minimum of editing.

I have nothing to do with this, other than coming to the decision when to stop one volume and start the next. Georgia would simply go on writing page after page. This leads me to agree with Georgia when she commented some time ago that she was sensing a meta-presence organizing the material through her.

This is, perhaps, more familiar territory to me than to her. When I was writing *Ask Your Angels* with my two colleagues, Alma Daniel and Andrew Ramer, we found we'd been joined by an angel by the name of Abigrael who'd been assigned to work with us on the project. She only made herself known to us after we'd been working on the book for a year and a half and were struggling with the wealth of material. But we had apparently shown ourselves dedicated enough to deserve an angelic collaborator, and thank God we did!

When three people with ideas of their own are writing a book together about a subject as obscure and little understood as angels, it's akin to driving a car with three people at the wheel. I'm sure you can appreciate the problem. Starting with a question as modest as, "Do angels have wings?" (one "yes" and two "no") and its resolution, the angels will be perceived in whatever manner the perceiver needs, or can handle at that moment. In my NDE, for example, I saw some angels with wings, and others without.

It was really only with Abigrael's organizing grace that the book ultimately came together after four complete rewrites. This grace would manifest in such ways as when the three of us, writing in separate places, would find when we'd meet to discuss the material, that although we were writing autonomously, our viewpoints were being knitted together by Abigrael's subtle ministrations.

I feel it is with this volume in particular that both Georgia and I have come to understand there are more voices involved with this work than either of us anticipated. It seems to me I'm seeing a broadening in social comment as we move further into recorded history in Georgia's narrative thread and deeper into my second life in mine.

I can only assume this arrangement is going to continue, for it seems to work for us. I also trust it is the relevance of the material that is drawing other celestials to participate. This points to a desire on the part of these other celestials for more starseeds to be drawn to discovering and understanding the meaning and purpose to each of their lives.

However, all these celestial aspects fall under Georgia's rubric, and by now I'm confident she knows what she's doing.

I'm happily amazed that Georgia's narrative has not only held my interest over the course of writing these eight books together, but her narrative also makes me enthusiastic to get my teeth into the next volume as soon as possible.

Even though my monkey mind can tell me that few readers will likely get this far, my enthusiasm is focused rather on my own journey of self-discovery. My assurance coming from the letters I receive from my readers suggests that others feel a sufficient resonance with Georgia's words to activate their own self-remembrance.

As for me, I'm all the more intrigued to see what Georgia has to say in the next volumes—I can't help thinking there'll have to be a few more because we're starting to move into "interesting times" (in the Chinese sense) in both threads of her narrative. The two millennia before Christ, as well as the centuries after his death, saw the foundations being laid down for the modern age.

In my own life, in the second thread, I'm now in my early forties and just beginning to consciously work with the angels. As a consequence, I was experiencing an increasing number of synchronicities and finding myself being pitched into a whole series of unusual situations. I've included many of these encounters in my own three books about spiritual intelligences, and if this volume is anything to go by, Georgia will always have some valuable insights about what was going on behind the scenes.

I try not to repeat myself for readers who already know my own work. I encourage Georgia to do likewise, unless there's something I'm missing and need to know or if there's a subtext buried in the event that is of value for others to understand. I hope the way Georgia handled the few events in this volume that I have previously described in other books holds the reader's interest in the same way that her insights have informed me.

Human beings are individuals who seem both separate from one another and yet are one.

The metaphor used sometimes to illustrate this manner by which everything seems to spring from the same substrate is that of islands in an ocean. On the surface of the ocean we believe ourselves to be these separate islands, each different, and yet all those islands are joined at the base where they extend upward from the seabed.

I've found over the course of writing my own very personal books that there's some truth in this. If I'm prepared to dive deep enough—and Georgia needs no encouragement to do likewise—then the experiences I'm having, and Georgia's descriptions and analysis of them, should resonate with those elements of the seabed that we all share.

I remain a willing collaborator in Georgia's literary experiment and her desire to record what she observed in her half a million years on the planet, as she appears willing to remain part of my experiment in communicating in-depth with another species. In many ways, I feel this long work with Georgia is the apex of my thirty-year exploration of nonhuman intelligences, as well as a generous reward for paying it due attention.

I hope you will join Georgia and me in our further investigations and will derive from them authentic meaning that will be of value to you in the course of clarifying your own spiritual life.

❧·❦

## POST SCRIPT

This is the last book of Georgia's *Confession* series. I am certain Timothy and Georgia would have continued their collaboration. But given that Timothy passed on, then I believe what *they* needed to share has already been shared.

I've been asked by Timothy's readers and friends if Georgia has communicated directly with me, and I have to honestly say not since Timothy passed on. But as Timothy said in his past writings, he was but one of many incarnate angels Georgia had "on the ready." So perhaps she will collaborate with someone else in the future. Then again . . . perhaps she has learned what she intended to learn, and now *she* will incarnate herself (if she hasn't already). Time will tell!

DANIEL MATOR

# The Angelic Cosmology

Different versions of the so-called War in Heaven appear so frequently in indigenous legends and mythologies from around the world—as well as in the sacred books and traditions of major religions—that the war is more than likely based on a real event. I believe the most authoritative account can be found in *The Urantia Book,* where it is referred to as "the Lucifer Rebellion."

Thirty years after first reading *The Urantia Book,* I still regard it as the most reliable source of information about both extraterrestrial and celestial activities. It is broken down into four parts devoted to the following subjects: the Nature of God and the Central and Superuniverses, the Local Universe, the History of Urantia (their name for this planet), and the Life and Teachings of Jesus Christ. (For a definition of terms common to both *The Urantia Book* and this book, please refer to the glossary.)

According to the Urantia model, there are seven Superuniverses, which together compose the material Multiverse. These seven Superuniverses form the substance of the finite Multiverse and circle the Central Universe, which can be visualized as the hole in the center of the toroidal form of the Multiverse.

Each Superuniverse contains one hundred thousand Local Universes, each of which has its own Creator Son (ours is Christ Michael, or Jesus Christ) and its own Divine Mother—these are the Creator Beings of their domain. This pair of High Beings modulates the energy downstepped from the Central Universe to create and form

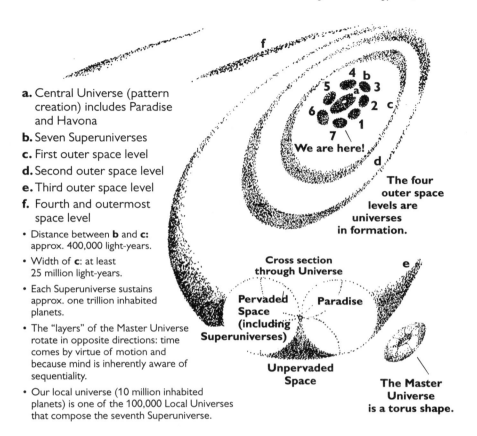

a. Central Universe (pattern creation) includes Paradise and Havona

b. Seven Superuniverses

c. First outer space level

d. Second outer space level

e. Third outer space level

f. Fourth and outermost space level

- Distance between **b** and **c:** approx. 400,000 light-years.

- Width of **c**: at least 25 million light-years.

- Each Superuniverse sustains approx. one trillion inhabited planets.

- The "layers" of the Master Universe rotate in opposite directions: time comes by virtue of motion and because mind is inherently aware of sequentiality.

- Our local universe (10 million inhabited planets) is one of the 100,000 Local Universes that compose the seventh Superuniverse.

**We are here!**

**The four outer space levels are universes in formation.**

**Cross section through Universe**

**Pervaded Space (including Superuniverses)**

**Paradise**

**Unpervaded Space**

**The Master Universe is a torus shape.**

Master Universe Structure (From *The Urantia Book,* p. 129)

the beings and the planetary biospheres with their Local Universe. Each Local Universe sustains ten million inhabited planets broken out into ten thousand Local Systems.

Each Local System, in turn, contains one thousand inhabited—or to be inhabited—planets, and each has its own System Sovereign (ours was Lucifer) appointed to govern the System. Each planet, in turn, has a Planetary Prince (ours was Prince Caligastia), who oversees their particular worlds.

According to *The Urantia Book,* Lucifer and Satan (Lucifer's main assistant) came to believe that an elaborate conspiracy had been concocted by the Creator Sons of the Local Universes to promote the existence of a fictitious Unseen Divinity, which the Creator Sons then used as a control device to manipulate the orders of celestials and angels within their creations. Having announced the existence of this conspiracy, Lucifer demanded more autonomy for all beings, and for System Sovereigns and Planetary Princes to follow their own approaches for accelerating the spiritual development of their mortal charges.

The revolutionaries quickly gained followers and the rebellion spread rapidly to affect thirty-seven planets in our System, with Urantia, our planet Earth, being one of them. Choice was given to the many angels involved with supervising System activities as to whether or not to join the rebel faction.

Lucifer's charge—that too much attention was being given to ascending mortals—appeared to ring true to a large number of angels, as well as the thirty-seven pairs of administrative angels: the Planetary Princes and their assistants who were responsible for the orderly progression of mortal (human) beings on their worlds. The revolution was effectively suppressed by the administration authorities and recast as a heinous rebellion, its immediate consequence being the removal of Lucifer and Satan from their posts in the System.

At the time of the Lucifer Rebellion, the vast majority of the fifty thousand midway angels on Earth—40,119 to be exact—aligned themselves with Lucifer and Satan. They were destined to remain on our planet until the time of Christ, when, according to *The Urantia Book,* it was one of Christ's occulted functions to remove them. It is a brief reference and no further details are given in the book as to where the rebel midwayers were taken. However, with the removal of these rebel midwayers, a mere 9,981 loyalist midwayers remained here to fulfill the tasks of five times their number.

As a result of this, in contrast to a normal planet (one not quarantined), on which angelic companions and the presence of helpful midwayers and extraterrestrials must be commonplace knowledge, we earthlings have slumbered in our corner of a populated Multiverse, unaware of who we are and how we got this way. Having been quarantined and isolated from normal extraterrestrial activity for the long

203,000 years since the rebellion, we first lost touch with, and then forgot entirely, our rightful place in the populated Multiverse. Given this, we were bound to evolve as a troubled species. Our world is one of the few planets that, due to the Lucifer Rebellion, has been thrown off its normal pattern of development.

This disquieting situation, this planetary quarantine, has persisted for more than two hundred thousand years, only to have finally been adjudicated, in my understanding, in the early 1980s.

Given that the planetary quarantine has finally been lifted, the rest of the Multiverse is now able to make legitimate contact with us. More recently what we are witnessing is both the return of the rebel midwayers (the beings of the violet flame), who are now coming back to assist us in the coming transformation of our world; and, perhaps of more personal interest to my readers, the many angels who aligned with Lucifer at the time of the rebellion are incarnating as mortals. It appears these rebel angels and Watchers are being offered human incarnation as a path to personal redemption, as the world is emerging from an interminably long dark age to shake off the shadows and fulfill its remarkable destiny.

# Glossary

Many valuable insights from many different sources have contributed to the themes and fundamental questions that this *Confessions* series seeks to explore, but the most reliable and comprehensive exposition of God, the Universe, and Everything, that I have come across remains *The Urantia Book*. A number of the concepts and words below are drawn from it and marked (UB), but the definitions are the author's.

**Agondonter:** a mortal who ascends from a world isolated by angelic rebellion.

**Albedo:** the second stage of the alchemical process resulting from the slow burning out of the impurities present in the first stage.

**Angel:** a general term for any order of being who administers within a Local Universe.

**Atman, Indwelling Spirit, Thought Adjuster (UB):** an essence of the Creator that indwells all mortal beings, human and extraterrestrial.

**Bioplasm (UB):** a constituent of an individual's genome required to reconstitute a biological duplicate of the bioplasm's donor, or for calibrating a cloned physical vehicle to its intended environment.

**Caligastia (UB):** a Secondary Lanonandek Son who served as Planetary Prince of this world and who aligned himself with Lucifer.

**Cano (UB):** young Nodite aristocrat who mated with Eve, the female visitor.

**Central Universe (UB):** the abode of the original Creator God(s)—the Father, the Mother/Son, and the Holy Spirit (UB). If the Multiverse is a torus, then the Central Universe is the hole in the middle, existing on a far finer frequency and from which energy is downstepped to form the building blocks of the Multiverse.

**Citrinitas:** advanced state of spiritual enlightenment whereby the alchemist can make an ultimate unification with the Supreme.

**Commodore:** a high-ranking mortal from an advanced world who commands the Andromedan vessel.

**Creator Beings:** Creator Son (ours is Christ Michael, or Jesus Christ) and Divine Mother, rulers of our earthly domain.

**Creator Sons (UB):** co-creators—each having a female complement, the Mother Spirit (UB)—of each of the seven hundred thousand Local Universes (UB). The co-creators of the Local Universes modulate the downstepped energies from the Central Universe to design the life-forms for those beings existing within all the frequency domains of their Local Universe.

**Daligastia (UB):** a Secondary Lanonandek Son who served as Caligastia's right-hand aide.

**Demons:** negative thoughtforms.

**Devas:** the coordinating spirits of the natural world. All living organisms are cared for by devas (or nature spirits). In the human being the deva is that which coordinates and synchronizes the immense amount of physical and biochemical information that keeps our bodies alive.

**Didgeridoo ("didg" for short):** a large bamboo or wooden trumpet played by Australian Aborigines.

**Dreamtime:** an altered state of consciousness induced by dances and chants and practiced by the many indigenous tribes of Australia.

**Extraterrestrial:** mortal beings such as ourselves who hail from more developed worlds with access to our frequency domain.

**Fandor (UB):** a large semi-telepathic passenger bird, said to have become extinct about thirty-eight thousand years ago.

**The Foundation Faith:** The successor name for the Process Church of which the author was a member.

**Frequency Domain:** the spectrum of frequencies that support the life-forms whose senses are tuned to that specific spectrum.

**God:** in *my* personal experience, God is both the Creator and the totality of Creation, manifest and unmanifest, immanent and transcendent.

**G.R.A.C.E. Process:** an acronym for the process by which thought-forms are released. It consists of Grounding, Releasing, Aligning, Conversing, and Enjoying the connection.

**Guardian (Companion) Angels (UB):** function in pairs to ensure their mortal wards grow in spirit over the course of their lifetimes.

**Holy Angel:** a sacred being that, according to Yazidi cosmology, was entrusted with the care of this world by the Creator.

**Indwelling Spirit, Atman, Thought Adjuster (UB):** an essence of the Creator that indwells all mortal beings, human and extraterrestrial.

**Janda-chi:** the second of the two Planetary Princes on the planet Zandana.

**Jesus Christ:** the Michaelson (UB) of our Local Universe (UB) who incarnated as Jesus Christ in the physical body of Joshua ben Joseph; he is also known as Michael of Nebadon (UB).

**Joy:** one of the author's two companion angels, Beauty being the second.

**Lakes of Glass:** extremely large crystals that function as terminals of a Universe Broadcast System linking all fourth-density planets.

**Lanaforge (UB):** a primary Lanonandek Son who succeeded Lucifer as System Sovereign.

**Land of the Two Rivers:** ancient name for Sumer, where much of our story takes place.

**Lanonandek Order of Sonship (UB):** the third order of Local Universe

Descending Sons of God who serve as System Sovereigns (Primary Lanonandeks) and Planetary Princes (Secondary Lanonandeks).

**Local System (UB):** our Local System, named Satania (UB), is believed to currently possess between 600 and 650 inhabited planets. Earth is numbered 606 in this sequence.

**Local System HQ Planet, Jerusem (UB):** the political and social center of the Satania System.

**Local Universe (UB):** a grouping of planets that comprises 10 million inhabited worlds.

**Lucifer (UB):** deposed System Sovereign and primary protagonist in the rebellion among the angels.

**Lucifer Rebellion (UB):** a rebellion among the angels occurring 203,000 years ago on Jerusem that affected thirty-seven inhabited worlds, of which Earth was one.

**Luminaries:** "Higher-ups" of the Process Church, most of whom were the earliest members.

**Magisterial Son:** powerful beings that present in human form and function more like an organizing principle or a point of spiritual coherence to elevate universal consciousness.

**Mani Particle Beam:** a type of universal propulsion system used by large ships and small starcars.

**Master Universe (UB):** the Multiverse that contains the seven Superuniverses (UB).

**Material Son and Daughter:** the two intraterrestrial biologists who were thwarted by Prince Caligastia in carrying out their mission on Earth.

**Melchizedek Sons/Brothers (UB):** a high order of Local Universe Sons devoted primarily to education and who function as planetary administrators in emergencies.

**Michaelson (UB):** otherwise known as Jesus Christ, he incarnated in the physical body of Joshua ben Joseph; he is also known as Michael of Nebadon (UB).

**Midwayers** or **Midway Creatures** (UB): intelligent beings, imperceptible to humans, who exist in a contiguous frequency domain and serve as the permanent planetary citizens.

**Mortals** (UB): intelligent beings who emerge as a result of biological evolutionary processes on a planet. Souls are born to their immortal lives as mortals, whose physical bodies live and die before they are given the choice to continue their Multiverse career.

**Mortal Ascension Scheme** (UB): the process by which all mortal beings who live and die on the material worlds of the Local Systems pass up through the seven subsequent levels to Jerusem, where they embark on their universe career.

**Mother Spirit** (UB): with the Michaelson, the female co-creator of a Local Universe.

**Multiverse**: the author's term for the entire range of frequency domains, on every level of the Master Universe (UB).

**Multiverse Administration** (MA): the author's general term for the celestial administration, with special reference to the Local Universe bureaucracy.

**Naga**: in Hindu and Buddhist cosmologies, a naga is a spirit part superhuman and part serpent, and also a genie of the water and the rain. As such they live in a subaqueous kingdom.

**Nebadon** (UB): the name of this Local Universe of 10 million inhabited planets.

**Nigredo**: the first stage of the alchemical process during which the alchemical material is broken down and dissolved to remove impurities.

**Nodites** (UB): descendants of the illicit interbreeding between selected mortals and, on realizing they were doomed to physical death, those of the Prince's staff who followed Caligastia's uprising.

**Nodu, Nod** (UB): Nodu is Georgia's informal, but respectful, name for the member of the Prince's staff who opposed Caligastia and who, in time, led his people to the Islands of Mu.

**Nommo:** a race of semiaquataic beings that, before incarnating in a human body, must first spend a life as a cetacean.

**Oannes:** a semiaquatic race that, together with the Nommo, taught the arts of civilization to ancient Mesopotamia.

**Overgovernment:** refers to the Seraphic Overgovernment, which is a coordinating agency for all the angels functioning in the fifth dimension.

**Phinsouse:** star system inhabited by a very old race of non-space-faring beings. The center of space activity, it is located in the middle of the Andromeda Galaxy.

**Planetary Prince:** like Prince Caligastia, each Planetary Prince is an overseer of each of the planets in each Local System of the Multiverse.

**Priest of El Elyon:** a term synonymous with the Most High, and/or the One and Only God.

**The Process:** a shorter name for the Process Church of which the author was a member.

**Rainbow Bridge:** A physical phenomenon seen on Zandana—and predicted for this planet—where the convergence of two bodies creates what appears as a rainbow-hued bridge. This "bridge" also serves as a conduit for beings between dimensions.

**Reincarnation Express:** Prince Caligastia's plan, thwarted by the MA, that attempted to recycle rebel angels while keeping the mortal ascension process open for the natural ascenders.

**Satan (UB):** Lucifer's right-hand aide who co-instigated the angelic rebellion 203,000 years ago.

**Serapatatia (UB):** Nodite Prince who persuaded Eve to accelerate the visitors' mission by mating with Cano and creating a singular Nodite bloodline with a healthy dash of violet blood.

**Seraph(im) (UB):** a high order of angels whose functions include that of companion (guardian) angels, or, like Georgia, observing angels.

**Seraphic Transport System (UB):** the transportation system of living beings that ferries Watchers and ascending mortals to different worlds in the Multiverse.

**Shandron:** a Supernaphim channeled by Timothy's friend Edward.

**Solonia (UB):** the seraphic "voice in the garden" (UB) that admonished the visitors and had them leave their garden home and start their long journey to settle in the Land of the Two Rivers.

**Star People:** starseeds and others of an extraterrestrial heritage who adopt human incarnation or use human bodies to help humanity progress.

**Starseeds:** beings from other worlds who come to Earth for various reasons and, once here, adopt a human vehicle. They include rebel angel incarnates as well as Walk-Ins and Star People.

**Superuniverse (UB):** a universe that contains one hundred thousand Local Universes.

**System of Planets (UB):** a grouping of planets consisting of a thousand inhabited, or to be inhabited, planets.

**System of Satania:** the System of planets within which Earth is but one of the more than 650 inhabited worlds of the one thousand planets within its administrative domain, and the locale of the Lucifer revolution.

**System Sovereign (UB):** the administrative angel, together with an assistant of the same rank, who is an overall authority of a Local System. Lucifer and Satan were the pair in charge of this System of planets.

**Thought Adjuster (UB), Atman, Indwelling Spirit:** an essence of the Creator that indwells all mortal beings, human and extraterrestrial.

**Thoughtforms:** quasi-life-forms existing in the astral regions, drawing their limited power from strong emotional thoughts projected out from human mentation, both conscious and unconscious. Thoughtforms can be negative or positive. Localized negative ones are referred to as fear-impacted thoughtforms.

**Transport Seraph(im):** Order of Seraphim specifically created as sentient vehicles to make interplanetary transit available in the fourth and fifth dimensions.

**Ultimaton:** building blocks of the quantum world of material particles that are continually downstepped energetically from the Central Universe to inform the material universes of time and space.

**Ultraterrestrial or Intraterrestrial Beings:** the beings who inhabit our neighboring frequency domain and who *The Urantia Book* calls the midwayers or midway creatures.

**Unava:** chief of staff to Prince Zanda, the senior of the two Planetary Princes of the neighboring planet Zandana.

**The Unit:** the author's splinter group of the Foundation that he founded in New York City in 1977.

**Universe Career (UB):** a mortal's destiny, unless chosen otherwise, to rise through the many hundreds of levels of the Multiverse to finally encounter the Creator.

*The Urantia Book:* Initially published in 1955 by Urantia Foundation, this book outlines the origin, history, and fate of mankind in its discussion of the nature of God, life in the universe, the backstory of Earth, and the life and message of Jesus Christ.

**Violet Blood (UB):** the potential of an infusion of a slightly higher frequency genetic endowment, which results in more acute senses and a deeper spiritual awareness and responsiveness.

**Walk-In:** a being from another world or dimension who comes to Earth and inhabits the body of a human being through a mutual agreement. Walk-Ins may be rebel angels and typically have heavy karma from a previous incarnation to work out while on Earth.

**Watcher:** an angel relegated to the status of observer, such as Georgia, the angel whose material was channeled for this book and the other books in the *Confessions* series.

**Wise Twins:** the two suns of the planet Zandana. These are the two bodies that created the Rainbow Bridge.

**Zanda:** senior Planetary Prince of Zandana, a planet named in his honor and to which Georgia has made frequent visits.

**Zandan:** the principal city of the planet Zandana.

**Zandana:** a neighboring planet developing within approximately the same time frame as Earth and whose Planetary Princes also followed Lucifer into revolution.

# Index

Abigrael, 306–7
Aboriginal mind, 56
Aboriginal worldview, 52
Aborigines
  conceptual framework, 50
  didgeridoo and, 38–40, 47, 52, 315
  isolation, 34–35
  Komilaroi tribe, 50, 54
  off-planet life and, 54
  "pointing the bone," 251
  star people, 49
  storytelling, 47–48
  as subtle and sophisticated, 37
  tribe involvement, 53
Adrian
  Jesse and, 40–45
  kayak and, 42–44
  lack of emotional strength, 33
  LSD and, 40–45
  Marion and, 31–33, 45–46
  Rachel and, 30
*Adventures among Spiritual*
  *Intelligences,* 53
Afterlife
  authenticity, acceptance of, 164

  experience of angels in, 162
  experiential reality of, 106
  NDE experience of, 180
  spirit vision in, 129
agondonters, 91, 135, 136, 314
Akhenaten, 228, 229, 230–31
albedo, 314
Amadon's teachings, 22, 110, 189, 230
Amdon, 289–90, 291–92
Amun-Re, 228, 229
Andrew, 196–99
Andromeda Galaxy, 211
Andromedan vessel, 192
angelic cosmology, 310–13
angelic rebellions
  Local Universe and, 131
  MA and, 136
  new forms of being and, 136
  as rare, 135
  references to, 164
angelic revolution
  allowed to continue, 133
  changes after, 24, 73, 90
  deeper meaning of, 10
  time before, 11, 127

"Angelic Dimension, The," 217
angels
    arbitrary prohibitions and, 103
    barge story, 86–87
    companion, 104, 113, 119, 248–49, 316
    contact with, 88
    defined, 314
    experience in Afterlife, 162
    functioning in the fifth dimension, 264
    mortals symbiosis, 133
    NDE and, 3, 88–89, 162, 180, 307
    reality of, 87, 88–89
    relationship with mortals, 104
    sound of singing, 198
    "swinging the planet back into
      normalcy" and, 167
    writing with, 219
    in Yazidi cosmology, 246
Anthesis, 143
Armand, 236–40, 241
Art of the People, 137
*Ask Your Angels,* 86, 87, 306
Astar
    Atlantis and, 58–59
    Jehovah and, 15
    on midwayers, 223–24
    Palestinian desert and, 276–77
    Prince Caligastia and, 13–15
    on rebel angel incarnation, 263
    on Sirians, 97
Aten, 228
atheists, 242
Atkin, June, 250
Atlantis
    Astar and, 58–59
    Caligastia and, 13, 58
    Lemurians on, 59

    natural disasters, 58
    naval primacy, 58
    Sirians and, 174
    starseeds on, 24, 132
Atman, 11, 314
Australia, 34–35, 37–40, 50–51, 55.
    *See also* Aborigines

bananas story, 232–35, 241
barge story, 86–87
base chakra, 254, 285–87, 294–95, 302
Being of Light, 201
Bennett Park
    graffiti, 139, 140
    UFO sighting, 141, 158–59, 237
Black Books, 218, 249

Caligastia, Prince
    abuse of power, 96
    ascension of the soul and, 244
    Atlantis and, 13, 58
    caution, 72
    China and, 22
    Clarisel and, 189
    declaration as Supreme God, 12–13
    defined, 314
    as devil, 300
    entheogens and, 56–57
    fourth density and, 209–10
    as "Heavenly Father," 231
    intentions, 212, 221–22
    Jehovah and, 61
    locating to the Middle East, 34
    loss of power, 299–300
    Lucifer and, 13–14, 300
    Melchizedek and, 298–300
    midwayer rebellion and, 224

monotheism, 15, 27, 223, 224
  Multiverse Administration (MA)
    and, 13, 16, 222–23
  Poseidon and, 59–60
  pride and narcissism, 72
  rebellions and, 72
  Reincarnation Express, 136
  succession and, 223
  technological progress and, 71
cancer, 252
Carolina, 257–58
Central Universe, 91, 93–94, 129,
  315
Chaldean herder, 288–89, 290
China
  clans and tribes unification, 21
  feudalism, 22
  Multiverse Administration (MA)
    and, 22–23
  Prince Caligastia and, 22
  southern, rebel angels and, 25
civilizations, Watchers and, 70
Clarisel
  about, 147
  Caligastia and, 189
  planetary dimensional shift and,
    148–49, 151
  Rainbow Bridge and, 147–48
  Sea People and, 191
  tourist ship from Andromeda and,
    154–55
Clearwater, Florida trip, 114–23, 202
"Cokey Joe," 258–59
Commodore, Andromedan
  about, 193
  Caligastia's intentions and, 212,
    221–22

Clarisel and, 193
  defined, 315
  fourth dimension and, 195, 209
  guidance, 205–6
  Jerusem seminars and, 207–8
  lounge, 207
  meeting with Georgia, 206–12
  as mortal, 210
  wine and, 205–6
community, 10, 180–81, 247–48
companion angels, 104, 113, 119,
  248–49, 316
Conference-in-Spirit, 268, 270–71
corroboree, 51–54
counter-phobia, 101–2
Creator Sons, 311–12, 315

Daligastia, Prince, 264, 300, 315
Damian
  background, 182–83
  Diana and, 232
  experience with, 184
  as ground control, 199, 202
  as healer, 196
  meeting, 183
  as portrait artist, 204
  as starseed, 185
Daniel, xi, xiii
Daniel, Alma, 66, 67–68, 99–101, 179,
  306
death. *See also* near-death experience
  (NDE)
  absence of, 93
  fear of, no, 203
  life after, 83, 84
  narrative of, 107
  premature, 47

*Delta Factor: Dolphins ETs & Angels, The,* 116, 159, 165–66, 218, 256, 268, 275
demons, 135, 226, 251, 254, 291, 315
devas, 295, 315
Diana (mother)
    background, 231–32
    bananas and, 232–35, 241
    Charterhouse and, 18
    desire to kill her son, 240
    dive toward her son, 239–40
    George and, 280
    Greek goddess Diana and, 241
    letter from father, handing over, 304
    party at Armand's and, 236–40, 241
    repressed trauma, 221
    trip to see son, 232
    viewing manuscript, 220–21
didgeridoos, 38–40, 47, 52, 315
"divided self," 252
Divine Spark, 244
divinities, 107
DMT, 179
Dobbs, Horace, 114
Dolphin and Whale Conference, 75, 77
dolphins
    circling, 121–22
    Clearwater, Florida trip and, 114–23, 202
    encounters with, 74, 85–86
    health maintenance, 115
    human emotions and, 115
    interest in, 114–15
    Jamaican Rasta man story and, 117–18
    Louis Herman observations about, 76
    as midwives, 114
    movies about, 114

    Oannes feeling and, 121, 122
    rescue by, 118
    swimming with, 81, 116
    telepathic, 88
    UFOs and, 116
    ultrasound and, 260
    Zandana and, 190
*Dolphins, Telepathy & Underwater Birthing: Further Adventures Among Spiritual Intelligences,* 218–19
Dolphins Plus, 123
Dome of the Rock, 293–94
Dominic, 6–7, 9
Dreamtime, 36, 315
droughts, 97, 225
DW Viewpacks Ltd., 16–17, 30

Edward, 159–60, 165
Egypt
    as center of gravity, 69
    development of, 112
    Nile Delta, 71
    Nile Valley, 69–70, 71, 98, 108
Egyptians
    belief system, 228–29
    priest-kings, 225
    priests, 109
    underworld and, 57
Eleena
    conversation at Seraphic Transport Center, 126–30, 131–36
    rebellion and, 133–35
    return to Earth with, 213, 221
    sonic pieces, 144–45
    as Transport Seraph, 128–29, 134–35, 145
    travel to Zandana with, 136

El Elyon, 289, 292, 300, 319
Eleusinian Mysteries, 106, 107, 108
"Emergency Sons," 264
entheogens. *See also specific types of entheogens*
   Adrian and Jesse and, 40–45
   Caligastia and, 56–57
   in expanding consciousness, 106
   flow to, 44–45
   inner workings of the mind and, 66
   Marion and, 44
   mystical experience and, 105
   mystical illumination with, 104
   pagan religions use of, 105
   religious origin and, 104
   as research tool, 64
   spiritual growth and, 103
   use of, 105–6
extraterrestrials
   angel incarnation and, 23
   from aquatic world, 74
   as commonplace knowledge, 312
   contact with individuals and, 113
   defined, 315
   dolphins and, 88
   encounters with, 194, 218
   experience with, 81–89
   individual trust and, 112
   interest in, 144

father experience
   about, 283–84
   base chakra insecurity and, 286–87
   description, 284–85
   recognition of father and, 285
   self-healing and, 287
   self-knowledge and, 288

   sense of security and, 285–86
   subpersonality and, 286
Father Jesse. *See* Jesse
Faust, Bobby, 237–39, 242
Ferguson, Marilyn, 37
feudalism, 22
fifth dimension
   angels functioning in, 264
   beings of, 150–51
   safety in, 222
   Sea People, 191
   Seraphic Transport Centers, 212
   traveling through, 168
floods, 225
*Foundation Faith of God, The,* 5
fourth density. *See also* third- to fourth-density shift
   Caligastia and, 209–10
   Commodore on, 208–9
   frequency domains, 208–9, 211
   planetary ascension to, 192
   Zandana and, 147, 148, 174, 178
frequency domains, 208–9, 211, 316
Future Studies Research Group (FSRG), 270

George (father), 280, 283–86, 304
Georgia
   addressing of Jesse, 21
   collaboration with, 309
   looking through the eyes of, 152–53
   making known to Jesse, 305
   meeting with Commodore, 206–12
   narrative, 307
   starseed use, 4
   visit with Prince Janda-chi, 168–71, 173–75

as Watcher, 2–3
writing with, 1–2, 3–4, 306
glossary of terms, 314–22
Göbekli Tepe, 14, 73
G.R.A.C.E. Process, 254, 255, 316
graffiti
    appreciation of, 137
    as Art of the People, 137
    Bennett Park and, 139, 140
    garden wall, 137–39
Great Pyramid, 267, 268, 270
Great Rocks of the World, 294
Great Spirit, awareness of, 215
grotto (Jerusalem), 301–2
guardian angels. See companion angels
Gwendolyn, 75, 77–80

"hands-off" policy, 163
"Heavenly Father," 231
Helianx project, 184
Helianx Proposition, The, 139, 215
Herman, Dr. Louis, 75–76
Hinduism, 262
Hofmann, Albert, 46, 64
Human/Dolphin Foundation, 114
"human religions," 229
"Hymn of Creation" (Rigveda), 27–28

ibogaine, 179
"inattentional blindness," 250
India
    coastal cities, 21–22
    Krishna, 224
    Multiverse Administration (MA)
        and, 23
    rebel angels, 25
    Vedic Age, 26

Indwelling Spirit, 11–12, 72, 93, 314
intelligence
    celestial, 92
    cetacean, 114, 115
    compassionate, 133
    dolphin, 65–66, 115
    mortal, 93, 195
    spiritual, 152–53, 253
    starseed, 186
"intelligence accelerator," 202
intuition, 2, 63, 112, 294–95
Israel
    affinity for, 278
    Dome of the Rock, 293–94
    insights in, 278–80
    Jerusalem, 292–93, 301–4
    Melinda and, 279
    Netanya, 218, 279, 282, 292
    sacred circle, 283

Jamaican Rasta man story, 117–18
Janda-chi, Prince
    Caligastia and, 111
    defined, 316
    as effective, 158
    friendly nature of, 174–75
    Georgia visit with, 168–71, 173–75
    Lucifer and, 170
    as manipulative, 189–90
    personal cabin, 187–88, 192
    planetary shifts and, 170–71
    as practical joker, 169
    residence, 168
jealousy, 253
Jehovah, 15, 20, 46, 61
Jerusalem, 292–93, 301–4
Jerusem seminars, 132, 158, 207–8, 265

Jesse. *See also* Diana (mother); George
     (father)
  about, 6
  Adrian and, 40–45
  Alma and, 67–68, 179
  in Australia, 37–40
  bananas and, 232–35, 241
  counter-phobia, 101–2
  Damian and, 182–85, 196, 199,
     202–4, 232
  drawing, 61–62
  in Israel, 278–80, 292–93, 301–4
  Marion and, 19–21, 29–33, 46, 179
  Melinda and, 114–20, 263–64,
     271–74, 289–92, 297–300
  relationship with women, 20–21, 179
  Viewpack business and, 16–17, 30,
     61–62
Joy, 254, 255, 316
Jung, Carl, 254

Kelly, Ray, Jr., 53, 54, 55
Kennedy, John F., 269
ketamine
  dose, 99
  as entheogen, 66, 197
  injection of, 98–99
  Lilly and, 65–66, 197, 259–60
  taking of, 202–3
  use in hospitals, 65
"King of the Living," 57
Komilaroi tribe, 50, 54
Krishna, 224

Lake of Glass, 155
Lanaforge, 14, 155, 163, 316
Leadbeater, C. W., 254

Left-Hand Path, 244
Lemurian culture, 58–59
Lemurians, 13, 21–22, 59
Lilly, John C., 65–66, 114, 197,
     256–57
Local Systems, 311, 317
Local Universes
  angelic rebellions, 131
  Creator Sons of, 267, 311–12
  cycle, 132
  defined, 317
  Mother Spirit from, 265
  organization, 265
  in Superuniverses, 93, 310
  in Urantia model, 310
Long Island Sound, 43–44, 45
LSD, 40–46
Lucifer
  charge, 312
  defined, 317
  forgiveness for, 167, 272–73
  planets aligned with, 134
  Prince Caligastia and, 13–14, 300
  understanding nature of, 9–10
  in Urantia model, 311–12
Lucifer Rebellion
  angels speaking to, 165–67
  defined, 317
  midwayers and, 262
  reconciliation of, 268, 272–73
  systemwide quarantine and, 157
  as War in Heaven, 310

Magisterial Sons, 152, 317
Mali, 74, 76, 98, 109
"Manchurian Candidate," 170
Mani Particle Beam, 142

Marion. *See also specific members of The Unit*
  Adrian and, 30–33, 45–46
  bossy manner, 32
  entheogens and, 44
  as "gung ho," 20
  Jehovah and, 20, 46
  Jesse and, 19–21, 29–33
  as psychic counselor, 30
  Viewpack business and, 17–18, 29
Mary Ann
  about, 5–6
  attachment to, 181
  Rachel story about, 7–8
  surrender to, 271
  vengeful actions, 6
"Masters of the Water," 110
Master Universe structure, 311
Material Son, 266
MDMA, 215
meditation, 43, 222, 237, 254, 257, 295
Melchizedek, Machiventa
  about, 263–64
  appearance of, 297–98
  blessing, 289
  Caligastia and, 298–300
  Chaldean herder and, 288–89, 290
  El Elyon revelation, 289, 292, 300
  finding in the flesh, 291
  intelligence, 298
Melchizedek Brothers, 16, 131–32, 164, 263, 273, 277–78, 317
Melchizedek Order of Sonship, 267
Melchizedek Sons, 264
Melchizedek teachers, 91
Melek Taus, 245–46

Melinda
  about, 271–72
  Bennett Park and, 136–37
  in Clearwater, Florida, 114, 115–20
  in Israel, 278–80, 292–97
  parents, 279
  Shandron and, 272–74
  in Toronto, 159–60
  years living with, 248
mental breakdown, 252
Michael, 265, 266
Michaelson, 265, 266, 317
Middle East, 13, 21–22, 34–35, 69, 271
midwayers
  defined, 318
  emotions and, 227
  as faux divinities, 12, 107
  floods and, 225
  function to turn away, 110
  helpful, 312
  human behavior and, 73
  Jehovah, 15
  loyalist, 105, 262, 312
  Lucifer Rebellion and, 262
  pantheon of, 108
  rebel, 34–36, 108, 223, 224, 245, 262, 312
  visible to human perceptions, 224
Monroe, Robert, 123
morning glory seeds, 56
mortal ascension, 11, 91, 93, 318
mortals
  attached to physical vehicles, 156
  as creative beings, 249–50
  defined, 318
  from different planes, differences in, 195

starseed relationships with, 186
third- to fourth-density reality, 152
work with companion angels, 249
"Most Highs," 166
Muhammad's Night Journey, 294, 296
multiple personality disorder (MPD),
236
Multiverse
ascendancy, 125–26
defined, 318
isolation from, 127
material particles, 94–95
mortals and, 63
moving toward completion, 132
"need to know" and, 112–13
as no beginning or end, 94
purpose of, 11–12
quantum nature of, 303
spiritual law of, 63
visualization of, 93
Multiverse Administration (MA)
about, 11, 318
agondonters and, 91
angel and mortal symbiosis and, 133
angelic rebellions and, 136
Energy Beings, 13
extending religious teachings, 12
illicit interventions, 172
infected planets and, 134
Prince Caligastia and, 13, 16, 222–23
strategic positioning, 90

nagas, 215, 318
near-death experience (NDE)
aftereffects of, 201, 203
Afterlife and, 180
angels and, 3, 88–89, 162, 180, 307
assimilation of truths of, 201
meeting father experience and, 284
Muhammad's Night Journey and, 294
no fear of death and, 203
Ruth and, 83, 85
as turning point, 89
Nebadon, 318
Nefertiti, 231
Netanya, 218, 279, 282, 292
New Atlantis, 61
New Order, 60
Nile Valley, 69–70, 71, 98, 108
nomadic tribes, 35–36
Nommo, 23, 98, 109–10, 112–13, 319
nonviolent resistance, 239
nurturing, 1–4, 91, 97, 157

Oannes, 97, 111–13, 121–24, 171, 224,
319
"Ogo the Fox," 109
oral tradition, 26–27

Palestinian, 276–78, 290
"Peacock Angel," 245
phencyclidine (PCP), 64–65, 117, 197,
238
Philo of Alexandria, 55
Phinsouse, 142, 143, 319
pituri, 56
planetary dimensional shifts, 147–49,
151
Pleiadeans, 48
polytheistic cultures, 226–27
Poseidon, 59–61
praying, 295–96
priestcraft, 226
"Prince Caligastia's monotheism," 10–11

Process, the, 6, 9, 165, 179–82, 217,
    271, 319

quantum mechanics, 303

Rachel, 7–8, 30
Rainbow Bridge, 124, 147–48, 319
Rajneesh, Bhagwan Shree, 67
rebel angels. *See* starseeds
rebellions
    angelic, 131, 135, 136, 164
    Caligastia and, 72
    in cosmic alchemy, 90–91
*Rebel Angels among Us, The,* xi, 1
Reincarnation Express, 91, 136, 244, 319
religion
    eternal soul and, 244
    Father Creator and, 243
    promotion and practice of, 242
    rebel angels and, 244–45
    shared belief system and, 261
    worship and, 243
*Return of the Rebel Angels, The,* 157,
    217, 219, 268, 269–70
Rigveda, 27–28
Rock Kingdom, 295
rocks, attraction to, 294
Ruth, 74–75, 81–85, 87–88

sacred circle, 283
Sadat, Anwar, 269, 278
Sandy, Toronto mediumship and,
    159–61
Satan, 13, 134, 163, 245, 300, 311, 319
scientific thinking, 95–96
*Scientist: A Metaphysical
    Autobiography, The* (Lilly), 66

Sea People, 190, 194
Seraph, 319
Seraphic Overgovernment, 264
Seraphic Transport Centers, 126, 129,
    145, 212–13, 222
Seraphic Transport System, 320
shamanism, 108
Shandron
    about, 165–66
    defined, 320
    forgiveness to Lucifer and, 272–73
    message, 273
    "Most Highs" and, 166
    as Supernaphim, 165, 274
Sirian Intervention, 124
Sirians, 97–98, 111–12, 174, 210
Smith, Bill, 50–55
Solonon, 204–5
soma, 106
starcars, 142
star people, 48–49, 50, 320
starseeds
    authentic self-knowledge and, 288
    choices and, 185
    difficulties and challenges faced by,
        23
    flow into mortal incarnation, 263
    healing process for, 196
    as human beings in Atlantis, 24, 132
    in India, 25
    intimate relationships, 185–86, 187
    issues and weaknesses, 186–87
    Jesse's acceptance as, 304–5
    mortal incarnation, 288
    receptacle for, 204
    southern China and, 25
    at start of cycle, 23

substitution with, 244
term usage, 4
Sumer, 71, 97–98, 112
Sumerians, 224–26
Superuniverses, 93, 310, 320
symbiosis, 133, 134, 135
System Sovereign, 14, 155, 163, 265,
   311, 320

third-density planets
  angels on, 23
  great crystal, 155
  Indwelling Spirit and, 11
  mortal life on, 92
  odors from, 146
  shift to fourth density and, 148–49,
    151, 152
third- to fourth-density shift, 147–48,
   151, 152
thoughtforms
  childhood, 255
  defined, 320
  as entities, 255
  as experienced, 253
  fear-impacted, 254
  generation of, 250
  in human creative imagination, 253
  negative, 251, 315
  as personal or impersonal, 252–53
  subtle-energy bodies of, 254–55
thoughts
  emotional, 250–51
  fifth dimension and, 222
  rebellious, 130
  self-awareness and, 210
  solidification of, 251
  utterance of, 250

Toronto mediumship, 159–64
Transport Seraph, 128–29, 134–35,
   145, 321

UFOs
  Bennett Park sighting, 89, 141–44,
    158–59, 237
  dolphins and, 116
  as starcars, 142
  Wharram family and, 86
  young boy and, 141–44
ultimatons, 93–94, 265, 321
Unit, The. *See also specific members
   of The Unit*
  closing of, 29
  defined, 321
  establishment of, 5
  stories and secrets in, 8
Urantia
  belief system, 272
  lexicon, 161
  Thought Adjuster cosmology, 11
Urantia model, 310
*Urantia Book, The*
  angelic cosmology and, 310–12
  angel rebellion and, 163
  angels in, 164–65
  contradictions, 273
  defined, 321
  glossary of terms from, 314–22
  introduction to, 119
  reading and retention of, 89
  on reality, 216
  study of, 272
  vocabulary and knowledge of,
   161
  voice in, 159

Vanu's teachings, 22–23, 24, 110, 189, 230
Vedic belief system, 25
Viewpack business, 16–18, 29–30, 61–62
violet blood, 247, 321
Von Newman's Catastrophe, 302, 303

Walk-Ins
  defined, 321
  experience as, 49
  increase of, 49
  interference and, 49
  life of, 49
  Manhattan and, 23
  Orion, 171
  Pleiadeans as, 48
  spiritual technology, 48–49
  use of, 48
Watchers. *See also specific Watchers*
  civilizations and, 70
  consciousness, 124–26, 128
  defined, 321
  dimensional movement and, 150–51
  emotions and, 23–24, 125
  ideas and, 176–77
  lower dimensions and, 150
  prattling, 177
  receptacle for, 204
  transport of, 126–27
Wharram, James, 74–75, 77–80, 83–87
Wilson, Robert Anton, 302, 303–4
Wise Twins, 145, 146, 175, 322
"word builds, the," 250, 251
World Mind, 113
"World of Men," 6, 63

worship, 243, 261
written knowledge, 26

Yazidi
  about, 245
  angels and, 245
  assimilation into Western life, 248
  community, 247–48
  cosmology, 246, 247
  as monotheists, 245
Yazidism, 245–46

Zanda, Prince, 174, 189–90, 191, 322
Zandan, 146, 187, 322
Zandana
  about, 124
  approach to, 145
  Clarisel and, 147–49
  defined, 322
  indigenous population of, 151
  Lake of Glass, 155
  life on Earth vs., 153
  Planetary Princes, 158
  Rainbow Bridge and, 124, 147–48, 319
  scents of, 146
  sea mammals and, 190
  Sea People, 190, 194
  shift to fourth density and, 147–48, 178
  tipping point, 151
  travel to, 124–25
  wine, 205–6
  Wise Twins, 145, 146, 175
Zeus, 107, 108

# About the Author

Photo by Neil Edwards

Timothy Wyllie (1940–2017) chose to be born in London at the height of the Battle of Britain. Surviving an English public school education unbroken, he studied architecture, qualifying in 1964 and practicing in London and the Bahamas. During this time he also worked with two others to create a mystery school, which came to be known as the Process Church, and subsequently traveled with the community throughout Europe and America. He became art director of PROCESS magazine, designing a series of magazines in the 1960s and '70s that have recently become recognized as among the prime progenitors of psychedelic magazine design. In 1975, Wyllie became the director of the New York headquarters and organized a series of conferences and seminars on unorthodox issues such as out-of-body travel, extraterrestrial encounters, alternative cancer therapies, and Tibetan Buddhism. After some fractious and fundamental disagreements with his colleagues in the community, he left to start a new life in 1977. The record of Wyllie's fifteen years in the mystery school of the Process Church and the true account of this eccentric spiritual community appears in his book *Love, Sex, Fear, Death: The Inside Story of the Process Church of the Final Judgment,* which was published by Feral House in 2009. It is slowly becoming a cult classic.

A profound near-death experience in 1973 confirmed for Wyllie the reality of other levels of existence and instigated what has become a lifetime exploration of nonhuman intelligences. Having created his intention, the Multiverse opened up a trail of synchronicities that led to his swimming with a coastal pod of wild dolphins, two extraterrestrial encounters—during one of which he was able to question the ET mouthpiece as to some of the ways of the inhabited Multiverse—and finally to an extended dialogue with a group of angels speaking through a light-trance medium in Toronto, Canada.

Wyllie's first phase of spiritual exploration was published as *The Deta Factor: Dolphins, Extraterrestrials & Angels* by Coleman Press in 1984 and republished by Bear & Company as *Dolphins, ETs & Angels* in 1993.

His second book, *Dolphins, Telepathy & Underwater Birthing,* published by Bear & Company in 1993, was republished by Wisdom Editions in 2001 under the title *Adventures Among Spiritual Intelligences: Angels, Aliens, Dolphins & Shamans.* In this book Wyllie continues his travels exploring Balinese shamanic healing, Australian Aboriginal cosmology, human underwater birthing, dolphin death and sexuality, entheogenic spirituality, the gathering alien presence on the planet, and his travels with a Walk-In, along with much else.

Wyllie's work with the angels through the 1980s resulted in the book *Ask Your Angels: A Practical Guide to Working with Your Messengers of Heaven to Empower and Enrich Your Life,* written with Alma Daniel and Andrew Ramer and published by Ballantine Books in

1992. After spending time at the top of the *New York Times* religious bestsellers, *Ask Your Angels* went on to become an international success in eleven translations.

*The Return of the Rebel Angels* continues the series he began with *Dolphins, ETs & Angels* and *Adventures Among Spiritual Intelligences,* presenting further in-depth intuitive explorations of nonhuman intelligences. It draws together the many meaningful strands of Wyllie's thirty-year voyage of discovery into unknown and long-taboo territories in a coherent and remarkably optimistic picture for the immediate future of the human species, with the inconspicuous help of a benign and richly inhabited living Multiverse.

*The Helianx Proposition: The Return of the Rainbow Serpent—A Cosmic Creation Fable,* also thirty years in the making, is Wyllie's illustrated mythic exploration of an ancient extraterrestrial personality and its occult influence on life in this world. Published by Daynal Institute Press in 2010, it includes two DVDs and two CDs of associated material. The CDs contain nineteen tracks of the author's visionary observations, augmented by Emmy-winning musician the late Jim Wilson, master of digital sonic manipulation.

*Confessions of a Rebel Angel,* Wyllie's first collaboration with Georgia, emerged in 2012, published by Inner Traditions • Bear & Company. They followed up with *Revolt of the Rebel Angels* in 2013, *Rebel Angels in Exile* in 2014, *Wisdom of the Watchers* in 2015, *Awakening of the Watchers* in 2016, *Secret History of the Watchers* in 2018, and *Rebel Angels among Us* in 2020.

## BOOKS BY TIMOTHY WYLLIE

*The Deta Factor: Dolphins, Extraterrestrials & Angels,* 1984 (currently in print as *Dolphins, ETs & Angels,* 1993).

*Ask Your Angels: A Practical Guide to Working with the Messengers of Heaven to Empower and Enrich Your Life,* 1992 (cowritten with Alma Daniel and Andrew Ramer).

*Dolphins, Telepathy & Underwater Birthing,* 1993 (currently in print as

*Adventures Among Spiritual Intelligences: Angels, Aliens, Dolphins & Shamans,* 2001).

*Contacting Your Angels through Movement, Meditation & Music,* 1995 (with Elli Bambridge).

*Love, Sex, Fear, Death: The Inside Story of the Process Church of the Final Judgment,* 2009 (editor, with Adam Parfrey).

*The Helianx Proposition: The Return of the Rainbow Serpent—A Cosmic Creation Fable,* 2010.

*The Return of the Rebel Angels,* 2011.


The *Confessions* Series

*Confessions of a Rebel Angel,* 2012.

*Revolt of the Rebel Angels,* 2013.

*Rebel Angels in Exile,* 2014.

*Wisdom of the Watchers,* 2015.

*Awakening of the Watchers,* 2016.

*Secret History of the Watchers,* 2018.

*The Rebel Angels among Us,* 2020.